ISBN 978-1-331-13436-7
PIBN 10148886

1 MONTH OF
FREE
READING

at

www.ForgottenBooks.com

By purchasing this book you are eligible for one month membership to ForgottenBooks.com, giving you unlimited access to our entire collection of over 700,000 titles via our web site and mobile apps.

To claim your free month visit: www.forgottenbooks.com/free148886

English
Français
Deutsche
Italiano
Español
Português

www.forgottenbooks.com

Mythology Photography **Fiction**
Fishing Christianity **Art** Cooking
Essays Buddhism Freemasonry
Medicine **Biology** Music **Ancient**
Egypt Evolution Carpentry Physics
Dance Geology **Mathematics** Fitness
Shakespeare **Folklore** Yoga Marketing
Confidence Immortality Biographies
Poetry **Psychology** Witchcraft
Electronics Chemistry History **Law**
Accounting **Philosophy** Anthropology
Alchemy Drama Quantum Mechanics
Atheism Sexual Health **Ancient History**
Entrepreneurship Languages Sport
Paleontology Needlework Islam
Metaphysics Investment Archaeology
Parenting Statistics Criminology
Motivational

PIONEER SERMONS

=== AND ===

ADDRESSES

From the writings of Barton W. Stone, Thomas and Alexander Campbell, Walter Scott, John Smith, Wm. Hayden, Wm. Baxter, Moses E. Lard, Dr. A. Wliford Hall, Benj. Franklin and Jas. M. Mathes.

COMPILED BY

F. L. ROWE

ASSISTED BY

M. A. C.

F. L. ROWE, Publisher

CINCINNATI, OHIO

1908

Copyright, 1908
BY
F. L. ROWE
Cincinnati, O.

PREFACE

Some months ago I had occasion to write to about twenty-five of our representative brethren, embracing educators, preachers, and the common people, asking for information about matters relating to the early work of the pioneers. To my surprise, not more than six of the twenty-five appealed to acknowledged any familiarity with the early writings; in fact, not much knowledge of their early works as individuals. This discovery convinced me that something was needed. It occurred to me that a collection of sermons gathered through a period of fifty years would prove not only helpful to the present and future generations, but would familiarize our brethren, present and future, with the character of the sermons and addresses uttered or written by some of the pioneers of the faith. To this end I scanned the writings of the pioneers and collected the twelve sermons and addresses which make up this present collection. The ones included in this volume are only a few writings from a few of the early writers. It would require many volumes like this one to contain the valuable sermons that can still be collected from these pioneer works.

It has been the aim of the compilers of this volume

to have the subjects of a diversified character, so that not only first principles would be treated but also sermons given on Christian growth and character.

We consider the "Declaration and Address," by Thomas Campbell, to be a most valuable historical document. In connection with that address we also call special attention to one by Barton W. Stone, which antedates the Campbell address by five years, clearly proving that the reform work that is generally spoken of as the "Reformation of the Nineteenth Century," had its inception in the mind and conduct of Barton W. Stone and his followers.

March, 1908.   F. L. R.

TABLE OF CONTENTS

Pioneer Sermons and Addresses

LAST WILL AND TESTAMENT OF SPRINGFIELD PRESBYTERY.

The Presbytery of Springfield, just before it expired, made its last will and testament, which is quite a curiosity in its way. But it shows what advancement the Presbytery had made in the knowledge of the truth and the principles of reformation. For the satisfaction of such of our readers as may not have seen this remarkable document, we here insert it, together with the witnesses' address:

THE LAST WILL AND TESTAMENT OF SPRINGFIELD PRESBYTERY.

For where a testament is, there must of necessity be the death of the testator; for a testament is of force after men are dead, otherwise it is of no strength at all while the testator liveth. Thou fool, that which thou sowest is not quickened except it die. Verily, verily, I say unto you, except a corn of wheat fall into the ground and die, it abideth alone; but if it die, it bringeth forth much fruit. Whose voice then shook the earth; but now he hath promised, saying, yet once more I shake not the earth only, but also heaven. And this word, yet once more, signifies the removing of those things that are shaken as of things that are made, that those things which can not be shaken may remain.—*Scripture.*

LAST WILL AND TESTAMENT, ETC.

THE PRESBYTERY OF SPRINGFIELD, sitting at Cane Ridge, in the county of Bourbon, being, through a gracious Providence, in more than ordinary bodily health, growing in strength and size daily; and in perfect soundness and composure of mind; but knowing that it is appointed for all delegated bodies once to die; and considering that the life of every such body is very uncertain, do make and ordain this our last will and testament, in manner and form following, viz.:

Imprimis. We *will,* that this body die, be dissolved. and sink into union with the body of Christ at large; for there is but one body, and one spirit, even as we are called in one hope of our calling.

Item. We *will,* that our name of distinction, with its *Reverend* title, be forgotten, that there be but one Lord over God's heritage, and his name one.

Item. We *will,* that our power of making laws for the government of the church, and executing them by delegated authority, forever cease; that the people may have free course to the Bible, and adopt the *law of the spirit of life in Jesus Christ.*

Item. We *will,* that candidates for the gospel ministry henceforth study the Holy Scriptures with fervent prayer, and obtain license from God to preach the simple gospel, *with the Holy Ghost sent down from heaven,* without any mixture of philosophy, vain deceit, traditions of men, or the rudiments of the world. And let none henceforth take *this honor to himself, but he that is called of God, as was Aaron.*

Item. We *will,* that the Church of Christ resume her native right of internal government, try her candidates for the ministry, as to their soundness in the faith, acquaintance with experimental religion, gravity and aptness to teach; and admit no other proof of their authority but Christ speaking in them. We will, that the Church of Christ look up to the Lord of the harvest to send forth laborers into his harvest; and that she resume her primitive right of trying those *who say they are apostles and are not.*

Item. We *will,* that each particular church, as a body, actuated by the same spirit, choose her own preacher and support him by a free-will offering, without a written *call* or *subscription,* admit members, remove offenses; and never henceforth *delegate* her right of government to any man or set of men whatever.

Item. We *will,* that the people henceforth take the Bible as the only sure guide to heaven; and as many as are offended with other books, which stand in competition with it, may cast them into the fire if they choose; for it is better to enter into life having one book, than having many to be cast into hell.

Item. We *will,* that preachers and people cultivate a spirit of mutual forbearance; pray more and dispute less; and while they behold the signs of the times, look up, and confidently expect that redemption draweth nigh.

Item. We *will,* that our weak brethren, who may have been wishing to make the Presbytery of Springfield their king, and wot not what is now become of it, betake themselves to the Rock of Ages, and follow Jesus for the future.

Item. We *will,* that the Synod of Kentucky examine every member who may be suspected of having departed from the Confession of Faith, and suspend every such suspected heretic immediately, in order that the oppressed may go free, and taste the sweets of gospel liberty.

Item. We *will,* that Ja—— ————, the author of two letters lately published in Lexington, be encouraged in his zeal to destroy *partyism.* We will, moreover, that our past conduct be examined into by all who may have correct information; but let foreigners beware of speaking evil of things which they know not.

Item. Finally, we *will,* that all our *sister bodies* read their Bibles carefully, that they may see their fate there determined, and prepare for death before it is too late.

SPRINGFIELD PRESBYTERY, } L. S.
June 28th, 1804.

ROBERT MARSHALL,
JOHN DUNLAVY,
RICHARD MCNEMAR,   } Witnesses.
B. W. STONE,
JOHN THOMPSON,
DAVID PURVIANCE,

THE WITNESSES' ADDRESS.

We, the above named witnesses of the Last Will and Testament of the Springfield Presbytery, knowing that there will be many conjectures respecting the causes which have occasioned the dissolution of that body, think proper to testify, that from its first existence it was knit together in love, lived in peace and concord, and died a voluntary and happy death.

Their reasons for dissolving that body were the following: With deep concern they viewed the divisions and party spirit among professing Christians, principally owing to the adoption of human creeds and forms of government. While they were united under the name of a Presbytery, they endeavored to cultivate a spirit of love and unity with all Christians, but found it extremely difficult to suppress the idea that they themselves were a party separate from others. This difficulty increased in proportion to their success in the ministry. Jealousies were excited in the minds of other denominations; and a temptation was laid before those who were connected with the various parties to view them in the same light. At their last meeting they undertook to prepare for the press a piece entitled, "Observations on Church Government," in which the world will see the beautiful simplicity of Christian church government, stript of human inventions and lordly traditions.

As they proceeded in the investigation of that subject, they soon found that there was neither precept nor example in the New Testament for such confederacies as modern Church Sessions, Presbyteries, Synods, General Assemblies, etc. Hence they concluded that while they continued in the connection in which they then stood, they were off the foundation of the Apostles and the Prophets, of which Christ himself is the chief corner-stone. However just, therefore, their views of church government might have been, they would have gone out under the name and sanction of a self-constituted body. Therefore, from a principle of love to Christians of every name, the precious cause of Jesus, and dying sinners who are kept from the Lord by the existence of sects and parties in the church, they have cheerfully consented to retire from the din and fury of conflicting parties—sink out of the view of fleshy minds, and die the death. They believe their death will be great gain to the world. But though dead, as above, and stript of their mortal frame which only served to keep them too near the confines of Egyptian bondage, they yet live and speak in the land of gospel liberty; they blow the trumpet of jubilee, and willingly devote themselves to the help of the Lord against the mighty. They will aid the brethren, by their counsel, when required; assist in ordaining elders or pastors, seek the divine blessing, unite with all Christians, commune together, and strengthen each others' hands in the work of the Lord.

We design, by the grace of God, to continue in the exercise of those functions which belong to us as ministers of the gospel, confidently trusting in the Lord, that he will be with us. We candidly acknowledge, that in some things we may err, through human infirmity; but he will correct our wanderings and preserve his church. Let all Christians join with us, in crying to God day and night, to remove the obstacles which stand in the way of his work, and give him no rest till he make Jerusalem a praise in the earth. We heartily unite with our Christian brethren of every name, in thanksgiving to God for the display of his goodness in the glorious work he is carrying on in our western country, which we hope will terminate in the universal spread of the gospel.

Thus far the witnesses of the last will and testament of the Springfield Presbytery.

Why the work alluded to above, on the subject of church government, never made its appearance, the writer is not advised. Perhaps the Shaker difficulty, which shortly after this time arose, was the cause, as it is known that Dunlavy and McNemar, two of the witnesses, were carried away with that miserable delusion; and also, that shortly after their defection from the cause, Marshall and Thompson began to look back, and subsequently joined the Presbyterians again.

DECLARATION AND ADDRESS.

OF THE

CHRISTIAN ASSOCIATION OF WASHINGTON, PENN.

(Published A. D. 1809.)

Thomas Campbell was born in County Down, Ireland, February 1, 1763. Came to America in 1807. Died January 4, 1854.

[At a meeting held at Buffalo, August 17, 1809, consisting of persons of different religious denominations, most of them in an unsettled state as to a fixed Gospel ministry, it was unanimously agreed, upon the considerations, and for the purposes hereinafter declared, to form themselves into a religious association, designated as above, which they accordingly did, and appointed twenty-one of their number to meet and confer together, and, with the assistance of Elder Thomas Campbell, minister of the Gospel, to determine upon the proper means to carry into effect the important ends of their Association; the result of which conference was the following Declaration and Address, agreed upon and ordered to be printed at the expense, and for the benefit of the society.—SEPTEMBER 7, 1809.

DECLARATION, ETC.*

From the series of events which have taken place in the Churches for many years past, especially in this Western country, as well as from what we know in general of the present state of things in the Christian world, we are persuaded that it is high time for us

---

* This "Declaration and Address" was not the constitution of any Church existing then or now, but a "Declaration" of a purpose to institute a society of "Voluntary Advocates for Church

not only to think, but also to act, for ourselves; to
see with our own eyes, and to take all our measures
directly and immediately from the Divine Standard;
to this alone we feel ourselves Divinely bound to be
conformed, as by this alone we must be judged. We
are also persuaded that as no man can be *judged* for
his brother, so no man can *judge* for his brother;
every man must be allowed to judge for himself, as
every man must bear his own judgment—must give
account of himself to God. We are also of opinion
that as the Divine word is equally binding upon all,
so all lie under an equal obligation to be bound by it,
and it alone; and not by any human interpretation
of it; and that, therefore, no man has a right to
judge his brother, except in so far as he manifestly
violates the express letter of the law. That every
such judgment is an express violation of the law of
Christ, a daring usurpation of his throne, and a gross
intrusion upon the rights and liberties of his subjects.
We are, therefore, of opinion that we should beware
of such things; that we should keep at the utmost
distance from everything of this nature; and that,
knowing the judgment of God against them that commit such things, we should neither do the same our-

---

Reformation." Its sole purpose was to promote "simple Evangelical Christianity," and for this end resolved to countenance
and support such ministers, and such only, as exhibited a manifest
conformity to the original standard, in conversation, doctrine, zeal,
and diligence; such as practiced that original simple form of
Christianity expressly exhibited upon the sacred page; without
inculcating anything of human authority, of private opinion or of
inventions of men, as having any place in the constitution, faith,
or worship of the Christian Church; or anything as matter of
Christian faith or duty for which there cannot be expressly produced a *"Thus saith the Lord, either in express terms, or by
approved precedent."*

selves, nor take pleasure in them that do them. Moreover, being well aware, from sad experience, of the heinous nature and pernicious tendency of religious controversy among Christians; tired and sick of the bitter jarrings and janglings of a party spirit, we would desire to be at rest; and, were it possible, we would also desire to adopt and recommend such measures as would give rest to our brethren throughout all the Churches: as would restore unity, peace, and purity to the whole Church of God. This desirable rest, however, we utterly despair either to find for ourselves, or to be able to recommend to our brethren, by continuing amid the diversity and rancor of party contentions, the veering uncertainty and clashings of human opinions: nor, indeed, can we reasonably expect to find it anywhere but in Christ and his simple word, which is the same yesterday, to-day, and forever. Our desire, therefore, for ourselves and our brethren would be, that, rejecting human opinions and the inventions of men as of any authority, or as having any place in the Church of God, we might forever cease from further contentions about such things; returning to and holding fast by the original standard; taking the Divine word alone for our rule; the Holy Spirit for our teacher and guide, to lead us into all truth; and Christ alone, as exhibited in the word, for our salvation; that, by so doing, we may be at peace among ourselves, follow peace with all men, and holiness, without which no man shall see the Lord. Impressed with these sentiments, we have resolved as follows:

I. That we form ourselves into a religious association under the denomination of the Christian Association of Washington, for the sole purpose of promoting simple evangelical Christianity, free from all mixture of human opinions and inventions of men.

II. That each member, according to ability, cheerfully and liberally subscribe a certain specified sum, to be paid half yearly, for the purpose of raising a fund to support a pure Gospel ministry, that shall reduce to practice that whole form of doctrine, worship, discipline, and government, expressly revealed and enjoined in the word of God. And, also, for supplying the poor with the holy Scriptures.

III. That this Society consider it a duty, and shall use all proper means in its power, to encourage the formation of similar associations; and shall for this purpose hold itself in readiness, upon application, to correspond with, and render all possible assistance to, such as may desire to associate for the same desirable and important purposes.

IV. That this Society by no means considers itself a Church, nor does at all assume to itself the powers peculiar to such a society; nor do the members, as such, consider themselves as standing connected in that relation; nor as at all associated for the peculiar purposes of Church association; but merely as voluntary advocates for Church reformation; and, as possessing the powers common to all individuals, who may please to associate in a peaceable and orderly manner, for any lawful purpose, namely, the disposal of their time, counsel, and property, as they may see cause.

V. That this Society, formed for the sole purpose of promoting simple evangelical Christianity, shall, to the utmost of its power, countenance and support such ministers, and such only, as exhibit a manifest conformity to the original standard in conversation and doctrine, in zeal and diligence; only such as reduce to practice that simple original form of Christianity, expressly exhibited upon the sacred page; without attempting to inculcate anything of human authority, of private opinion, or inventions of men, as having any place in the constitution, faith, or worship, of the Christian Church, or anything as matter of Christian faith or duty, for which there can not be expressly produced a "Thus saith the Lord, either in express terms, or by approved precedent."*

VI. That a Standing Committee of twenty-one members of unexceptionable moral character, inclusive of the secretary and treasurer, be chosen annually to superintend the interests, and transact the business of

---

* On reading the proof-sheets of this "Declaration," as they issued from the press immediately after my arrival in Washington, Pennsylvania, direct from Scotland, I observed to its author: *"Then, sir, you must abandon and give up infant baptism, and some other practices for which it seems to me you can not produce an express precept or an example in any book of the Christian Scriptures."*

After a considerable pause, his response was to this effect: *"To the law and to the testimony"* we make our appeal. If not found therein, we, of course, must abandon it. But," he added, "we could not unchurch ourselves now, and go out into the world and then turn back again and enter the church, merely for the sake of form or decorum.

"But," we replied, "if there be any virtue, privilege, or blessing in submitting to any ordinance, of course we can not enjoy that virtue, privilege, or blessing whatever it may be, of which it is an ordained, a Divinely-appointed instrumentality or medium. 'Without faith it is impossible to please God' in any act, or in any formal obedience to any precept, ordinance, or institution; and equally true that without this faith we can not enjoy any act of obedience to either a moral, a positive, or a religious ordinance of any class whatever. There is a promised reward, or, rather, an immediate blessing attendant on every act of obedience to the Divine precepts; and, as you have taught, 'the blessings attached to, or connected with the moral *positive,* are superior to those connected with the moral *negative.*' And, as for an assent to an opinion, there is no virtue in it."

the Society.   And that said Committee be invested
with full powers to act and do, in the name and behalf of their constituents, whatever the Society had
previously determined, for the purpose of carrying into
effect the entire object of its institution, and that
in case of any emergency, unprovided for in the existing determinations of the Society, said Committee be
empowered to call a special meeting for that purpose.

VII. That this Society meet at least twice a year,
viz.: on the first Thursday of May and of November,
and that the collectors appointed to receive the half-
yearly quotas of the promised subscriptions, be in
readiness, at or before each meeting, to make their
returns to the treasurer, that he may be able to report
upon the state of the funds.   The next meeting to
be held at Washington on the first Thursday of November next.

VIII. That each meeting of the Society be opened
with a sermon, the constitution and address read, and
a collection lifted for the benefit of the Society; and
that all communications of a public nature be laid
before the Society at its half-yearly meetings.

IX. That this Society, relying upon the all-sufficiency of the Church's Head; and, through his grace,
looking with an eye of confidence to the generous
liberality of the sincere friends of genuine Christianity, holds itself engaged to afford a competent support to such ministers as the Lord may graciously
dispose to assist, at the request, and by invitation
of the Society, in promoting a pure evangelical reformation, by the simple preaching of the everlasting
Gospel, and the administration of its ordinances in an
exact conformity to the Divine standard as aforesaid;
and that, therefore, whatever the friends of the institution shall please to contribute toward the support

of ministers in connection with this Society, who may
be sent forth to preach at considerable distances, the
same shall be gratefully received and acknowledged
as a donation to its funds.

ADDRESS, Etc.

*To all that love our Lord Jesus Christ, in sincerity throughout
all the Churches, the following Address is most respectfully
submitted.*

DEARLY BELOVED BRETHREN:

That it is the grand design and native tendency of
our holy religion to reconcile and unite men to God,
and to each other, in truth and love, to the glory of
God, and their own present and eternal good, will
not, we presume, be denied by any of the genuine
subjects of Christianity. The nativity of its Divine
author was announced from heaven, by an host of
angels, with high acclamations of "Glory to God in
the highest, and on earth peace and good-will toward
men." The whole tenor of that Divine book which
contains its institutes, in all its gracious declarations,
precepts, ordinances, and holy examples, most express-
ively and powerfully inculcates this. In so far, then,
as this holy unity and unanimity in faith and love is
attained, just in the same degree is the glory of God
and the happiness of men promoted and secured. Impressed with those sentiments, and, at the same time,
grievously affected with those sad divisions which
have so awfully interfered with the benign and gracious intention of our holy religion, by exciting its
professed subjects to bite and devour one another, we
can not suppose ourselves justifiable in withholding

the mite of our sincere and humble endeavors to heal and remove them.

What awful and distressing effects have those sad divisions produced! what aversions, what reproaches, what backbitings, what evil surmisings, what angry contentions, what enmities, what excommunications, and even persecution!!! And, indeed, this must, in some measure, continue to be the case so long as those schisms exist; for, saith the apostle, where envying and strife is, *there* is confusion and every evil work. What dreary effects of those accursed divisions are to be seen, even in this highly favored country, where the sword of the civil magistrate has not as yet learned to serve at the altar. Have we not seen congregations broken to pieces, neighborhoods of professing Christians first thrown into confusion by party contentions, and, in the end, entirely deprived of Gospel ordinances; while in the meantime, large settlements and tracts of country remain to this day entirely destitute of a Gospel ministry, many of them in little better than a state of heathenism, the Churches being either so weakened with divisions that they can not send them ministers, or the people so divided among themselves that they will not receive them. Several, at the same time, who live at the door of a preached Gospel, dare not in conscience go to hear it, and, of course, enjoy little more advantage, in that respect, than if living in the midst of heathens. How seldom do many in those circumstances enjoy the dispensations of the Lord's Supper, that great ordinance of unity and love. How sadly, also, does this broken and confused state of things interfere with that spiritual intercourse among Christians, one with another, which is so essential to their edification and comfort, in the midst of a present evil world; so divided in sentiment, and, of course, living at such distances, that but few of the same opinion,* or party, can conveniently and frequently assemble for religious purposes, or enjoy a due frequency of ministerial atten-

---

*"Opinions" were, in those days, and even yet are very popular in the pulpits and in the presses of religious sectaries of all the denominational religions of the living world. Yet the word "opinion" is not once found in the Christian Scriptures, nor even in the Jewish records, except once by Elijah, in a case pending between the worshipers of Baal and those of Jehovah. No man ever believed an opinion or a doctrine! He may assent to them, but to believe an opinion or a doctrine is simply absurd.

The discriminating reason has to do with opinions. They are tried by reasoning upon them, pro or con. Hence, they are debatable alone in the court of reason. But faith has to do with testimony, as hope has to do with a promise and fear with a threatening. We believe, when reported, well authenticated facts and events. We hope in promises believed. We fear and tremble at threatenings enunciated. We obey precepts when propounded, and not before, and only when they emanate from legitimate authority.

Such is a practical view of the constitution of the human mind, as God created it. And such is the well-authenticated meaning of these words in the currency of those who properly appreciate and understand our language.

The corrupt language of Ashdod has fearfully invaded the pulpit and the press of the living world. It is well illustrated by Nehemiah, chapter xii, in his history of the Jewish captivity. One passage will suffice: "In those days also, I saw Jews who had married wives of Ashdod, of Ammon, and of Moab. And their children spoke half in the speech of Ashdod, and could not speak in the Jewish language; but, according to the language of each people." "And," says Nehemiah the reformer, "I contended with them and reviled them."

Babylon the great, is the antitype of old Babylon. And most Protestants that have come out of her still speak, and preach, and teach in a mixed and confused dialect.

No one of Elder Campbell's cotemporaries known to me more earnestly contended and labored than he for "a pure speech," a Scriptural dialect, or the calling of Bible themes by Bible names.

tions. And even where things are in a better state with respect to settled Churches, how is the tone of

---

"The restoration of a pure speech" was with him a cardinal theme, and a petition in many a prayer.

How many debates, schisms, and alienations of heart and life have grown out of "the articles of faith," or "the doctrines" of the present generation. "Doctrines," like "articles of faith," are wholly uncanonical. In the Christian Scriptures we never read of the "doctrines of Christ." It is always singular, never plural, "Doctrines," like "articles of faith," are unprecedented in the New Testament, except in the case of *demons,* and those under their influence. And how many more in the generations past and gone! According to the apostolic style the Christian faith is called *"The doctrine of Christ,"* and all other faiths or theories are called "the doctrines of men," or "of demons."

There is a pride of opinion more subtile, and more permeating the religious world than is generally supposed or imagined. A zeal wholly sectarian and selfish is more easily detected in others than in ourselves. Our premises and our observations of the religious world, for at least one-half a century, more than justify this opinion.

The strength or *spiritual power* of the apostolic Gospel is now, has been heretofore, and will till time shall end, continue to be, "the power of God to salvation," to every one who clearly appreciates and embraces it in his affections, and consequently acts in harmony with its spiritual and eternal obligations. Indeed, we can not conceive of higher claims and demand on the heart, the life, the devotion of man to his Creator and Redeemer, than are found in the doctrine of Christ, duly appreciated and cordially embraced.

It presents to us transcendent facts to be believed, precepts to be obeyed, threatenings to be feared, promises to be hoped for, and an ineffably beautiful person and character to be loved, admired, and adored. It effectually addresses all the rudimental elements and cravings of our nature, and ministers to them all; as light to the eye, music to the ear, peace to the conscience, and joy to the heart, so it meets and provides for every rational, moral, and religious appetency of our nature in all its conditions and circumstances. It is, indeed, infinitely worthy of God to be the author of it, and of man to be the subject and the object of it.

discipline relaxed under the influence of a party spirit;
many being afraid to exercise it with due strictness,
lest their people should leave them, and, under the
cloak of some specious pretense, find refuge in the
bosom of another party; while, lamentable to be
told, so corrupted is the Church with those accursed
divisions, that there are but few so base as not to find
admission into some professing party or other. Thus,
in a great measure, is that Scriptural purity of communion banished from the Church of God, upon the
due preservation of which much of her comfort, glory,
and usefulness depends. To complete the dread result
of our woful divisions, one evil yet remains, of a very
awful nature: the Divine displeasure justly provoked
with this sad perversion of the Gospel of peace, the
Lord withholds his gracious influential presence from
his ordinances, and not unfrequently gives up the
contentious authors and abettors of religious discord
to fall into grievous scandals, or visits them with
judgments, as he did the house of Eli. Thus, while
professing Christians bite and devour one another,
they are consumed one of another, or fall a prey to
the righteous judgments of God; meantime, the truly
religious of all parties are grieved, the weak stumbled,
the graceless and profane hardened, the mouths of
infidels opened to blaspheme religion, and thus the
only thing under heaven divinely efficacious to promote and secure the present spiritual and eternal good
of man, even the Gospel of the blessed Jesus, is reduced to contempt, while multitudes, deprived of a
Gospel ministry, as has been observed, fall an easy
prey to seducers, and so become the dupes of almost
unheard-of delusions. Are not such the visible effects
of our sad divisions, even in this otherwise happy
country. Say, dear brethren, are not these things so?
Is it not then your incumbent duty to endeavor, by all

Scriptural means, to have those evils remedied. Who will say that it is not? And does it not peculiarly belong to *you,* who occupy the place of Gospel ministers, to be leaders in this laudable undertaking? Much depends upon *your* hearty concurrence and zealous endeavors. The favorable opportunity which Divine Providence has put into your hands, in this happy country, for the accomplishment of so great a good, is, in itself, a consideration of no small encouragement. A country happily exempted from the baneful influence of a civil establishment of any peculiar form of Christianity; from under the direct influence of the antichristian hierarchy; and, at the same time, from any formal connection with the devoted nations that have given their strength and power unto the beast; in which, of course, no adequate reformation can be accomplished, until the word of God be fulfilled, and the vials of his wrath poured out upon them. Happy exemption, indeed, from being the object of such awful judgments. Still more happy will it be for us if we duly esteem and improve those great advantages, for the high and valuable ends for which they are manifestly given, and sure where much is given, much also will be required. Can the Lord expect, or require, anything less from a people in such unhampered circumstances—from a people so liberally furnished with all means and mercies, than a thorough reformation in all things, civil and religious, according to his word? Why should we suppose it? And would not such an improvement of our precious privileges be equally conducive to the glory of God, and our own present and everlasting good? The auspicious phenomena of the times furnish collateral arguments of a very encouraging nature, that our dutiful and pious endeavors shall not be in vain in the Lord. Is it not the day of the Lord's vengeance upon the antichristian world—the year of recompenses for the controversy of Zion? Surely, then, the time to favor her is come; even the set time. And is it not said that Zion shall be built in troublous times? Have not greater efforts been made, and more done, for the promulgation of the Gospel among the nations, since the commencement of the French revolution, than had been for many centuries prior to that event? And have not the Churches, both in Europe and America, since that period, discovered a more than usual concern for the removal of contentions, for the healing of divisions, for the restoration of a Christian and brotherly intercourse one with another, and for the promotion of each other's spiritual good, as the printed documents upon those subjects amply testify? Should *we* not, then, be excited by these considerations to concur with all our might, to help forward this good work; that what yet remains to be done, may be fully accomplished. And what though the well-meant endeavors after union have not, in some instances, entirely succeeded to the wish of all parties, should this dissuade us from the attempt! Indeed, should Christians cease to contend earnestly for the sacred articles of faith and duty once delivered to the saints, on account of the opposition and scanty success which, in many instances, attend their faithful and honest endeavors, the Divine cause of truth and righteousness might have long ago been relinquished. And is there anything more formidable in the Goliath schism, than in many other evils which Christians have to combat? Or, has the Captain of Salvation sounded a desist from pursuing, or proclaimed a truce with this deadly enemy that is sheathing its sword in the very bowels of his Church, rending and mangling his mystical body into pieces? Has he said to his servants, Let it alone? If not, where is the warrant for a cessation of endeavors to have it removed? On the other hand, are we not the better instructed by sage experience, how to proceed in this business, having before our eyes the inadvertencies and mistakes of others, which have hitherto, in many instances, prevented the desired success? Thus taught by experience, and happily furnished with the accumulated instructions of those that have gone before us, earnestly laboring in this good cause, let us take unto ourselves the whole armor of God, and, having our feet shod with the preparation of the Gospel of peace, let us stand fast by this important duty with all perseverance. Let none that love the peace of Zion be discouraged, much less offended, because that an object of such magnitude does not, in the first instance, come forth recommended by the express suffrage of the mighty or the many. This consideration, if duly weighed, will neither give offense, nor yield discouragement to any one that considers the nature of the thing in question in connection with what has been already suggested. Is it not a matter of universal right, a duty equally belonging to every citizen of Zion, to seek her good? In this respect, no one can claim a preference above his fellows, as to any peculiar, much less exclusive obligation. And, as for authority, it can have no place in this business; for, surely, none can suppose themselves invested with a Divine right, as to anything peculiarly belonging to them, to call the attention of their brethren to this dutiful and important undertaking. For our part, we entertain no such arrogant presumption; nor are we inclined to impute the thought to any of our brethren, that this good work should be let alone till such time as they may think proper to come forward and sanction the attempt, by their invitation and example. It is an open field, an extensive work, to which all are equally welcome, equally invited.

Should we speak of competency, viewing the greatness of the object, and the manifold difficulties which lie in the way of its accomplishment, we would readily exclaim, with the apostle, Who is sufficient for these things? But, upon recollecting ourselves, neither would *we* be discouraged; persuaded with him, that, as the work in which we are engaged, so, likewise, *our* sufficiency is of God. But, after all, both the mighty and the many are with us. The Lord himself, and all that are truly his people, are declaredly on our side. The prayers of all the Churches, nay, the prayers of Christ himself, (John xvii: 20, 23,) and of all that have ascended to his heavenly kingdom, are with us. The blessing out of Zion is pronounced upon our undertaking. "Pray for the peace of Jerusalem; they shall prosper that love thee." With such encouragements as these, what should deter us from the heavenly enterprise, or render hopeless the attempt of accomplishing, in due time, an entire union of all the Churches in faith and practice, according to the word of God? Not that we judge ourselves competent to effect such a thing; we utterly disclaim the thought; but we judge it our bounden duty to make the attempt, by using all due means in our power to promote it; and also, that we have sufficient reason to rest assured that our humble and well-meant endeavors shall not be in vain in the Lord.

The cause that we advocate is not our own peculiar cause, nor the cause of any party, considered as such; it is a common cause, the cause of Christ and our brethren of all denominations. All that we presume, then, is to do what we humbly conceive to be *our* duty, in connection with our brethren; to each of whom it equally belongs, as to us, to exert himself for this blessed purpose. And as we have no just reason to doubt the concurrence of our brethren to accomplish an object so desirable in itself, and fraught with such happy consequences, so neither can we look forward to that happy event which will forever put an end to our hapless divisions, and restore to the Church its primitive unity, purity, and prosperity, but in the pleasing prospect of their hearty and dutiful concurrence.

Dearly beloved brethren, why should *we* deem it a thing incredible that the Church of Christ, in this highly favored country, should resume that original unity, peace, and purity which belongs to its constitution, and constitutes its glory? Or, is there anything that can be justly deemed necessary for this desirable purpose, both to conform to the model and adopt the practice of the primitive Church, expressly exhibited in the New Testament? Whatever alterations this might produce in any or in all of the Churches, should, we think, neither be deemed inadmissible nor ineligible. Surely such alteration would be every way for the better, and not for the worse, unless we should suppose the divinely-inspired rule to be faulty, or defective. Were we, then, in our Church constitution and managements, to exhibit a complete conformity to the apostolic Church, would we not be, in that respect, as perfect as Christ intended we should be? And should not this suffice us?

It is, to us, a pleasing consideration that all the Churches of Christ which mutually acknowledge each other as such, are not only agreed in the great doctrines of faith and holiness, but are also materially agreed as to the positive ordinances of Gospel institution; so that our differences, at most, are about the things in which the kingdom of God does not consist, that is, about matters of private opinion or human invention. What a pity that the kingdom of God should be divided about such things! Who, then, would not be the first among us to give up human inventions in the worship of God, and to cease from imposing his private opinions upon his brethren, that our breaches might *thus* be healed? Who would not willingly conform to the original pattern laid down in the New Testament, for *this* happy purpose? Our dear brethren of all denominations will please to consider that we have our educational prejudices and particular customs to struggle against as well as they. But this we do sincerely declare, that there is nothing we have hitherto received as matter of faith or practice which is not expressly taught and enjoined in the word of God, either in express terms or approved precedent, that we would not heartily relinquish, that so we might return to the original constitutional unity of the Christian Church; and, in this happy unity, enjoy full communion with all our brethren, in peace and charity. The like dutiful condescension we candidly expect of all that are seriously impressed with a sense of the duty they owe to God, to each other, and to their perishing brethren of mankind. To this we call, we invite, our brethren of all denominations, by all the sacred motives which we have avouched as the impulsive reasons of our thus addressing them.

You are all, dear brethren, equally included as the objects of our love and esteem. With you all we desire to unite in the bonds of an entire Christian unity—Christ alone being the *head,* the center, his word the *rule;* an explicit belief of, and manifest conformity to it, in all things—*the terms.* More than this, you will not require of us; and less we can not require of you; nor, indeed, can we reasonably suppose any would desire it, for what good purpose would it serve? We dare neither assume nor propose the trite indefinite distinction between essentials and non-essentials, in matters of revealed truth and duty; firmly persuaded, that, whatever may be their comparative importance, simply considered, the high obligation of the Divine authority revealing, or enjoining them, renders the belief or performance of them absolutely essential to us, in so far as we know them. And to be ignorant of anything God has revealed, can neither be our duty nor our privilege. We humbly presume, then, dear brethren, you can have no relevant objection to meeting us upon this ground. And, we again beseech you, let it be known that it is the invitation of but few; by your accession we shall be many; and whether few or many, in the first instance, it is all one with respect to the event which must ultimately await the full information and hearty concurrence of all. Besides, whatever is to be done, must begin, some time, somewhere; and no matter where, nor by whom, if the Lord puts his hand to the work, it must surely prosper. And has he not been graciously pleased, upon many signal occasions, to bring to pass the greatest events from very small beginnings, and even by means the most unlikely. Duty then is ours; but events belong to God.

We hope, then, what we urge will neither be deemed an unreasonable nor an unseasonable undertaking. Why should it be thought unseasonable? Can any time be assigned, while things continue as they are, that would prove more favorable for such an attempt, or what could be supposed to make it so? Might it be the approximation of parties to a greater nearness, in point of public profession and similarity of customs? Or might it be expected from a gradual decline of bigotry? As to the former, it is a well-known fact, that where the difference is least, the opposition is always managed with a degree of vehemence inversely

proportioned to the merits of the cause. With respect
to the latter, though we are happy to say, that in some
cases and places, and, we hope, universally, bigotry is
upon the decline; yet we are not warranted, either
by the past or present, to act upon that supposition.
We have, as yet, by this means seen no such effect
produced; nor indeed could we reasonably expect it;
for there will always be multitudes of weak persons
in the Church, and these are generally most subject
to bigotry; add to this, that while divisions exist,
there will always be found interested men who will
not fail to support him; nor can we at all suppose
that Satan will be idle to improve an advantage so
important to the interests of his kingdom. And, let
it be further observed upon the whole, that, in matters
of similar importance to our secular interests, we
would by no means content ourselves with such kind
of reasoning. We might further add, that the attempt
here suggested not being of a partial, but of general
nature, it can have no just tendency to excite the
jealousy, or hurt the feelings of any party. On the
contrary, every effort toward a permanent Scriptural
unity among the Churches, upon the solid basis of
universally acknowledged and self-evident truths,
must have the happiest tendency to enlighten and con-
ciliate, by thus manifesting to each other their mutual
charity and zeal for the truth: "Whom I love in the
truth," saith the apostle, "and not I only, but also all
they that have known the truth; for the truth's sake,
which is in us, and shall be with us forever." Indeed,
if no such Divine and adequate basis of union can be
fairly exhibited as will meet the approbation of every
upright and intelligent Christian, nor such mode of
procedure adopted in favor of the weak as will not
oppress their consciences, then the accomplishment of
this grand object upon principle must be forever im-

possible. There would, upon this supposition, remain no other way of accomplishing it but merely by voluntary compromise, and good-natured accommodation. That such a thing, however, will be accomplished, one way or other, will not be questioned by any that allow themselves to believe that the commands and prayers of our Lord Jesus Christ will not utterly prove ineffectual. Whatever way, then, it is to be effected, whether upon the solid basis of Divinely-revealed truth, or the good-natured principle of Christian forbearance and gracious condescension, is it not equally practicable, equally eligible to us, as ever it can be to any; unless we should suppose ourselves destitute of that Christian temper and discernment which is essentially necessary to qualify us to do the will of our gracious Redeemer, whose express command to his people is, that there be "no divisions among them; but that they all walk by the same rule, speak the same thing, and be perfectly joined together in the same mind, and in the same judgment?" We believe then it is as practicable as it is eligible. Let us attempt it. "Up, and be doing, and the Lord will be with us."

Are we not all praying for that happy event, when there shall be but one fold, as there is but one chief Shepherd? What! shall we pray for a thing, and not strive to obtain it11 not use the necessary means to have it accomplished!! What said the Lord to Moses upon a piece of conduct somewhat similar? "Why criest thou unto me? Speak unto the children of Israel that they go forward, but lift thou up thy rod, and stretch out thine hand." Let the ministers of Jesus but embrace this exhortation, put their hand to the work, and encourage the people to go forward upon the firm ground of obvious truth, to unite in the bonds of an entire Christian unity; and who will venture to say that it would not soon be accomplished? "Cast ye up, cast ye up, prepare the way, take up the stumbling-block out of the way of my people," saith your God. To you, therefore, it peculiarly belongs, as the professed and acknowledged leaders of the people, to go before them in this good work, to remove human opinions and the inventions of men out of the way, by carefully separating this chaff from the pure wheat of primary and authentic revelation; casting out that assumed authority, that enacting and decreeing power by which those things have been imposed and established. To the ministerial department, then, do we look with anxiety. Ministers of Jesus, you can neither be ignorant of nor unaffected with the divisions and corruptions of his Church. His dying commands, his last and ardent prayers for the visible unity of his professing people, will not suffer you to be indifferent in this matter. You will not, you can not, therefore, be silent upon a subject of such vast importance to his personal glory and the happiness of his people—consistently you can not; for silence gives consent. You will rather lift up your voice like a trumpet to expose the heinous nature and dreadful consequences of those unnatural and antichristian divisions, which have so rent and ruined the Church of God. Thus, in justice to your station and character, honored of the Lord, would we hopefully anticipate your zealous and faithful efforts to heal the breaches of Zion; that God's dear children might dwell together in unity and love; but if otherwise * * * we forbear to utter it. (See Mal. ii: 1-10.)

Oh, that ministers and people would but consider that there are no divisions in the grave, nor in that world which lies beyond it! there our divisions must come to an end! we must all unite there! Would to God we could find in our hearts to put an end to our

short-lived divisions here; that so we might leave a
blessing behind us; even a happy and united Church.
What gratification, what utility, in the mean time, can
our divisions afford either to ministers or people?
Should they be perpetuated till the day of judgment,
would they convert one sinner from the error of his
ways, or save a soul from death? Have they any tendency to hide the multitude of sins that are so dishonorable to God, and hurtful to his people? Do
they not rather irritate and produce them? How innumerable and highly aggravated are the sins they
have produced, and are at this day producing, both
among professors and profane. We entreat, we beseech you then, dear brethren, by all those considerations, to concur in this blessed and dutiful attempt.
What is the work of all, must be done by all. Such was
the work of the tabernacle in the wilderness. Such
is the work to which you are called, not by the authority of man, but by Jesus Christ, and God the Father,
who raised him from the dead. By this authority are
you called to raise up the tabernacle of David, that
is fallen down among us, and to set it up upon its own
base. This you can not do, while you run every man
to his own house, and consult only the interests of his
own party. Until you associate, consult, and advise
together, and in a friendly and Christian manner ex-
plore the subject, nothing can be done. We would
therefore, with all due deference and submission, call
the attention of our brethren to the obvious and important duty of association. Unite with us in the
common cause of simple evangelical Christianity; in
this glorious cause we are ready to unite with you.
United we shall prevail. It is the cause of Christ, and
of our brethren throughout all the Churches, of
catholic unity, peace, and purity; a cause that must
finally prosper in spite of all opposition. Let us unite

to promote it. Come forward, then, dear brethren, and help with us. Do not suffer yourselves to be lulled asleep by that siren song of the slothful and reluctant professor: "The time is not yet come, the time is not come, saith he; the time that the Lord's house should be built." Believe him not. Do ye not discern the signs of the times? Have not the two witnesses arisen from their state of political death, from under the long proscription of ages? Have they not stood upon their feet, in the presence, and to the consternation and terror of their enemies? Has not their resurrection been accompanied with a great earthquake? Has not the tenth part of the great city been thrown down by it? Has not this event aroused the nations to indignation? Have they not been angry, yea, very angry? Therefore, O Lord, is thy wrath come upon them, and the time of the dead that they should be avenged, and that thou shouldst give reward to thy servants the prophets, and to them that fear thy name, both small and great; and that thou shouldst destroy them that have destroyed the earth. Who among us has not heard the report of these things, of these lightnings and thunderings and voices; of this tremendous earthquake and great hail; of these awful convulsions and revolutions that have dashed and are dashing to pieces the nations, like a potter's vessel? Yea, have not the remote vibrations of this dreadful shock been felt even by us, whom God has graciously placed at so great a distance?

What shall we say to these things? Is it time for us to sit still in our corruptions and divisions, when the Lord, by his word and providence, is so loudly and expressly calling us to repentance and reformation? "Awake, awake; put on thy strength, O Zion, put on thy beautiful garments, O Jerusalem, the holy city; for henceforth there shall no more come unto thee the uncircumcised and the unclean. Shake thyself from the dust, O Jerusalem; arise, loose thyself from the *bands* of thy neck, O captive daughter of Zion." Resume that precious, that dear-bought liberty, wherewith Christ has made his people free; a liberty from subjection to any authority but his own, in matters of religion. Call no man father, no man master on earth; for one is your master, even Christ, and all ye are brethren. Stand fast, therefore, in this precious liberty, and be not entangled again with the yoke of bondage. For the vindication of this precious liberty have we declared ourselves hearty and willing advocates. For this benign and dutiful purpose have we associated, that by so doing we might contribute the mite of our humble endeavors to promote it, and thus invite our brethren to do the same. As the first-fruits of our efforts for this blessed purpose we respectfully present to their consideration the following propositions, relying upon their charity and candor that they will neither despise nor misconstrue our humble and adventurous attempt. If they should in any measure serve, as a perliminary, to open up the way to a permanent Scriptural unity among the friends and lovers of truth and peace throughout the Churches, we shall greatly rejoice at it. We by no means pretend to dictate, and could we propose anything more evident, consistent, and adequate, it should be at their service. Their pious and dutiful attention to an object of such magnitude will induce them to communicate to us their emendations; and thus what is sown in weakness will be raised up in power. For certainly the collective graces that are conferred upon the Church, if duly united and brought to bear upon any point of commanded duty, would be amply sufficient for the right and successful performance of it. "For to one is given by the Spirit the word of wisdom;

to another the word of knowledge by the same Spirit; to another faith by the same Spirit; to another the discerning of spirits: but the manifestation of the Spirit is given to every man to profit withal. As every man, therefore, hath received the gift, even so minister the same one to another as good stewards of the manifold grace of God." In the face, then, of such instructions, and with such assurances of an all-sufficiency of Divine grace, as the Church has received from her exalted Head, we can neither justly doubt the concurrence of her genuine members; nor yet their ability, when dutifully acting together, to accomplish anything that is necessary for his glory and their own good; and certainly their visible unity in truth and holiness, in faith and love, is, of all things, the most conducive to both these, if we may credit the dying commands and prayers of our gracious Lord. In a matter, therefore, of such confessed importance, our Christian brethren, however unhappily distinguished by party names, will not, can not, withhold their helping hand. We are as heartily willing to be their debtors, as they are indispensably bound to be our benefactors. Come, then, dear brethren, we most humbly beseech you, cause your light to shine upon our weak beginnings, that we may see to work by it. Evince your zeal for the glory of Christ, and the spiritual welfare of your fellow-Christians, by your hearty and zealous co-operation to promote the unity, purity, and prosperity of his Church.

Let none imagine that the subjoined propositions are at all intended as an overture toward a new creed or standard for the Church, or as in any wise designed to be made a term of communion; nothing can be further from our intention. They are merely designed for opening up the way, that we may come fairly and firmly to original ground upon clear and certain premises, and take up things just as the apostles left them; that thus disentangled from the accruing embarrassments of intervening ages, we may stand with evidence upon the same ground on which the Church stood at the beginning. Having said so much to solicit attention and prevent mistake, we submit as follows:

PROP. 1. That the Church of Christ upon earth is essentially, intentionally, and constitutionally one; consisting of all those in every place that profess their faith in Christ and obedience to him and in all things according to the Scriptures, and that manifest the same by their tempers and conduct, and of none else; as none else can be truly and properly called Christians.

2. That although the Church of Christ upon earth must necessarily exist in particular and distinct societies, locally separate one from another, yet there ought to be no schism, no uncharitable divisions among them. They ought to receive each other as Christ Jesus hath also received them, to the glory of God. And for this purpose they ought all to walk by the same rule, to mind and speak the same thing; and to be perfectly joined together in the same mind, and in the same judgment.

3. That in order to this, nothing ought to be inculcated upon Christians as articles of faith; nor required of them as terms of communion, but what is expressly taught and enjoined upon them in the word of God. Nor ought anything to be admitted, as of Divine obligation, in their Church constitution and managements, but what is expressly enjoined by the authority of our Lord Jesus Christ and his apostles upon the new Testament Church; either in express terms or by approved precedent.

4. That although the Scriptures of the Old and New Testaments are inseparably connected, making

together but one perfect and entire revelation of the Divine will, for the edification and salvation of the Church, and therefore in that respect can not be separated; yet as to what directly and properly belongs to their immediate object, the New Testament is as perfect a constitution for the worship, discipline, and government of the New Testament Church, and as perfect a rule for the particular duties of its members, as the Old Testament was for the worship, discipline, and government of the Old Testament Church, and the particular duties of its members.

5. That with respect to the commands and ordinances of our Lord Jesus Christ, where the Scriptures are silent as to the express time or manner of performance, if any such there be, no human authority has power to interfere, in order to supply the supposed deficiency by making laws for the Church; nor can anything more be required of Christians in such cases, but only that they *so* observe these commands and ordinances as will evidently answer the declared and obvious end of their institution. Much less has any human authority power to impose new commands or ordinances upon the Church, which our Lord Jesus Christ has not enjoined. Nothing ought to be received into the faith or worship of the Church, or be made a term of communion among Christians, that is not as old as the New Testament.

6. That although inferences and deductions from Scripture premises, when fairly inferred, may be truly called the doctrine of God's holy word, yet are they not formally binding upon the consciences of Christians further than they perceive the connection, and evidently see that they are so; for their faith must not stand in the wisdom of men, but in the power and veracity of God. Therefore, no such deductions can be made terms of communion, but do properly belong

to the after and progressive edification of the Church. Hence, it is evident that no such deductions or inferential truths ought to have any place in the Church's confession.

7. That although doctrinal exhibitions of the great system of Divine truths, and defensive testimonies in opposition to prevailing errors, be highly expedient, and the more full and explicit they be for those purposes, the better, yet, as these must be in a great measure the effect of human reasoning, and of course must contain many inferential truths, they ought not to be made terms of Christian communion; unless we suppose, what is contrary to fact, that none have a right to the communion of the Church but such as possess a very clear and decisive judgment, or are come to a very high degree of doctrinal information; whereas the Church from the beginning did, and ever will, consist of little children and young men, as well as fathers.

8. That as it is not necessary that persons should have a particular knowledge or distinct apprehension of all Divinely-revealed truths in order to entitle them to a place in the Church; neither should they, for this purpose, be required to make a profession more extensive than their knowledge; but that, on the contrary, their having a due measure of Scriptural self-knowledge respecting their lost and perishing condition, by nature and practice, and of the way of salvation through Jesus Christ, accompanied with a profession of their faith in and obedience to him, in all things, according to his word, is all that is absolutely necessary to qualify them for admission into his Church.

9. That all that are enabled through grace to make such a profession, and to manifest the reality of it in their tempers and conduct, should consider each other

as the precious saints of God, should love each other as brethren, children of the same family and Father, temples of the same Spirit, members of the same body, subjects of the same grace, objects of the same Divine love, bought with the same price, and joint-heirs of the same inheritance. Whom God hath thus joined together no man should dare to put asunder.

10. That division among the Christians is a horrid evil, fraught with many evils. It is antichristian, as it destroys the visible unity of the body of Christ; as if he were divided against himself, excluding and ex-communicating a part of himself. It is antiscriptural, as being strictly prohibited by his sovereign authority; a direct violation of his express command. It is anti-natural, as it excites Christians to contemn, to hate, and oppose one another, who are bound by the highest and most endearing obligations to love each other as brethren, even as Christ has loved them. In a word, it is productive of confusion and of every evil work.

11. That (in some instances) a partial neglect of the expressly revealed will of God, and (in others) an assumed authority for making the approbation of human opinions and human inventions a term of com-munion, by introducing them into the constitution, faith, or worship of the Church, are, and have been, the immediate, obvious, and universally-acknowledged causes of all the corruptions and divisions that ever have taken place in the Church of God.

12. That all that is necessary to the highest state of perfection and purity of the Church upon earth is, first, that none be received as members but such as having that due measure of Scriptural self-knowledge described above, do profess their faith in Christ and obedience to him in all things according to the Scrip-tures; nor, secondly, that any be retained in her com-munion longer than they continue to manifest the

reality of their profession by their temper and conduct. Thirdly, that her ministers, duly and Scripturally qualified, inculcate none other things than those very articles of faith and holiness expressly revealed and enjoined in the word of God. Lastly, that in all their administrations they keep close by the observance of all Divine ordinances, after the example of the primitive Church, exhibited in the New Testament; without any additions whatsoever of human opinions or inventions of men.

13. Lastly. That if any circumstantials indispensable necessary to the observance of Divine ordinances be not found upon the page of express revelation, such, and such only, as are absolutely necessary for this purpose should be adopted under the title of human expedients, without any pretense to a more sacred origin, so that any subsequent alteration or difference in the observance of these things might produce no contention nor division in the Church.

From the nature and construction of these propositions, it will evidently appear, that they are laid in a designed subserviency to the declared end of our association; and are exhibited for the express purpose of performing a duty of previous necessity, a duty loudly called for in existing circumstances at the hand of every one that would desire to promote the interests of Zion; a duty not only enjoined, as has been already observed from Isaiah lvii: 14, but which is also there predicted of the faithful remnant as a thing in which they would voluntarily engage. "He that putteth his trust in me shall possess the land, and shall inherit my holy mountain; and shall say, Cast ye up, cast ye up, prepare the way; take up the stumbling-block out of the way of my people." To prepare the way for a permanent Scriptural unity among Christians, by calling up to their consideration fundamental truths, directing their attention to first principles, clearing the way before them by removing the stumbling-blocks—the rubbish of ages, which has been thrown upon it, and fencing it on each side, that in advancing toward the desired object they may not miss the way through mistake or inadvertency, by turning aside to the right hand or to the left—is, at least, the sincere intention of the above propositions. It remains with our brethren now to say how far they go toward answering this intention. Do they exhibit truths demonstrably evident in the light of Scripture and right reasoning, so that to deny any part of them the contrary assertion would be manifestly absurd and inadmissible? Considered as a preliminary for the above purpose, are they adequate, so that if acted upon, they would infallibly lead to the desired issue? If evidently defective in either of these respects, let them be corrected and amended, till they become sufficiently evident, adequate, and unexceptionable. In the meantime let them be examined with rigor, with all the rigor that justice, candor, and charity will admit. If we have mistaken the way, we shall be glad to be set right; but if, in the mean time, we have been happily led to suggest obvious and undeniable truths, which, if adopted and acted upon, would infallibly lead to the desired unity, and secure it when obtained, we hope it will be no objection that they have not proceeded from a General Council. It is not the voice of the multitude, but the voice of truth, that has power with the conscience, that can produce rational conviction and acceptable obedience. A conscience that awaits the decision of the multitude, that hangs in suspense for the casting vote of the majority, is a fit subject for the man of sin. This, we are persuaded, is the uniform sentiment of real Christians of every denomination. Would to God that all professors were such; then should our eyes soon behold the prosperity of Zion; we should soon see Jerusalem a quiet habitation. Union in truth has been, and ever must be, the desire and prayer of all such; "Union in truth" is our motto. The Divine word is our standard; in the Lord's name do we display our banners. Our eyes are upon the promises, "So shall they fear the name of the Lord from the west, and his glory from the rising of the sun." "When the enemy shall come in like a flood the Spirit of the Lord shall lift up a standard against him." Our humble desire is to be his standard-bearers, to fight under *his* banner, and with *his* weapons, "which are not carnal, but mighty through God to the pulling down of strongholds;" even all these strongholds of division, those partition walls of separation, which, like the walls of Jericho, have been built up, as it were, to the very heavens, to separate God's people, to divide *his* flock and so to prevent them from entering into their promised rest, at least in so far as it respects this world. An enemy hath done this, but he shall not finally prevail; "for the meek shall inherit the earth, and shall delight themselves in the abundance of peace." "And the kingdom and dominion, even the greatness of the kingdom under the whole heaven, shall be given to the people of the saints of the Most High, and they shall possess it forever." But this can not be in their present broken and divided state; "for a kingdom or a house divided against itself can not stand; but cometh to desolation." Now this has been the case with the Church for a long time. However, "the Lord will not cast off his people, neither will he forsake his heritage; but judgment shall return unto righteousness, and all the upright in heart shall follow it." To all such, and such alone, are our expectations directed. Come, then, ye blessed of the Lord, we have your prayers, let us also have your actual assistance. What, shall we pray for a thing and not strive to obtain it!

We call, we invite you again, by every consideration in these premises. You that are near, associate with us; you that are at too great a distance, associate as we have done. Let not the paucity of your number in any given district prove an insuperable discouragement. Remember Him that has said, "If two of you shall agree on earth as touching anything that they shall ask, it shall be done for them of my Father who is in heaven: for where two or three are gathered together in my name, there am I in the midst of them." With such a promise as this, for the attainment of every possible and promised good, there is no room for discouragement. Come on then, "ye that fear the Lord; keep not silence, and give him no rest till he make Jerusalem a joy and a praise in the earth." Put on that noble resolution dictated by the prophet, saying, "For Zion's sake will we not hold our peace, and for Jerusalem's sake we will not rest, until the righteousness thereof go forth as brightness, and the salvation thereof as a lamp that burneth." Thus impressed, you will find means to associate at such convenient distances as to meet at least once a month, to beseech the Lord to put an end to our lamentable divisions; to heal and unite his people, that his Church may resume her original constitutional unity and purity, and thus be exalted to the enjoyment of her promised prosperity, that the Jews may be speedily converted, and the fullness of the Gentiles brought in. Thus associated, you will be in a capacity to investigate the evil causes of our sad divisions; to consider and bewail their pernicious effects; and to mourn over them before the Lord—who hath said: "I will go and return to my place, till they acknowledge their offense and seek my face." Alas! then, what reasonable prospect can we have of being delivered from those sad calamities, which have so long afflicted the Church of God; while a party spirit, instead of bewailing, is everywhere justifying, the bitter principle of these pernicious evils; by insisting upon the right of rejecting those, however unexceptionable in other respects, who can not see with them in matters of private opinion, of human inference, that are nowhere expressly revealed or enjoined in the word of God. Thus associated, will the friends of peace, the advocates for Christian unity, be in a capacity to connect in larger circles, where several of those smaller societies may meet semi-annually at a convenient center; and thus avail themselves of their combined exertions for promoting the interests of the common cause. We hope that many of the Lord's ministers in all places will volunteer in this service, forasmuch as they know it is his favorite work, the very desire of his soul.

You lovers of Jesus, and beloved of him, however scattered in this cloudy and dark day, you love the truth as it is in Jesus; (if our hearts deceive us not) so do we. You desire union in Christ with all them that love him; so do we. You lament and bewail our sad divisions; so do we. You reject the doctrines and commandments of men, that you may keep the law of Christ; so do we. You believe the alone sufficiency of his word; so do we. You believe that the word itself ought to be our rule, and not any human explication of it; so do we. You believe that no man has a right to judge, to exclude, or reject his professing Christian brother, except in so far as he stands condemned or rejected by the express letter of the law; so do we. You believe that the great fundamental law of unity and love ought not to be violated to make way for exalting human opinions to an equality with express revelation, by making them articles of faith and terms of communion; so do we. You sincere and impartial followers of Jesus, friends of truth and peace, we dare not, we can not think otherwise of you; it would be doing violence to your character; it would be inconsistent with your prayers and profession so to do. We shall therefore have *your* hearty concurrence. But if any of our dear brethren, from whom we should expect better things, should, through weakness or prejudice, be in anything otherwise minded than we have ventured to suppose, we charitably hope that, in due time, God will reveal even this unto them; only let such neither refuse to come to the light, nor yet, through prejudice, reject it when it shines upon them. Let them rather seriously consider what we have thus most seriously and respectfully submitted to their consideration; weigh every sentiment in the balance of the sanctuary, as in the sight of God, with earnest prayer for, and humble reliance upon, his Spirit, and not in the spirit of self-sufficiency and party zeal; and, in so doing, we rest assured, the consequence will be happy, both for their own and the Church's peace. Let none imagine, that in so saying, we arrogate to ourselves a degree of intelligence superior to our brethren; much less superior to mistake. So far from this, our confidence is entirely founded upon the express Scripture and matter-of-fact evidence of the things referred to; which may, nevertheless, through inattention or prejudice, fail to produce their proper effect, as has been the case with respect to some of the most evident truths, in a thousand instances. But charity thinketh no evil; and we are far from surmising, though we must speak. To warn, even against possible evils, is certainly no breach of charity, as to be confident of the certainty of some things is no just argument of presumption. We by no means claim the approbation of our breth-

ren as to anything we have suggested for promoting
the sacred cause of Christian unity, further than it
carries its own evidence along with it; but we humbly
claim a fair investigation of the subject, and solicit
the assistance of our brethren in carrying into effect
what we have thus weakly attempted. It is our consolation, in the mean time, that the desired event, as
certain as it will be happy and glorious, admits of no
dispute, however we may hesitate or differ about the
proper means of promoting it. All we shall venture
to say as to this is, that we trust we have taken the
proper ground; at least, if we have not, we despair
of finding it elsewhere. For, if holding fast in profession and practice whatever is expressly revealed and
enjoined in the Divine standard does not, under the
promised influence of the Divine Spirit, prove an
adequate basis for promoting and maintaining unity,
peace, and purity, we utterly despair of attaining those
invaluable privileges by adopting the standard of any
party. To advocate the cause of unity, while espous-
ing the interests of a party, would appear as absurd
as for this country to take part with either of the bel-
ligerents in the present awful struggle, which has con-
vulsed and is convulsing the nations, in order to maintain her neutrality and secure her peace. Nay, it
would be adopting the very means by which the bewildered Church has, for hundreds of years past, been
rending and dividing herself into factions, for Christ's
sake, and for the truth's sake; though the first and
foundation truth of our Christianity is union with
him, and the very next to it in order, union with
each other in him—"that we receive each other, as
Christ has also received us, to the glory of God."
"For this is his commandment: That we believe in
his Son Jesus Christ, and love one another, as he gave
us commandment. And he that keepeth his command-

ments dwelleth in him, and he in him; and hereby we know that he dwelleth in us, by the Spirit which he hath given us," even the spirit of faith, and of love, and of a sound mind. And surely this should suffice us. But how to love and receive our brother, as we believe and hope Christ has received both him and us, and yet refuse to hold communion with him, is, we confess, a mystery too deep for us. If this be the way that Christ hath received us, then woe is unto us. We do not here intend a professed brother transgressing the express letter of the law, and refusing to be reclaimed. Whatever may be our charity in such a case, we have not sufficient evidence that Christ has received him, or that he has received Christ as his teacher and Lord. To adopt means, then, apparently subversive of the very end proposed, means which the experience of ages has evinced successful only in overthrowing the visible interests of Christianity, in counteracting, as far as possible, the declared intention, the express command of its Divine author, would appear in no wise a prudent measure for removing and preventing those evils. To maintain unity and purity has always been the plausible pretense of the compilers and abettors of human systems, and we believe, in many instances, their sincere intention; but have they at all answered the end? Confessedly, demonstrably, they have not; no, not even in the several parties which have most strictly adopted them; much less to the catholic professing body. Instead of her catholic constitutional unity and purity, what does the Church present us with, at this day, but a catalogue of sects and sectarian systems—each binding its respective party, by the most sacred and solemn engagements, to continue as it is to the end of the world; at least, this is confessedly the case with many of them. What a sorry substitute these for Christian unity and love! On the other hand, what a mercy is it that no human obligation that man can come under is valid against the truth. When the Lord the healer descends upon his people, to give them a discovery of the nature and tendency of those artificial bonds wherewith they have suffered themselves to be bound in their dark and sleepy condition, they will no more be able to hold them in a state of sectarian bondage than the withes and cords with which the Philistines bound Samson were able to retain him their prisoner, or than the bonds of Antichrist were to hold in captivity the fathers of the Reformation. May the Lord soon open the eyes of his people to see things in their true light, and excite them to come up out of their wilderness condition, out of this Babel of confusion, leaning upon their Beloved, and embracing each other in him, holding fast the unity of the spirit in the bond of peace. This gracious unity and unanimity in Jesus would afford the best external evidence of their union with him, and of their conjoint interest in the Father's love. "By this shall all men know that you are my disciples," says he, "if you have love one to another." And "This is my commandment, That you love one another as I have loved you; that you also love one another." And again, "Holy Father, keep through thine own name those whom thou hast given me, that they may be one, as we are;" even "all that shall believe in me; that they all may be one; as thou, Father, art in me and I in thee, that they also may be one in us: that the world may believe that thou hast sent me. And the glory which thou gavest me, I have given them; that they may be one, even as we are one; I in them, and thou in me, that they may be made perfect in one; and that the world may know that thou hast sent me, and hast loved them as thou hast loved me." May the Lord hasten it in his time. Farewell.

Peace be with all them that love our Lord Jesus Christ in sincerity. Amen.   THOMAS CAMPBELL,
THOMAS ACHESON.

APPENDIX.

To prevent mistakes, we beg leave to subjoin the following explanations. As to what we have done, our reasons for so doing, and the grand object we would desire to see accomplished, all these, we presume, are sufficiently declared in the foregoing pages. As to what we intend to do in our associate capacity, and the ground we have taken in that capacity, though expressly and definitely declared, yet these, perhaps, might be liable to some misconstruction. First, then, we beg leave to assure our brethren that we have no intention to interfere, either directly or indirectly, with the peace and order of the settled Churches, by directing any ministerial assistance with which the Lord may please to favor us, to make inroads upon such; or by endeavoring to erect Churches out of Churches, to distract and divide congregations. We have no nostrum, no peculiar discovery of our own to propose to fellow-Christians, for the fancied importance of which they should become followers of us. We propose to patronize nothing but the inculcation of the express word of God, either as to matter of faith or practice; but every one that has a Bible, and can read it, can read this for himself. Therefore, we have nothing new. Neither do we pretend to acknowledge persons to be ministers of Christ, and, at the same time, consider it our duty to forbid or discourage people to go to hear them, merely because they may hold some things disagreeable to us; much less to encourage their people to leave them on that account.

And such do we esteem all who preach a free, unconditional* salvation through the blood of Jesus to perishing sinners of every description, and who manifestly connect with this a life of holiness and pastoral diligence in the performance of all the duties of their sacred office, according to the Scriptures, of even all of whom, as to all appearance, it may be truly said to the objects of their charge: "They seek not *yours*, but *you*." May the good Lord prosper all such, by whatever name they are called, and hasten that happy period when Zion's watchmen shall see eye to eye, and all be called by the same name. *Such*, then, have nothing to fear from our association, were our resources equal to our utmost wishes. But all others we esteem as hirelings, as idle shepherds, and

---

* *"Unconditional"* salvation. There is neither *conditional* nor *unconditional* salvation so designated in holy Scripture. As respects procurement, there is no condition. *It is of grace.* But, like *life* and *health*, there are conditions of enjoyment. We could not procure, merit, or purchase it at any price. But when justified by faith and not by works, sanctified by the Spirit, or separated from the world, we are commanded to give "all diligence to make our calling and election sure."

There are means of spiritual life and health, as well as means of temporal or animal life and health. The latter are not more necessary than the former. God's whole universe is one great system of means and ends—physical, intellectual, moral, and religious. The means and the ends are alike of Divine institution, and are, therefore, inseparable.

The word *means* is found in the common version of the Christian Scriptures, only *twenty-one times*. Two-thirds of these are found in Paul's writings. *Poos* or *cipoos*—"how," or *by what means*—are equivalent terms. The *how* case and the *why* case are quite dissimilar. The *why* case demands the *cause*. The *how* case demands the *means*. Our English dictionaries authenticate these distinctions. They are, however, frequently unheeded in the pulpit and in the press.

should be glad to see the Lord's flock delivered from
their mouth, according to his promise. Our principal
and proper design, then, with respect to ministerial
assistants, such as we have described in our fifth resolution, is to direct their attention to those places
where there is manifest need for their labors; and
many such places there are; would to God it were
in our power to supply them. As to creeds and confessions, although we may appear to our brethren to
oppose them, yet this is to be understood only in *so
far* as they oppose the unity of the Church, by containing sentiments not expressly revealed in the word
of God; or, by the way of using them, become the
instruments of a human or implicit faith, or oppress
the weak of God's heritage. Where they are liable
to none of those objections, we have nothing against
them. It is the *abuse* and not the *lawful use* of such
compilations that we oppose. See Proposition 7.
Our intention, therefore, with respect to all the
Churches of Christ is perfectly amicable. We heartily
wish their reformation, but by no means their hurt or
confusion. Should any affect to say that our coming
forward as we have done, in advancing and publishing such things, has a manifest tendency to distract
and divide the Churches, or to make a new party, we
treat it as a confident and groundless assertion, and
must suppose they have not duly considered, or, at
least, not well understood the subject.

All we shall say to this at present, is, that if the
Divine word be not the standard of a party, then are
we not a party, for we have adopted no other. If to
maintain its alone sufficiency be not a party principle,
then are we not a party. If to justify this principle
by our practice, in making a rule of it, and of *it alone,*
and not of our own opinions, nor of those of others,
be not a party principle, then are we not a party. If

to propose and practice neither more nor less than it expressly reveals and enjoins be not a partial business, then are we not a party. These are the very sentiments we have approved and recommended, as a society formed for the express purpose of promoting Christian unity, in opposition to a party spirit. Should any tell us that to do these things is impossible without the intervention of human reason and opinion, we humbly thank them for the discovery. But who ever thought otherwise? Were we not rational subjects, and of course capable of understanding and forming opinions, would it not evidently appear that, to us, revelation of any kind would be quite useless, even supposing it as evident as mathematics? We pretend not, therefore, to divest ourselves of reason, that we may become quiet, inoffensive, and peaceable Christians; nor yet, of any of its proper and legitimate operations upon Divinely-revealed truths. We only pretend to assert, what every one that pretends to reason must acknowledge, namely, that there is a manifest distinction between an express Scripture declaration, and the conclusion or inference which may be deduced from it; and that the former may be clearly understood, even where the latter is but imperfectly if at all perceived; and that we are at least as certain of the declaration as we can be of the conclusion we draw from it; and that, after all, the conclusion ought not to be exalted above the premises, so as to make void the declaration for the sake of establishing our own conclusion; and that, therefore, the express commands to preserve and maintain inviolate Christian unity and love, ought not to be set aside to make way for exalting our inferences above the express authority of God. Our inference, upon the whole, is, that where a professing Christian brother opposes or refuses nothing either in faith or practice for which there can be expressly produced a "Thus saith the Lord," that we ought not to reject him because he can not see with our eyes as to matters of human inference, of private judgment. "Through thy knowledge shall the weak brother perish? How walkest thou not charitably?" Thus we reason, thus we conclude, to make no conclusion of our own, nor of any other fallible fellow-creature, a rule of faith or duty to our brother. Whether we refuse reason, then, or abuse it, in our so doing, let our brethren judge. But, after all, we have only ventured to suggest what, in other words, the apostle has expressly taught; namely, that the strong ought to bear with the infirmities of the weak, and not to please themselves; that we ought to receive him that is weak in the faith, because God has received him. In a word, that we ought to receive one another, as Christ hath also received us to the glory of God. We dare not, therefore, patronize the rejection of God's dear children, because they may not be able to see alike in matters of human inference— of private opinion; and such we esteem all things not expressly revealed and enjoined in the word of God. If otherwise, we know not what private opinion means. On the other hand, should our peaceful and affectionate overture for union in truth prove offensive to any of our brethren, or occasion distrubances in any of the Churches, the blame can not be attached to us. We have only ventured to persuade, and, if possible, to excite to the performance of an important duty—a duty equally incumbent upon us all. Neither have we pretended to dictate to *them* what *they* should do. We have only proposed what appeared to *us* most likely to promote the desired event, humbly submitting the whole premises to their candid and impartial investigation, to be altered, corrected, and amended, as they see cause, or to adopt any other plan that may appear more just and unexceptionable. As for ourselves, we have taken all due care, in the mean time, to take no step that might throw a stumbling-block in the way, that might prove now, or at any future period, a barrier to prevent the accomplishment of that most desirable object, either by joining to support a party, or by patronizing anything as articles of faith or duty not expressly enjoined in the Divine standard; as we are sure, whatever alterations may take place, *that* will stand. That considerable alterations must and will take place, in the standards of all the sects, before that glorious object can be accomplished, no man, that duly considers the matter, can possibly doubt. In so far, then, we have at least endeavored to act consistently; and with the same consistency would desire to be instrumental in erecting as many Churches as possible throughout the desolate places of God's heritage, upon the same catholic foundation, being well persuaded that every such erection will not only in the issue prove an accession to the general cause, but will also, in the mean time, be a step toward it, and, of course, will reap the first-fruits of that blissful harvest that will fill the face of the world with fruit. For if the first Christian Churches, walking in the fear of the Lord in holy unity and unanimity, enjoyed the comforts of the Holy Spirit, and were increased and edified, we have reason to believe that walking in their footsteps will everywhere and at all times insure the same blessed privileges. And it is in an exact conformity to their recorded and approved example, that we, through grace, would be desirous to promote the erection of Churches; and this we believe to be quite practicable, if the legible and authentic records of *their* faith and practice be handed down to *us* upon the page of New Testament Scripture; but if otherwise, we can not help it. Yet, even in this case, might we not humbly presume that the Lord would take the will for the deed? for if there be first a willing mind, we are told, "it is accepted according to what a man hath, and not according to what he hath not." It would appear, then, that sincerely and humbly adopting this model, with an entire reliance upon promised grace, we can not, we shall not, be disappointed. By this, at least, we shall get rid of two great evils, which, we fear, are at this day grievously provoking the Lord to plead a controversy with the Churches: we mean the taking and giving of unjust offenses; judging and rejecting each other in matters wherein the Lord hath not judged, in a flat contradiction to his expressly-revealed will. But, according to the principle adopted, we can neither take offense at our brother for his private opinions, if he be content to hold them as such, nor yet offend him with ours, if he do not usurp the place of the lawgiver; and even suppose he should, in this case we judge him, not for his *opinions,* but for his *presumption.* "There is one Lawgiver, who is able to save and to destroy: who art thou that judgest another?" But further, to prevent mistakes, we beg leave to explain our meaning in a sentence or two, which might possibly be misunderstood. In the first page we say, that no man has a right to judge his brother, except in so far as he manifestly violates the express letter of the law. By the law here, and elsewhere, when taken in this latitude, we mean that whole revelation of faith and duty expressly declared in the Divine word, taken together, or in its due connection, upon every article, and not any detached sentence. We understand it as extending to all prohibitions, as well as to all requirements. "Add thou not unto his words, lest he reprove thee, and thou be found a liar." We dare, therefore, neither do nor receive anything as of Divine obligation for

which there can not be expressly produced a "Thus
saith the Lord," either in express terms or by approved precedent. According to this rule we judge,
and beyond it we dare not go. Taking this sentiment
in connection with the last clause of the fifth resolution, we are to be understood, of all matters of faith
and practice, of primary and universal obligation;
that is to say, of express revelation; that nothing be
inculcated, as such, for which there can not be expressly produced a "Thus saith the Lord," as above, without, at the same time, interfering directly or indirectly
with the private judgment of any individual, which
does not expressly contradict the express letter of the
law, or add to the number of its institutions. Every
sincere and upright Christian will understand and do
the will of God, in every instance, to the best of his
skill and judgment; but in the application of the
general rule to particular cases there may, and doubtless will, be some variety of opinion and practice.
This, we see, was actually the case in the apostolic
Churches, without any breach of Christian unity; and
if this was the case at the erection of the Christian
Church from among Jews and Gentiles, may we not
reasonably expect that it will be the same at her restoration from under her long antichristian and sectarian desolations?

With a direct reference to this state of things, and,
as we humbly think, in a perfect consistency with the
foregoing explanations, have we expressed ourselves
in the twenty-ninth page, wherein we declare ourselves
ready to relinquish whatever we have hitherto received
as matter of faith or practice, not expressly taught and
enjoined in the word of God, so that we and our brethren might, by this mutual concession, return together
to the original constitutional unity of the Christian
Church, and dwell together in peace and charity. By

this proposed relinquishment we are to be understood in the first instance, of our manner of holding those things, and not simply of the things themselves; for no man can relinquish his opinions or practices till once convinced that they are wrong; and this he may not be immediately, even supposing they were so. One thing, however, he may do: when not bound by an express command, he need not impose them upon others, by anywise requiring their approbation; and when this is done, the things, to them, are as good as dead, yea, as good as buried, too, being thus removed out of the way. Has not the apostle set us a noble example of this in his pious and charitable zeal for the comfort and edification of his brother, in declaring himself ready to forego his rights (not indeed to break commandments) rather than stumble, or offend, his brother? And who knows not that the Hebrew Christians abstained from certain meats, observed certain days, kept the passover, circumcised their children, etc., etc., while no such things were practiced by the Gentile converts, and yet no breach of unity while they charitably forbore one with the other. But had the Jews been expressly prohibited, or the Gentiles expressly enjoined, by the authority of Jesus, to observe these things, could they, in such a case, have lawfully exercised this forbearance? But where no express law is, there can be no formal, no intentional transgression, even although its implicit and necessary consequences had forbid the thing, had they been discovered. Upon the whole, we see one thing is evident: the Lord will bear with the weaknesses, the involuntary ignorances, and mistakes of his people, though not with their presumption. Ought they not, therefore, to bear with each other—"to preserve the unity of the Spirit in the bond of peace; forbearing one with another in love?" What says the Scripture? We say, then, the declaration referred to is to be thus understood in the first instance; though we do not say but something further is intended. For certainly we may lawfully suspend both declaration and practice upon any subject, where the law is silent; vhen to do otherwise must prevent the accomplish- nent of an expressly-commanded and highly-impor- tant duty; and such, confessedly, is the thing in ques- tion. What says the apostle? "All things are lawful for me; but all things are not expedient. All things are lawful for me; but all things edify not." It seems, then, that among lawful things which might be forborne—that is, as we humbly conceive, things not expressly commanded—the governing principle of the apostle's conduct was the edification of his brethren of the Church of God. A Divine principle this, in- deed! May the Lord God infuse it into all his people. Were all those nonperceptive opinions and practices which have been maintained and exalted to the de- struction of the Church's unity, counterbalanced with the breach of the express law of Christ, and the black catalogue of mischiefs which have necessarily ensued, on which side, think you, would be the preponderance? When weighed in the balance with this monstrous complex evil, would they not all appear lighter than vanity? Who, then, would not relinquish a cent to obtain a kingdom! And here let it be noted, that it is not the renunciation of an opinion or practice as sinful that is proposed or intended, but merely a ces- sation from the publishing or practicing it, so as to give offense; a thing men are in the habit of doing every day for their private comfort or secular emol- ument, where the advantage is of infinitely less im- portance. Neither is there here any clashing of duties, as if to forbear was a sin and also to practice was sin; the thing to be forborne being a matter of private opinion, which, though not expressly forbidden, yet are we by no means expressly commanded to practice; whereas we are expressly commanded to endeavor to maintain the unity of the Spirit in the bond of peace. And what says the apostle to the point in hand? "Hast thou faith," says he; "have it to thyself before God. Happy is the man that condemneth not himself in the thing which he alloweth."

It may be further added, that a still higher and more perfect degree of uniformity is intended, though neither in the first nor second instance, which are but so many steps toward it; namely, the utter abolition of those minor differences, which have been greatly increased, as well as continued, by our unhappy manner of treating them, in making them the subject of perpetual strife and contention. Many of the opinions which are now dividing the Church, had they been let alone, would have been long since dead and gone; but the constant insisting upon them, as articles of faith and terms of salvation, have so beaten them into the minds of men, that, in many instances, they would as soon deny the Bible itself as give up one of those opinions. Having thus embraced contentions and preferred divisions to that constitutional unity, peace, and charity so essential to Christianity, it would appear that the Lord, in righteous judgment, has abandoned his professing people to the awful scourge of those evils; as, in an instance somewhat similar, he formerly did his highly-favored Israel. "My people," says he, "would not hearken to my voice. So I gave them up to their own hearts' lusts, and they walked in their own counsels." "Israel hath made many altars to sin: therefore altars shall be unto him to sin." Thus, then, are we to be consistently understood as fully and fairly intending, on *our* part, what we have declared and proposed to our brethren, as, to *our* ap-

prehension, incumbent upon *them* and *us,* for putting
an end forever to our sad and lamentable schisms.
Should any object and say that, after all, the fullest
compliance with everything proposed and intended
would not restore the Church to the desired unity, as
there might remain differences of opinion and practice, let such but duly consider what properly belongs
to the unity of the Church, and we are persuaded this
objection will vanish. Does not the visible Scriptural
unity of the Christian Church consist in the unity of
her public profession and practice, and, under this, in
the manifest charity of her members, one toward
another, and not in the unity of private opinion and
practice of every individual? Was not this evidently
the case in the apostles' days, as has been already observed? If so, the objection falls to the ground. And
here let it be noted, (if the hint be at all necessary,)
that we are speaking of the unity of the Church considered as a great, visible, professing body, consisting
of many co-ordinate associations; each of these, in
its aggregate or associate capacity, walking by the
same rule, professing and practicing the same things.
That this visible Scriptural unity be preserved without
corruption, or breach of charity, throughout the whole,
and in every particular worshiping society or Church,
is the grand desideratum—the thing strictly enjoined
and greatly to be desired. An agreement in the expressly-revealed will of God is the adequate and firm
foundation of this unity; ardent prayer, accompanied
with prudent, peaceable, and persevering exertion, in
the use of all Scriptural means for accomplishing it,
are the things humbly suggested and earnestly recommended to our brethren. If we have mistaken the
way, their charity will put us right; but if otherwise,
their fidelity to Christ and his cause will excite them

to come forth speedily, to assist with us in this blessed work.

After all, should any impeach us with the vague charge of Latitudinarianism, (let none be startled at this gigantic term,) it will prove as feeble an opponent to the glorious cause in which we, however weak and unworthy, are professedly engaged, as the Zamzummins did of old, to prevent the children of Lot from taking possession of their inheritance. If we take no greater latitude than the Divine law allows, either in judging of persons or doctrines—either in profession or practice, (and this is the very thing we humbly propose and sincerely intend,) may we not reasonably hope that such a latitude will appear, to every upright Christian, perfectly innocent and unexceptionable? If this be Latitudinarianism, it must be a good thing, and, therefore, the more we have of it the better; and may be it is, for we are told, "the commandment is exceeding broad;" and we intend to go just as far as it will suffer us, but not one hair-breadth further; so, at least, says our profession. And surely it will be time enough to condemn our practice, when it appears manifestly inconsistent with the profession we have thus precisely and explicitly made. We here refer to the whole of the foregoing premises. But were this word as bad as it is long, were it stuffed with evil from beginning to end, may be it better belongs to those that brandish it so unmercifully at their neighbors, especially if they take a greater latitude than their neighbors do, or than the Divine law allows. Let the case, then, be fairly submitted to all that know their Bible, to all that take upon them to see with their own eyes, to judge for themselves. And here let it be observed once for all, that it is only to such we direct our attention in the foregoing pages. As for those that either can not or will not see and judge for themselves, they must be content to follow their leaders till they come to their eyesight, or determine to make use of the faculties and means of information which God has given them; with such, in the mean time, it would be useless to reason, seeing that they either confessedly can not see, or have completely resigned themselves to the conduct of their leaders, and are therefore determined to hearken to none but them. If there be none such, however, we are happily deceived; but, if so, we are not the only persons that are thus deceived; for this is the common fault objected by almost all the parties to each other, namely, that they either can not or will not see; and it would be hard to think they were all mistaken; the fewer there be, however, of this description, the better. To all those then that are disposed to see and think for themselves, to form their judgment by the Divine word itself, and not by any human explication of it, humbly relying upon and looking for the promised assistance of Divine teaching, and not barely trusting to their own understanding—to all such do we gladly commit our cause, being persuaded that, at least, they will give it a very serious and impartial consideration, as being truly desirous to know the truth. To you, then, we appeal, in the present instance, as we have also done from the beginning. Say, we beseech you, to whom does the charge of Latitudinarianism, when taken in a bad sense, (for we have supposed it may be taken in a good sense,) most truly and properly belong, whether to those that will neither add nor diminish anything as to matter of faith and duty, either to or from what is expressly revealed and enjoined in the holy Scriptures, or to those who pretend to go further than this, or to set aside some of its express declarations and injunctions, to make way for their own opinions, inferences, and conclusions? Whether to those who profess their willingness to hold communion with their acknowledged Christian brethren, when they neither manifestly oppose nor contradict anything expressly revealed and enjoined in the sacred standard, or to those who reject such, when professing to believe and practice whatever is expressly revealed and enjoined therein, without, at the same time, being *alleged,* much less *found* guilty, of anything to the contrary, but instead of this asserting and declaring their hearty assent and consent to everything for which there can be expressly produced a "Thus saith the Lord," either in express terms or by approved precedent? To which of these, think you, does the odious charge of Latitudinarianism belong? Which of them takes the greatest latitude? Whether those that expressly judge and condemn where they have no express warrant for so doing, or those that absolutely refuse so to do? And we can assure our brethren, that such things are and have been done, to our own certain knowledge, and even where we least expected it; and that it is to this discovery, as much as to many other things, that we stand indebted for that thorough conviction of the evil state of things in the Churches, which has given rise to our association. As for our part, we dare no longer give our assent to such proceedings; we dare no longer concur in expressly asserting or declaring anything in the name of the Lord, that he has not expressly declared in his holy word. And until such time as Christians come to see the evil of doing otherwise, we see no rational ground to hope that there can be either unity, peace, purity, or prosperity, in the Church of God. Convinced of the truth of this, we would humbly desire to be instrumental in pointing out to our fellow-Christians the evils of such conduct. And if we might venture to give our opinion of such proceedings, we would not hesitate to say, that they appear to include three great evils—evils truly great in themselves, and at the same time productive of most evil consequences.

First, to determine expressly, in the name of the Lord, when the Lord has not expressly determined, appears to us a very great evil. (See Deut. xviii: 20) : "The prophet that shall presume to speak a word in my name, which I have not. commanded him to speak, even that prophet shall die." The apostle Paul, no doubt, well aware of this, cautiously distinguishes between his own judgment and the express injunctions of the Lord. (See 1 Cor. vii: 25 and 40.) Though, at the same time, it appears that he was as well convinced of the truth and propriety of his declarations, and of the concurrence of the Holy Spirit with his judgment, as any of our modern determiners may be; for "I think," said he, "that I have the Spirit of God;" and we doubt much, if the best of them could honestly say more than this; yet we see that, with all this, he would not bind the Church with his conclusions; and, for this very reason, as he expressly tells us, because, as to the matter on hand, he had no commandment of the Lord. He spoke by permission, and not by commandment, as one that had obtained mercy to be faithful, and therefore would not forge his Master's name by affixing it to his own conclusions, saying, "The Lord saith," when the Lord had not spoken.

A second evil is, not only judging our brother to be absolutely wrong, because he differs from our opinions, but more especially, our judging him to be a transgressor of the law in so doing, and, of course, treating him as such by censuring or otherwise exposing him to contempt, or, at least, preferring ourselves

before him in our own judgment, saying, as it were,
Stand by, I am holier than thou.

A third and still more dreadful evil is, when we not
only, in this kind of way, judge and set at naught our
brother, but, moreover, proceed as a Church, acting
and judging in the name of Christ, not only to determine that our brother is wrong because he differs
from our determinations, but also, in connection with
this, proceed so far as to determine the merits of the
cause by rejecting him, or casting him out of the
Church, as unworthy of a place in her communion, and
thus, as far as in our power, cutting him off from the
kingdom of heaven. In proceeding thus, we not only
declare that, in our judgment, our brother is in an
error, which we may sometimes do in a perfect con-
sistence with charity, but we also take upon us to
judge, as acting in the name and by the authority of
Christ, that his error cuts him off from salvation;
that continuing such, he has no inheritance in the kingdom of Christ and of God. If not, what means our
refusing him—our casting him out of the Church,
which is the kingdom of God in this world? For
certainly, if a person have no right, according to the
Divine word, to a place in the Church of God upon
earth, (which we say he has not, by thus rejecting
him,) he can have none to a place in the Church in
heaven—unless we should suppose that those whom
Christ by his word rejects here, he will nevertheless
receive hereafter. And surely it is by the word that
every Church pretends to judge; and it is by this rule,
in the case before us, that the person in the judgment
of the Church stands rejected. Now is not this, to
all intents and purposes, determining the merits of the
cause? Do we not conclude that the person's error
cuts him off from all ordinary possibility of salvation,
by thus cutting him off from a place in the Church, out

of which there is no ordinary possibility of salvation? Does he not henceforth become to us as a heathen man and a publican? Is he not reckoned among the number of those that are without, whom God judgeth? If not, what means such a solemn determination? Is it anything, or is it nothing, for a person to stand rejected by the Church of God? If such rejection confessedly leave the man still in the same safe and hopeful state as to his spiritual interests, then, indeed, it becomes a matter of mere indifference; for as to his civil and natural privileges, it interferes not with them. But the Scripture gives us a very different view of the matter; for there we see that those that stand justly rejected by the Church on earth, have no room to hope for a place in the Church of heaven. "What ye bind on earth shall be bound in heaven" is the awful sanction of the Church's judgment, in justly rejecting any person. Take away this, and it has no sanction at all. But the Church rejecting, always pretends to have acted justly in so doing, and, if so, whereabouts does it confessedly leave the person rejected, if not in a state of damnation? that is to say, if it acknowledge itself to be a Church of Christ, and to have acted justly. If, after all, any particular Church acting thus should refuse the foregoing conclusion, by saying: We meant no such thing concerning the person rejected; we only judged him unworthy of a place among *us,* and therefore put him away, but there are other Churches that may receive him;—we would be almost tempted to ask such a Church, if those other Churches be Churches of Christ, and if so, pray what does it account itself? Is it anything more or better than a Church of Christ? And whether, if those other Churches do their duty as faithful Churches, any of them would receive the person it had rejected? If it be answered that, in acting

faithfully, none of those other Churches either could
or would receive him, then, confessedly, in the judgment of this particular Church, the person ought to be
universally rejected; but if otherwise, it condemns itself of having acted unfaithfully, nay cruelly, toward
a Christian brother, a child of God, in thus rejecting
him from the heritage of the Lord, in thus cutting him
òff from his Father's house, as the unnatural brethren
did the beloved Joseph.   But even suppose some one
or other of those unfaithful Churches should receive
the outcast, would their unfaithfulness in so doing
nullify, in the judgment of this more faithful Church,
its just and faithful decision in rejecting him?   If not,
then, confessedly, in its judgment, the person still remains under the influence of its righteous sentence,
debarred from the kingdom of heaven;   that is to say,
if it believe the Scriptures, that what it has righteously done upon earth is ratified in heaven.   We see no
way that a Church acting *thus* can possibly get rid of
this *awful conclusion,* except it acknowledge that the
person it has rejected from its communion still has a
right to the communion of the Church; but if it
acknowledge *this,* whereabout does it leave itself, in
thus shutting out a fellow-Christian, an acknowledged
brother, a child of God?   Do we find any parallel for
such conduct in the inspired records, except in the
case of Diotrephes, of whom the apostle says, "Who
loveth to have the pre-eminence among them, receiveth
us not, prating against us with malicious words: and
not content therewith, neither doth he himself receive
the brethren, and forbiddeth them that would, and
casteth them out of the Church."
   But further, suppose another Church should receive
this castaway, this person which this faithful Church
supposed itself to have righteously rejected, would
not the Church so doing incur the displeasure, nay,

even the *censure* of the Church that had rejected him? and, we should think, justly too if he deserved to be rejected. And would not this naturally produce a schism between the Churches? Or, if it be supposed that a schism did already exist, would not this manifestly tend to perpetuate and increase it? If one Church, receiving those whom another puts away, will not be productive of schism, we must confess we can not tell what would. That Church, therefore, must surely act very schismatically, very unlike a Church of Christ, which necessarily presupposes or produces schism in order to shield an oppressed fellow-Christian from the dreadful consequences of its unrighteous proceedings. And is not this confessedly the case with every Church which rejects a person from its communion while it acknowledges him to be a fellow-Christian; and, in order to excuse this piece of cruelty, says he may find refuge some place else, some other Church may receive him? For, as we have already observed, if no schism did already exist, one Church receiving those whom another has rejected must certainly make one. The same evils also will as justly attach to the conduct of an individual who refuses or breaks communion with a Church because it will not receive or make room for his private opinions or self-devised practices in its public profession and managements; for does he not, in this case, actually take upon him to judge the Church which he thus rejects as unworthy of the communion of Christians? And is not this, to all intents and purposes, declaring it, in his judgment, excommunicate, or at least worthy of excommunication?

Thus have we briefly endeavored to show our brethren what evidently appears to us to be the heinous nature and dreadful consequences of that truly Latitudinarian principle and practice which is the bitter root of

almost all our divisions, namely, the imposing of our
private opinions upon each other as articles of faith or
duty, introducing them into the public profession and
practice of the Church, and acting upon them as if
they were the express law of Christ, by judging and
rejecting our brethren that differ from us in those
things, or at least by *so* retaining them in our public
profession and practice that our brethren can not join
with us, or we with them, without becoming actually
partakers in those things which they or we can not in
conscience approve, and which the word of God
nowhere expressly enjoins upon us. To cease from all
such things, by simply returning to the original standard of Christianity, the profession and practice of the
primitive Church, as expressly exhibited upon the
sacred page of the New Testament Scripture, is the
only possible way that we can perceive to get rid of
those evils. And we humbly think that a uniform
agreement in *that* for the preservation of charity would
be infinitely preferable to our contentions and divisions; nay, that such a uniformity is the very thing
that the Lord requires if the New Testament be a perfect model, a sufficient formula for the worship, discipline, and government of the Christian Church. Let
us do as we are there expressly told *they* did, say as
they said; that is, profess and practice as therein expressly enjoined by precept and precedent, in every
possible instance, after *their* approved example; and
in so doing we shall realize and exhibit all that unity
and uniformity that the primitive Church possessed,
or that the law of Christ requires. But if, after all,
our brethren can point out a better way to regain and
preserve that Christian unity and charity expressly enjoined upon the Church of God, we shall thank them
for the discovery, and cheerfully embrace it.

Should it still be urged that this would open a wide

door to Latitudinarianism, seeing all that profess
Christianity profess to receive the holy Scriptures, and
yet differ so widely in their religious sentiments, we
say, let them profess what they will, their difference in
religious profession and practice originates in their
departure from what is expressly revealed and enjoined, and not in their strict and faithful conformity to
it, which is the thing we humbly advise for putting an
end to those differences. But you may say, Do they
not already all agree in the letter, though differing so
far in sentiment? However this may be, have they
all agreed to make the letter their rule, or, rather, to
make it the subject-matter of their profession and
practice? Surely not, or else they would all profess
and practice the same thing. Is it not as evident as
the shining light that the Scriptures exhibit but one
and the self-same subject-matter of profession and
practice, at all times and in all places, and that, there--
fore, to say as it declares, and to do as it prescribes in
all its holy precepts, its approved and imitable examples, would unite the Christian Church in a holy
sameness of profession and practice throughout the
whole world? By the Christian Church throughout
the world, we mean the aggregate of such professors as we have described in Propositions 1 and
8, even all that mutually acknowledge each other
as Christians, upon the manifest evidence of their
faith, holiness, and charity. It is such only we
intend when we urge the necessity of Christian unity.
Had only such been all along recognized as the genuine subjects of our holy religion, there would not, in
all probability, have been so much apparent need for
human formulas to preserve an external formality of
professional unity and soundness in the faith, but artificial and superficial characters need artificial means
to train and unite them. A manifest attachment to our

Lord Jesus Christ in faith, holiness, and charity, was the original criterion of Christian character, the distinguishing badge of our holy profession, the foundation and cement of Christian unity. But now, alas! and long since, an external name, a mere educational formality of sameness in the profession of a certain standard or formula of human fabric, with a very moderate degree of what is called morality, forms the bond and foundation, the root and reason of ecclesiastical unity. Take away from such the technicalness of their profession, the shibboleth of party, and what have they more? What have they left to distinguish and hold them together? As for the Bible, they are but little beholden to it, they have learned little from it, they know little about it, and therefore depend as little upon it. Nay, they will even tell you it would be of no use to them without their formula; they could not know a Papist from a Protestant by *it;* that merely by *it* they could neither keep themselves nor the Church right for a single week. You might preach to them what you please, they could not distinguish truth from error. Poor people, it is no wonder they are so fond of their formula! Therefore they that exercise authority upon them and tell them what they are to believe and what they are to do, are called benefactors. These are the reverend and right reverend authors, upon whom they *can* and *do* place a more entire and implicit confidence than upon the holy apostles and prophets; those plain, honest, unassuming men, who would never venture to say or do anything in the name of the Lord without an express revelation from Heaven, and therefore were never distinguished by the venerable titles of Rabbi or Reverend, but just simple Paul, John, Thomas, etc. *These* were but servants. They did not assume to legislate, and, therefore, neither assumed nor received any hon-

orary titles among men, but merely such as were descriptive of their office. And how, we beseech you,
shall this gross and prevalent corruption be purged out
of the visible professing Church but by a radical reform, but by returning to the original simplicity, the
primitive purity of the Christian institution, and, of
course, taking up things just as we find them upon the
sacred page. And who is there that knows anything
of the present state of the Church who does not perceive that it is greatly overrun with the aforesaid
evils? Or who that reads his Bible, and receives the
impressions it must necessarily produce upon the re-
ceptive mind by the statements it exhibits, does not
perceive that such a state of things is as distinct from
genuine Christianity as oil is from water?

On the other hand, is it not equally as evident that
not one of all the erroneous tenets and corrupt practices which have so defamed and corrupted the public
profession and practice of Christianity, could ever
have appeared in the world had men kept close by the
express letter of the Divine law, had they thus held
fast that form of sound words contained in the holy
Scriptures, and considered it their duty so to do, unless they blame those errors and corruptions upon the
very form and expression of the Scriptures, and say
that, taken in their letter and connection, they immediately, and at first sight, as it were, exhibit the picture they have drawn? Should any be so bold as to
assert this, let them produce their performance, the
original is at hand; and let them show us line for
line, expression for expression, precept and precedent
for practice, without the torture of criticism, inference, or conjecture, and then we shall honestly blame
the whole upon the Bible, and thank those that will
give us an expurged edition of it, call it constitution,
or formula, or what you please, that will not be liable

to lead the simple, unlettered world into those gross
mistakes, those contentions, schisms, excommunications, and persecutions which have proved so detri-
mental and scandalous to our holy religion.

Should it be further objected, that even this strict
literal uniformity would neither infer nor secure unity
of sentiment; it is granted that, in a certain degree,
it would not; nor, indeed, is there anything either in
Scripture or the nature of things that should induce
us to expect an entire unity of sentiment in the present
imperfect state. The Church may, and we believe
will, come to such a Scriptural unity of faith and
practice, that there will be no schism in the body, no
self-preferring sect of professed and acknowledged
Christians rejecting and excluding their brethern. *This*
can not be, however, till the offensive and excluding
causes be removed; and every one knows what *these*
are. But that all the members should have the same
identical views of all Divinely-revealed truths, or that
there should be no difference of opinion among them,
appears to us morally impossible, all things considered. Nor can we conceive what desirable purpose such
a unity of sentiment would serve, except to render
useless some of those gracious, self-denying, and compassionate precepts of mutual sympathy and forbearance which the word of God enjoins upon his people.
Such, then, is the imperfection of our present state.
Would to God it might prove, as it ought, a just and
humbling counterbalance to our pride! Then, indeed,
we would judge one another no more about such matters. We would rather be conscientiously cautious to
give no offense; to put no stumbling-block or occasion
to fall in our brother's way. We would then no longer
exalt our own opinions and inferences to an equality
with express revelation, by condemning and rejecting
our brother for differing with us in those things.

But although it be granted that the uniformity we plead for would not secure unity of sentiment, yet we should suppose that it would be as efficacious for that purpose as any human expedient or substitute whatsoever. And here we would ask: Have all or any of those human compilations been able to prevent divisions, to heal breaches, or to produce and maintain unity of sentiment even among those who have most firmly and solemnly embraced them? We appeal for this to the history of all the Churches, and to the present divided state of the Church at large. What good, then, have those divisive expedients accomplished, either to the parties that have adopted them, or to the Church universal, which might not have been as well secured by holding fast in profession and practice that form of sound words contained in the Divine standard, without, at the same time, being liable to any of those dangerous and destructive consequences which have necessarily ensued upon the present mode? Or, will any venture to say that the Scriptures, thus kept in their proper place, would not have been amply sufficient, under the promised influence of the Divine Spirit, to have produced all that unity of sentiment which is necessary to a life of faith and holiness; and also to have preserved the faith and worship of the Church as pure from mixture and error as the Lord intended, or as the present imperfect state of his people can possibly admit? We should tremble to think that any Christian should say that they would not. And if to use them thus would be sufficient for those purposes, why resort to other expedients; to expedients which, from the beginning to this day, have proved utterly insufficient; nay, to expedients which have always produced the very contrary effects, as experience testifies? Let none here imagine that we set any certain limits to the Divine intention, or to the greatness of his power when we thus speak, as if a certain degree of purity from mixture and error were not designed for the Church in this world, or attainable by his people upon earth, except in so far as respects the attainment of an angelic or unerring perfection, much less that we mean to suggest that a very moderate degree of unity and purity should content us. We only take it for granted that such a state of perfection is neither intended nor attainable in this world as will free the Church from all those weaknesses, mistakes, and mismanagements from which she will be completely exempted in heaven, however sound and upright she may now be in her profession, intention, and practice. Neither let any imagine that we here or elsewhere suppose or intend to assert that human standards are intentionally set up in competition with the Bible, much less in opposition to it. We fairly understand and consider them as human expedients, or as certain doctrinal declarations of the sense in which the compilers understood the Scriptures, designed and embraced for the purpose of promoting and securing that desirable unity and purity which the Bible alone, without those helps, would be insufficient to maintain and secure. If this be not the sense of those that receive and hold them, for the aforesaid purpose, we should be glad to know what it is. It is, however, in this very sense that we take them up when we complain of them as not only unsuccessful, but also as unhappy expedients, producing the very contrary effects. And even suppose it were doubtful whether or not those helps have produced divisions, one thing, at least, is certain, they have not been able to prevent them; and now that divisions do exist, it is as certain that they have no fitness nor tendency to heal them, but the very contrary, as fact and experience clearly demonstrate. What shall we do, then,

to heal our divisions? We must certainly take some
other way than the present practice, if they ever be
healed; for it expressly says, they must and shall
be perpetuated forever. Let all the enemies of Christianity say Amen; but let all Christians continually
say: Forbid it, O Lord! May the good Lord subdue
the corruptions and heal the divisions of his people.
Amen, and amen.

After all that has been said, some of our timid
brethren may, possibly, still object, and say: we fear
that without the intervention of some definite creed or
formula, you will justly incur the censure of Latitudinarianism; for how otherwise detect and exclude
Arians, Socinians, etc? To such we would reply, that
if to profess, inculcate, and practice neither more nor
less, neither anything else nor otherwise than the
Divine word expressly declares respecting the entire
subject of faith and duty, and simply to rest in *that,*
as the expression of our faith and rule of our practice,
will not amount to the profession and practical exhibition of Arianism, Socinianism, etc., but merely to one
and the self-same thing, whatever it may be called,
then is the *ground* that we have taken, the *principle*
that we advocate, in nowise chargeable with Latitudinarianism. Should it be still further objected that all
these sects, and many more, profess to receive the
Bible, to believe it to be the word of God, and, therefore, will readily profess to believe and practice whatever is revealed and enjoined therein, and yet each
will understand it his own way, and of course practice
accordingly; nevertheless, according to the plan proposed, you receive them all. We would ask, then, do
all these profess and practice neither more nor less
than what we read in the Bible—than what is expressly revealed and enjoined therein? If so, they all profess and practice the same thing, for the Bible exhibits

but one and the self-same thing to all. Or, is it their own inferences and opinions that they, in reality, profess and practice? If so, then upon the ground that we have taken they stand rejected, as condemned of themselves, for thus professing one thing when in fact and reality they manifestly practice another. But perhaps you will say, that although a uniformity in profession, and it may be in practice too, might thus be produced, yet still it would amount to no more than a mere uniformity in words, and in the external formalities of practice, while the persons thus professing and practicing might each entertain his own sentiments, how different soever these might be. Our reply is, if so, they could hurt nobody but themselves. Besides, if persons thus united professed and practiced all the same things, pray who could tell that they entertained different sentiments, or even in justice suppose it, unless they gave some evident intimation of it? which, if they did, would justly expose them to censure or to rejection, if they repented not; seeing the offense, in this case, must amount to nothing less than an express violation of the expressly-revealed will of God—to a manifest transgression of the express letter of the law; for we have declared, that except in such a case, no man, in our judgment, has a right to judge, that is, to condemn or reject his professing brother. Here, we presume, there is no greater latitude assumed or allowed on either side than the law expressly determines. But we would humbly ask if a professed agreement in the terms of any standard be not liable to the very same objection? If, for instance, Arians, Socinians, Arminians, Calvinists, Antinomians, etc., might not all subscribe the Westminster Confession, the Athanasian Creed, or the doctrinal articles of the Church of England? If this be denied, we appeal to historical facts; and, in the mean time, venture to assert, that such things are and have been done. Or, will any say that a person might not with equal ease, honesty, and consistency, be an Arian or a Socinian in his heart while subscribing the Westminster Confession or the Athanasian Creed, as while making his unqualified profession to believe everything that the Scriptures declare concerning Christ? to put all that confidence in him, and to ascribe all that glory, honor, thanksgiving, and praise to him, professed and ascribed to him in the Divine word? If you say not, it follows, of undeniable consequence, that the wisdom of men, in those compilations, has effected what the Divine Wisdom either could not, would not, or did not do, in that all-perfect and glorious revelation of his will, contained in the Holy Scriptures. Happy emendation! Blessed expedient! Happy, indeed, for the Church that Athanasius arose in the fourth century to perfect what the holy apostles and prophets had left in such a rude and unfinished state. But if, after all, the Divine Wisdom did not think proper to do anything more, or anything else than is already done in the sacred oracles, to settle and determine those important points, who can say that he determined such a thing should be done afterward? Or has he anywhere given us any intimation of such an intention?

Let it here be carefully observed that the question before us is about human standards designed to be subscribed, or otherwise solemnly acknowledged, for the preservation of ecclesiastical unity and purity, and therefore, of course, by no means applies to the many excellent performances for the Scriptural elucidation and defense of Divinely-revealed truths, and other instructive purposes. These, we hope, according to their respective merit, we as highly esteem, and as thankfully receive, as our brethren. But further, with respect to unity of sentiment, even suppose it ever so desirable, it appears highly questionable whether such a thing can at all be secured, by any expedient whatsoever, especially if we consider that it necessarily presupposes in so far a unity or sameness of understanding. Or, will any say, that from the youth of seventeen to the man of fourscore—from the illiterate peasant up to the learned prelate—all the legitimate members of the Church entertain the same sentiments under their respective formulas? If not, it is still but a mere verbal agreement, a mere show of unity. They say an amen to the same forms of speech, or of sound words, as they are called, without having, at the same time, the same views of the subject; or, it may be, without any determinate views of it at all. And, what is still worse, this profession is palmed upon the world, as well as upon the too credulous professors themselves, for unity of sentiment, for soundness in the faith, when, in a thousand instances, they have, properly speaking, no faith at all; that is to say, if faith necessarily presupposes a true and satisfactory conviction of the Scriptural evidence and certainty of the truth of the propositions we profess to believe. A cheap and easy orthodoxy this, to which we may attain by committing to memory a catechism, or professing our approbation of a formula, made ready to our hand, which we may or may not have once read over; or even if we have, yet may not have been able to read it so correctly and intelligently as to clearly understand one single paragraph from beginnig to end, much less to compare it with, to search and try it by the holy Scriptures, to see if these things be so. A cheap and easy orthodoxy this, indeed, to which a person may thus attain, without so much as turning over a single leaf of his Bible, whereas Christ knew no other way of leading us to the knowledge of himself, at least has prescribed no other, but by searching the Scriptures, with reliance upon his Holy Spirit. A person may, however, by this short and easy method, become as orthodox as the apostle Paul (if such superficial professions, such mere hearsay verbal repetitions can be called orthodoxy) without ever once consulting the Bible, or so much as putting up a single petition for the Holy Spirit to guide him into all truth, to open his understanding to know the Scriptures; for, his form of sound words truly believed, if it happen to be right, must, without more ado, infallibly secure his orthodoxy. Thrice happy expedient! But is there no Latitudinarianism in all this? Is not this taking a latitude, in devising ways and means for accomplishing Divine and saving purposes, which the Divine law has nowhere prescribed, for which the Scriptures nowhere afford us either precept or precedent? unless it can be shown that making human standards to determine the doctrine, worship, discipline, and government of the Church for the purpose of preserving her unity and purity, and requiring an approbation of them as a term of communion, is a Scripture institution. Far be it from us, in the mean time, to allege that the Church should not make every Scriptural exertion in her power to preserve her unity and purity; to teach and train up her members in the knowledge of all divinely-revealed truth; or to say that the evils above complained of attach to all that are in the habit of using the aforesaid helps; or that this wretched state of things, however general, necessarily proceeds from the legitimate use of such; but rather and entirely from the abuse of them, which is the very and only thing that we are all along opposing when we allude to those subordinate standards. (An appellation this, by the by, which appears to us highly paradoxical, if not utterly inconsistent, and full of confusion.)

But, however this may be, we are by no means to be understood as at all wishing to deprive our fellow-Christians of any necessary and possible assistance to understand the Scriptures, or to come to a distinct and particular knowledge of every truth they contain, for which purpose the Westminster Confession and Catechisms may, with many other excellent performances, prove eminently useful. But, having served ourselves of these, let our profiting appear to all, by our manifest acquaintance with the Bible; by making our profession of faith and obedience; by declaring its Divine dictates, in which we acquiesce, as the subject-matter and rule of both; in our ability to take the Scripture in its connection upon these subjects, so as to understand one part of it by the assistance of another; and in manifesting our self-knowledge, our knowledge of the way of salvation and of the mystery of the Christian life, in the express light of Divine revelation, by a direct and immediate reference to, and correct repetition of what it declares upon those subjects. We take it for granted that no man either knows God, or himself, or the way of salvation, but in so far as he has heard and understood his voice upon those subjects, as addressed to him in the Scriptures, and that, therefore, whatever he has heard and learned of a saving nature, is contained in the express terms of the Bible. If so, in the express terms, in and by which "he hath heard and learned of the Father," let him declare it. This by no means forbids him to use helps, but, we humbly presume, will effectually prevent him from resting either in them or upon them, which is the evil so justly complained of; from taking up with the directory instead of the object to which it directs. Thus will the whole subject of his faith and duty, in so far as he has attained, be expressly declared in a "Thus saith the Lord." And is it not worthy of remark, that of whatever use other books may be, to direct and lead us to the Bible, or to prepare and assist us to understand it, yet the Bible never directs us to any book but itself. When we come forward, then, as Christians, to be received by the Church, which, properly speaking, has but one book, "For to it were committed the oracles of God," let us hear of none else. Is it not upon the credible profession of our faith in, and obedience to its Divine contents, that the Church is bound to receive applicants for admission? And does not a profession of our faith and obedience necessarily presuppose a knowledge of the dictates we profess to believe and obey? Surely, then, we can declare them, and as surely, if our faith and obedience be Divine, as to the subject-matter, rule, and reason of them, it must be a "Thus saith the Lord;" if otherwise, they are merely human, being taught by the precepts of men. In the case then before us, that is, examination for Church-membership, let the question no longer be, What does any human system say of the primitive or present state of man? of the person, offices, and relation of Christ, etc., etc.? or of this, that, or the other duty? but, What says the Bible? Were this mode of procedure adopted, how much better acquainted with their Bibles would Christians be? What an important alteration would it also make in the education of youth? Would it not lay all candidates for admission into the Church under the happy necessity of becoming particularly acquainted with the holy Scriptures? whereas, according to the present practice, thousands know little about them.

One thing still remains that may appear matter of difficulty or objection to some, namely, that such a close adherence to the express letter of the Divine word, as we seem to propose, for the restoration and

maintenance of Christian unity, would not only interfere with the free communication of our sentiments
one to another upon religious subjects, but must, of
course, also necessarily interfere with the public
preaching and expounding of the Scriptures for the
edification of the Church. Such as feel disposed to
make this objection, should justly consider that one of
a similar nature, and quite as plausible, might be
made to the adoption of human standards, especially
when made, as some of them confessedly are, "the
standard for all matters of doctrine, worship, discipline, and government." In such a case it might, with
as much justice, at least, be objected to the adopters:
You have now no more use for the Bible; you have got
another book, which you have adopted as a standard
for all religious purposes; you have no further use
for explaining the Scriptures, either as to matter of
faith or duty, for this you have confessedly done already in your standard, wherein you have determined
all matters of this nature. You also profess to hold
fast the form of sound words, which you have thus
adopted, and therefore you must never open your
mouth upon any subject in any other terms than those
of your standard. In the mean time, would any of
the parties which has thus adopted its respective standard, consider any of these charges just? If not, let
them do as they would be done by. We must confess,
however, that for our part, we can not see how, with
any shadow of consistency, some of them could clear
themselves, especially of the first; that is to say, if
words have any determinate meaning; for certainly
it would appear almost, if not altogether incontrovertible, that a book adopted by any party as its standard
for all matters of doctrine, worship, discipline, and
government, must be considered as the Bible of that
party. And after all that can be said in favor of

such a performance, be it called Bible, standard, or what it may, it is neither anything more nor better than the judgment or opinion of the party composing or adopting it, and, therefore, wants the sanction of a Divine authority, except in the opinion of the party which has thus adopted it. But can the opinion of any party, be it ever so respectable, give the stamp of a Divine authority to its judgments? If not, then every human standard is deficient in this leading, all-important, and indispensable property of a rule or standard for the doctrine, worship, discipline, and government of the Church of God. But, without insisting further upon the intrinsic and irremediable deficiency of human standards for the above purpose, (which is undeniably evident if it be granted that a Divine authority is indispensably necessary to constitute a standard or rule for Divine things, such as is the constitution and managements, the faith and worship of the Christian Church,) we would humbly ask, Would any of the parties consider as just the foregoing objections, however conclusive and well founded all or any of them may appear? We believe they would not. And may we not with equal consistency hold fast the expressly-revealed will of God, in the very terms in which it is expressed in his holy word, as the very expression of our faith and express rule of our duty, and yet take the same liberty that they do, notwithstanding their professed and steadfast adherence to their respective standards? We find they do not cease to expound, because they have already expounded, as before alleged, nor yet do they always confine themselves to the express terms of their respective standards, yet they acknowledge them to be their standards and profess to hold them fast. Yea, moreover, some of them profess, and, if we may conclude from facts, we believe each of them is disposed to defend by occasional vindications (or testimonies, as some call them) the sentiments they have adopted and engrossed in their standards, without at the same time requiring an approbation of those occasional performances as a term of communion. And what should hinder us, or any, adopting the Divine standard, as aforesaid, with equal consistency to do the same for the vindication of the Divine truths expressly revealed and enjoined therein? To say that we can not believe and profess the truth, understand one another, inculcate and vindicate the faith and law of Christ, or do the duties incumbent upon Christians or a Christian Church without a human standard, is not only saying that such a standard is quite essential to the very being of Christianity, and, of course, must have existed before a Church was or could be formed, but it is also saying, that without such a standard, the Bible would be quite inadequate as a rule of faith and duty, or, rather, of no use at all, except to furnish materials for such a work; whereas the Church of Ephesus, long before we have any account of the existence of such a standard, is not only mentioned, with many others, as in a state of existence, and of high attainments too, but is also commended for her vigilance and fidelity in detecting and rejecting false apostles. "Thou hast tried them which say they are apostles, and are not, and hast found them liars." But should any pretend to say that although such performances be not essential to the very being of the Church, yet are they highly conducive to its well-being and perfection. For the confutation of such an assertion, we would again appeal to Church history and existing facts and leave the judicious and intelligent Christian to determine.

If after all that has been said, any should still pretend to affirm that the plan we profess to adopt and recommend is truly Latitudinarian, in the worst and fullest sense of the term, inasmuch as it goes to make void all human efforts to maintain the unity and purity of the Church, by substituting a vague and indefinite approbation of the Scriptures as an alternative for creeds, confessions, and testimonies, and thereby opens a wide door for the reception of all sorts of characters and opinions into the Church, were we not convinced by experience, that nowithstanding all that has been said, such objections would likely be made, or that some weak persons might possibly consider them as good as demonstration, especially when proceeding from highly influential characters, (and there have not been wanting such in all ages to oppose, under various plausible pretenses, the unity and peace of the Church,) were it not for these considerations, we should content ourselves with what we have already advanced upon the whole of the subject, as being well assured *that* duly attended to, there would not be the least room for such an objection; but to prevent if possible such unfounded conclusions, or if this can not be done, to caution and assist the too credulous and unwary professor, that he may not be carried away all at once with the hightoned confidence of bold assertion, we would refer him to the overture for union in truth contained in the foregoing address. Union in truth, among all the manifest subjects of grace and truth, is what we advocate. We carry our views of union no further than *this,* nor do we presume to recommend it upon any other principle than truth alone. Now, surely, truth is something certain and definite; if not, who will take upon him to define and determine it? This we suppose God has sufficiently done already in his holy Word. That men therefore truly receive and make the proper use of the Divine word for walking together in truth and peace, in holiness and charity, is, no doubt, the ardent desire of all the genuine subjects of our holy religion. This, we see, however, they have not done, to the awful detriment and manifest subversion of what we might almost call the primary intention of Christianity. We dare not, therefore, follow their example, nor adopt their ruinous expedients. But does it therefore follow that Christians may not, or can not take proper steps to ascertain that desirable and preceptive unity which the Divine word requires and enjoins? Surely no; at least we have supposed no such thing; but, on the contrary, have overtured to our brethren what appears to us undeniably just and Scripturally evident, and which, we humbly think, if adopted and acted upon, would have the desired effect; adopted and acted upon, not indeed as a standard for the doctrine, worship, discipline, and government of the Church, for it pretends not to determine these matters, but rather supposes the existence of a fixed and certain standard of Divine original, in which everything that the wisdom of God saw meet to reveal and determine, for *these* and all other purposes, is expressly defined and determined; between the Christian and which, no medium of human determination ought to be interposed. In all this there is surely nothing like the denial of any lawful effort to promote and maintain the Church's unity, though there be a refusal of the unwarrantable interposition of an unauthorized and assuming power.

Let none imagine that we are here determining upon the merits of the overture to which, in the case before us, we find it necessary to appeal in our own defense against the injustice of the supposed charge above specified. To the judgment of our brethren have we referred that matter, and with them we leave it. All we intend, therefore, is to avail ourselves so far of what we have done, as to show that we have no intention whatsoever of substituting a vague, indefinite approbation of the Scriptures as an alternative for creeds, confessions, and testimonies, for the purpose of restoring the Church to her original constitutional unity and purity. In avoiding Scylla we would cautiously guard against being wrecked upon Charybdis. Extremes, we are told, are dangerous. We therefore suppose a middle way, a safe way, so plainly marked out by unerring wisdom, that if duly attended to under the Divine direction, wayfaring men, though fools, need not err therein, and of such is the kingdom of God: "For he hath chosen the foolish things of the world to confound the things that are wise." We therefore conclude it must be a plain way, a way most graciously and most judiciously adapted to the capacity of the subjects, and consequently not the way of subscribing or otherwise approving human standards as a term of admission into his Church, as a test and defense of orthodoxy, which even the compilers themselves are not always agreed about, and which nineteen out of twenty of the Lord's people can not thoroughly understand. It must be a way very far remote from logical subtilties and metaphysical speculations, and as such we have taken it up, upon the plainest and most obvious principles of Divine revelation and common sense—the common sense, we mean, of Christians, exercised upon the plainest and most obvious truths and facts divinely recorded for their instruction. Hence we have supposed, in the first place, the true descrimination of Christian character to consist in an intelligent profession of our faith in Christ and obedience to him in all things according to the Scriptures, the reality of which profession is manifested by the holy consistency of the tempers and conduct of the professors with the express dictates and approved examples of the Divine word. Hence we have humility, faith, piety, temperance, justice, charity, etc., professed and manifested, in the first instance, by the persons professing with self-application the convincing, humbling, encouraging, pious, temperate, just and charitable doctrines and precepts of the inspired volume, as exhibited and enforced in its holy and approved examples, and the sincerity of this profession evidently manifested by the consistency of the professor's temper and conduct with the entire subject of his profession, either by an irreprovable conformity, like good Zachariah and Elizabeth, which is of all things most desirable, or otherwise, in case of any visible failure, by an apparently sincere repentance and evident reformation. Such professors, and such only, have we supposed to be, by common consent, truly worthy the Christian name. Ask from the one end of heaven to the other, the whole number of such intelligent and consistent professors as we intend and have described, and, we humbly presume, there will not be found one dissenting voice. They will all acknowledge, with one consent, that the true discrimination of Christian character consists in these things, and that the radical or manifest want of any of the aforesaid properties completely destroys the character.

We have here only taken for granted what we suppose no rational professor will venture to deny; namely, that the Divine word contains an ample sufficiency upon every one of the foregoing topics to stamp the above character, if so be that the impressions which its express declarations are obviously calculated to produce be truly received; for instance, suppose a person profess to believe, with application to himself, that whole description of human depravity and wretchedness which the Scriptures exhibit of fallen man, in the express declarations and dismal examples of human

wickedness therein recorded, contrasted with the holy
nature, the righteous requirements, and inflexible justice of an infinitely holy, just, and jealous God, would
not the subject-matter of such a profession be amply
sufficient to impress the believing mind with the most
profound humility, self-abhorrence, and dreadful apprehension of the tremendous effects of sin? Again,
should the person profess to believe, in connection
with this, all that the Scriptures declare of the sovereign love, mercy, and condescension of God toward
guilty, depraved, rebellious man, as the same is manifested in Christ, and in all the gracious declarations,
invitations, and promises that are made in and through
him for the relief and encouragement of the guilty,
etc., would not all this, taken together, be sufficient to
impress the believing mind with the most lively confidence, gratitude, and love? Should this person,
moreover, profess that delight and confidence in the
Divine Redeemer—that voluntary submission to him
—that worship and adoration of him which the Scriptures expressly declare to have been the habits and
practice of his people, would not the subject-matter of
this profession be amply sufficient to impress the believing mind with that dutiful disposition, with that
gracious veneration and supreme reverence which the
word of God requires? And should not all this taken
together satisfy the Church, in so far, in point of profession? If not, there is no alternative but a new revelation; seeing that to deny this, is to assert that a
distinct perception and sincere profession of whatever
the word declares upon every point of faith and duty,
is not only insufficient, as a doctrinal means, to produce a just and suitable impression in the mind of the
believing subject, but is also insufficient to satisfy the
Church as to a just and adequate profession; if otherwise, then it will necessarily follow, that not every

sort of character, but that one sort only, is admissible upon the principle we have adopted; and that by the universal consent of all that we, at least, dare venture to call Christians, *this* is acknowledged to be, exclusively, the true Christian character. Here, then, we have a fixed point, a certain description of character, which combines in every professing subject the Scriptural profession, the evident manifestation of humility, faith, piety, temperance, justice, and charity, instructed by, and evidently answering to the entire declaration of the word upon each of those topics, which, as so many properties, serve to constitute the character. Here, we say, we have a fixed, and at the same time sweeping distinction, which, as of old, manifestly divides the whole world, however otherwise distinguished, into but two classes only. "We know," said the apostle, evidently speaking of such, "that we are of God, and the whole world lieth in wickedness."

Should it be inquired concerning the persons included in this description of character, whether they be Arminians or Calvinists, or both promiscuously huddled together? It may be justly replied, that according to what we have proposed, they can be nominally neither, and of course not both, for we call no man master on earth, for one is our Master, even Christ, and all we are brethren, are Christians by profession; and as such, abstract speculation and argumentative theory make no part either of our profession or practice. Such professors, then, as we intend and have described, are just what their profession and practice make them to be; and this we hope has been Scripturally, and we might add, satisfactorily defined, in so far, at least, as the limits of so brief a performance would admit. We also entertain the pleasing confidence that the plan of procedure which we have ventured to suggest, if duly attended to, if fully reduced to practice, would necessarily secure to the professing subject all the advantages of divinely-revealed truth, without any liability to conceal, to diminish, or to misrepresent it, as it goes immediately to ascribe everything to God respecting his sovereignty, independence, power, wisdom, goodness, justice, truth, holiness, mercy, condescension, love, and grace, etc., which is ascribed to him in his word, as also to receive whatever it declares concerning the absolute dependence of the poor, guilty, depraved, polluted creature, upon the Divine will, power, and grace for every saving purpose; a just perception and correspondent profession of which, according to the Scriptures, is supposed to constitute that fundamental ingredient in Christian character: true evangelical humility. And so of the rest. Having thus, we hope, Scripturally and evidently determined the character, with the proper mode of ascertaining it, to the satisfaction of all concerned, we next proceed to affirm, with the same Scriptural evidence, that among such, however situated, whether in the same or similar associations, there ought to be no schism, no uncharitable divisions, but that they ought all mutually to receive and acknowledge each other as brethren. As to the truth of this assertion, they are all likewise agreed, without one dissenting voice. We next suggest that for this purpose they ought all to walk by the same rule, to mind and speak the same thing, etc., and that this rule is, and ought to be, the Divine standard. Here again we presume there can be no objection; no, not a single dissenting voice. As to the rule itself, we have ventured to allege that the New Testament is the proper and immediate rule, directory, and formula for the New Testament Church, and for the particular duties of Christians, as the Old Testament was for the Old Testament Church, and for the particular duties of the subject under that dispensation; at the same time by no means excluding the Old as fundamental to, illustrative of, and inseparably connected with the New, and as being every way of equal authority, as well as of an entire sameness with it in every point of moral natural duty, though not immediately our rule, without the intervention and coincidence of the New, in which our Lord has taught his people, by the ministry of his holy apostles, all things whatsoever they should observe and do, till the end of the world. Thus we come to the one rule, taking the Old Testament as explained and perfected by the New, and the New as illustrated and enforced by the Old; assuming the latter as the proper and immediate directory for the Christian Church, as also for the positive and particular duties of Christians as to all things whatsoever they should observe and do. Further, that in the observance of this Divine rule, this authentic and infallible directory, all such may come to the desirable coincidence of holy unity and uniformity of profession and practice, we have overtured that they all speak, profess, and practice the very same things that are exhibited upon the sacred page of New Testament Scripture, as spoken and done by the Divine appointment and approbation; and that this be extended to every possible instance of uniformity, without addition or diminution, without introducing anything of private opinion or doubtful disputation into the public profession or practice of the Church. Thus and thus have we overtured to all intents and purposes, as may be clearly seen by consulting the overture itself; in which, however, should anything appear not sufficiently explicit, we flatter ourselves it may be fully understood by taking into consideration what has been variously suggested upon this important subject throughout the whole of these premises; so that if any due degree of attention be paid, we should think it next to impossible that we could be so far misunderstood as to be charged with Latitudinarianism in any usual sense of the word.   Here we have proposed but one description of character as eligible, or, indeed, as at all admissible to the rights and privileges of Christianity. This description of character we have defined by certain and distinguishing properties, which not only serve to distinguish it from every other, but in which all the real subjects themselves are agreed, without one exception, all such being mutually and reciprocally acknowledged by each other as legitimate members of the Church of God.   All these, moreover, agreeing in the indispensable obligation of their unity, and in the one rule by which it is instructed, and also in the preceptive necessity of an entire uniformity in their public profession and managements for promoting and preserving this unity, that there should be no schism in the body, but that all the members should have the same care one for another;   yet in many instances, unhappily, and, we may truly say, involuntarily differing through mistake and mismanagement, which it is our humble desire and endeavor to detect and remove, by obviating everything that causeth difference, being persuaded that as truth is one and indivisible wherever it exists, so all the genuine subjects of it, if disentangled from artificial impediments, must and will necessarily fall in together, be all on one side, united in one profession, acknowledge each other as brethren, and love as children of the same family.   For this purpose we have overtured a certain and determinate application of the rule, to which we presume there can be no reasonable objection, and which, if adopted and acted upon, must, we think, infallibly produce the desired effect;   unless we should suppose that to say and do what is expressly said and done before our eyes upon the sacred page, would offend the believer, or that a strict uniformity, an entire Scriptural sameness in profession and practice, would produce divisions and offenses among those who are already united in one spirit, one Lord, one faith, one baptism, one hope of their calling, and in one God and Father of all, who is above all, and through all, and in them all, as is confessedly the case with all of this character throughout all the Churches. To induce to this we have also attempted to call their attention to the heinnous nature and awful consequences of schism, and to that evil, antiscriptural principle from which it necessarily proceeds. We have likewise endeavored to show, we humbly think, with demonstrable evidence, that there is no alternative but either to adopt that Scriptural uniformity we have recommended, or else continue as we are, bewildered in schisms and overwhelmed with the accursed evils inseparable from such a state. It remains now with our brethren to determine upon the whole of these premises, to adopt or to reject, as they see cause; but, in the mean time, let none impeach us with the Latitudinarian expedient of substituting a vague, indefinite approbation of the holy Scriptures as an alternative for the present practice of making the approbation of human standards a term of communion; as it is undeniably evident that nothing can be further from our intention. Were we to judge of what we humbly propose and urge as indispensably necessary for the reformation and unity of the Church, we should rather apprehend that there was reason to fear a charge of a very different nature; namely, that we aimed at too much strictness, both as to the description of character which we say ought only to be admitted, and also as to the use and application of the rule. But should this be the case, we shall cheerfully bear with it, as being fully satisfied

that not only the common sentiment of all apparently
sincere, intelligent, and practical Christians is on our
side, but that also the plainest and most ample testimonies of the inspired volume sufficiently attest the
truth and propriety of what we plead for, as essential
to the Scriptural unity and purity of the Christian
Church, and this, we humbly presume, is what we
should incessantly aim at.   It would be strange, indeed, if, in contending earnestly for the faith once
delivered to the saints, we should overlook those fruits
of righteousness, that manifest humility, piety, temperance, justice, and charity, without which faith itself
is dead, being alone.   We trust we have not so learned
Christ;   if so be we have been taught by him as the
truth is in Jesus, we must have learned a very different
lesson indeed.   While we would, therefore, insist upon
an entire conformity to the Scriptures in profession,
that we might all believe and speak the same things,
and thus be perfectly joined together in the same mind
and in the same judgment, we would, with equal
scrupulosity, insist upon and look for an entire conformity to them in practice, in all those whom we
acknowledge as our brethren in Christ.   "By their
fruits ye shall know them."   "Not every one that
saith unto me, Lord, Lord, shall enter into the kingdom of heaven;   but he that doeth the will of my
Father which is in heaven.   Therefore whosoever
heareth those sayings of mine, and doeth them not,
shall be likened unto a foolish man which built his
house upon the sand.   Woe unto you scribes and
Pharisees, hypocrites, for ye say and do not."   We
therefore conclude that to advocate unity alone, however desirable in itself, without at the same time purg-
ing the Church of apparently unsanctified characters,
even of all that can not show their faith by their
works, would be, at best, but a poor, superficial, skin-

deep reformation. It is from such characters, then, as the proposed reformation, if carried into effect, would entirely deprive of a name and a place in the Church, that we have the greatest reason to apprehend a determined and obstinate opposition. And alas! there are very many of this description, and in many places, of considerable influence. But neither should this discourage us, when we consider the expressly-revealed will of God upon this point, Ezek. xliv: 6, 9, with Matt. xiii: 15, 17; 1 Cor. v: 6, 13, with many other scriptures. Nor, in the end, will the multitude of unsanctified professors which the proposed reformation would necessarily exclude, have any reason to rejoice in the unfaithfulness of those that either through ignorance, or for filthy lucre's sake, indulged them with a name and place in the Church of God. These unfaithful stewards, these now mistaken friends, will one day be considered by such as their most cruel and treacherous enemies. These, then, are our sentiments upon the entire subject of Church-reformation; call it Latitudinarianism, or Puritanism, or what you please; and *this* is the reformation for which we plead. Thus, upon the whole, have we briefly attempted to point out those evils, and to prevent those mistakes which we earnestly desire to see obviated for the general peace, welfare, and prosperity of the Church of God. Our dear brethren, giving credit to our sincere and well-meant intention, will charitably excuse the imperfections of our humble performance, and by the assistance of their better judgment correct those mistakes and supply those deficiencies which in a first attempt of this nature may have escaped our notice. We are sorry, in the mean time, to have left a necessity of approaching so near the borders of controversy, by briefly attempting to answer objections which we plainly foresaw would, through mistake or prejudice, be made against our proceedings; controversy making no part of our intended plan. But such objections and surmises having already reached our ears from different quarters, we thought it necessary to attend to them, that, by so doing, we might not only prevent mistakes, but also save our friends the trouble of entering into verbal disputes in order to remove them, and thus prevent, as much as possible, that most unhappy of all practices sanctioned by the plausible pretense of zeal for the truth—religious controversy among professors. We would, therefore, humbly advise our friends to concur with us in our professed and sincere intention to avoid this evil practice. Let it suffice to put into the hands of such as desire information what we hereby publish for that purpose. If this, however, should not satisfy, let them give in their objections in writing; we shall thankfully receive, and seriously consider, with all due attention, whatever comes before us in this way; but verbal controversy we absolutely refuse. Let none imagine that by so saying, we mean to dissuade Christians from affording all the assistance they can to each other as humble inquirers after truth. To decline this friendly office would be to refuse the performance of an important duty. But certainly there is a manifest difference between speaking the truth in love for the edification of our brethren, and attacking each other with a spirit of controversial hostility, to confute and prove each other wrong. We believe it is rare to find one instance of this kind of arguing that does not terminate in bitterness. Let us, therefore, cautiously avoid it. Our Lord says, Matt. xvii: 7: "Woe unto the world because of offenses." Scott, in his incomparable work lately published in this country, called his Family Bible, observes in his notes upon this place, "that our Lord here intends all these evils within the

Church which prejudice men's minds against his religion, or any doctrines of it. The scandalous lives, horrible oppressions, cruelties, and iniquities of men called Christians; their divisions and bloody contentions; their idolatries and superstitions, are at this day the *great offenses* and *causes of stumbling* to Jews, Mohammedans, and pagans in all the four quarters of the globe, and they furnish infidels of every description with their most dangerous weapons against the truth. The acrimonious controversies agitated among those who agree in the principal doctrines of the Gospel, and their mutual contempt and revilings of each other, together with the extravagant notions and wicked practices found among them, form the grand prejudice in the minds of multitudes against evangelical religion, and harden the hearts of heretics, Pharisees, disguised infidels, and careless sinners against the truths of the Gospel. In these and numberless other ways, it may be said: 'Woe unto the world because of offenses,' for the devil, the sower of these tares, makes use of them in deceiving the nations of the earth and in murdering the souls of men. In the present state of human nature, it must needs be that such offenses should intervene, and God has wise and righteous reasons for permitting them; yet we should consider it as the greatest of evils to be accessory to the destruction of souls; and an awful woe is denounced against every one whose delusions or crimes thus stumble men and set them against the only method of salvation." We conclude with an extract from the Boston Anthology, which, with too many of the same kind that might be adduced, furnish a mournful comment upon the text; we mean, upon the sorrowful subject of our woful divisions and corruptions. The following reply to the Rev. Mr. Cram, missionary from Massachusetts to the Senecas, was made by the principal chiefs and warriors of the Six Nations in council assembled at Buffalo creek, State of New York, in the presence of the agent of the United States for Indian affairs, in the summer of 1805: "I am come, brethren," said the missionary, "to enlighten your minds and to instruct you how to worship the Great Spirit agreeably to his will, and to preach to you the Gospel of his Son Jesus Christ. There is but one way to serve God, and if you do not embrace the right way, you can not be happy hereafter." To which they replied: "Brother, we understand that your religion is written in a book. You say that there is but one way to worship and serve the Great Spirit. If there be but one religion, why do you white people differ so much about it? Why not all agree, as you can all read the book? Brother, we do not understand these things. We are told your religion was given to your forefathers; we also have a religion which was given to our forefathers; it teaches us to be *thankful* for all the favors we receive; to *love* one another, and to be *united*. We never quarrel about religion. We are told you have been preaching to the white people in this place. Those people are our neighbors, we are acquainted with them. We will wait a little to see what effect your preaching has upon *them*. If we find it does them good, makes them *honest,* and *less* disposed to cheat Indians, we will then consider again of what you have said." Thus closed the conference. Alas, poor people! how do our divisions and corruptions stand in your way! What a pity that you find us not upon original ground, such as the apostles left the primitive Churches! Had we but exhibited to you their unity and charity; their humble, honest, and affectionate deportment toward each other and toward all men, you would not have had those evil and shameful things to object to our holy religion, and to prejudice your minds against it. But your conversion, it seems, awaits our reformation; awaits our return to primitive unity and love. To this may the God of mercy speedily restore us, both for your sakes and our own, that *his way* may be known upon earth, and his saving health among all nations. Let the people praise thee, O God; let all the people praise thee. Amen, and amen.

SERMON ON THE LAW.

By Alexander Campbell.

Alexander Campbell was born September 12, 1788, in County Antrim, Ireland. Came to America in 1809. Died at Bethany, W. Va., March 4, 1866.

Requests have occasionally, during several years, been made for the publication, in this work, of a discourse on the Law, pronounced by me at a meeting of the Regular Baptist Association on Cross Creek, Virginia, 1816.   Recently these requests have been renewed with more earnestness;   and, although much crowded for room, I have concluded to comply with the wishes of my friends.

It was rather a youthful performance,. and is in one particular, to my mind, long since exceptionable. Its views of the Atonement are rather commercial than evangelical.   But this· was only casually introduced, and does not affect the object of the discourse or the merits of the great question discussed in it.   I thought it better to let it go to the public again without the change of a sentiment in it.   Although precisely thirty years this month since I delivered it, and some two or three years after my union with the Baptist denomination, the intelligent reader will discover in it the elements of things which have characterized all our writings on the subject of modern Christianity from that day to the present.

But as this discourse was, because of its alleged heterodoxy by the Regular Baptist· Association, made the ground of my impeachment and trial for heresy at its next annual meeting, it is, as an item of ecclesiastic history, interesting. It was by a great effort on my part that this self-same Sermon on the Law had not proved my public excommunication from the denomination under the foul brand of "damnable heresy." But by a great stretch of charity on the part of two or three old men, I was saved by a decided majority.

This unfortunate sermon afterwards involved me in a seven years' war with some members of said Association, and became a matter of much debate. I found at last, however, that there was a principle at work in the plotters of said crusade, which Stephen assigns as the cause of the misfortunes of Joseph.

It is, therefore, highly probable to my mind, that but for the persecution begun on the alleged heresy of this sermon, whether the present reformation had ever been advocated by me. I have a curious history of many links on this chain of providential events, yet unwritten and unknown to almost any one living—certainly to but a very few persons—which, as the waves of time roll on, may yet be interesting to many. It may be gratifying to some, however, at present to be informed that but one of the prime movers of this presumptive movement yet lives; and, alas! he has long since survived his usefulness. I may further say at present, that I do not think there is a Baptist Association on the continent that would now treat me as did the Redstone Association of that day, which is some evidence, to my mind, that the Baptists are not so stationary as a few of them would have the world believe.

But the discourse speaks for itself. It was indeed, rather an extemporaneous address; for the same spirit that assailed the discourse when pronounced, and when printed, reversed the resolution of the Association passed on Saturday evening, inviting me to address the audience on Lord's day, and had another person appointed in my place. He providentially was suddenly seized by sickness, and I was unexpectedly called upon in the morning, two hours before the discourse was spoken. A motion was made in the interval, that same day, by the same spirit of jealousy or zealousy, that public opinion should be arrested by having a preacher appointed to inform the congregation on the spot that my "discourse was not Baptist doctrine."

One preacher replied that it might be "Christian doctrine;" for his part it was new to him, and desired time for examination. I was, therefore, obliged to gather it up from a few notes, and commit it to writing. It was instantly called for to be printed, and after one year's deliberation, at next association, a party was formed to indict me for heresy on the published discourse. A committee met; resolutions were passed on Friday night. The next day was fixed for my trial; and, after asking counsel of Heaven, my sermon was called for, and the suit commenced. I was taken almost by surprise. On my offering immediately to go into an investigation of the matter, it was partially discussed; but on the ground of having no jurisdiction in the case, the Association resolved to dismiss the sermon, without any fuller mark of reprobation, and leave every one to form his own opinion of it. I presume our readers, without any license from an Association, will form their own opinion of it; and therefore we submit it to their candid perusal.

A. C.

THE SUBSTANCE OF A SERMON.

Delivered before the Redstone Baptist Association, met on Cross Creek, Brook County, Va., on the 1st of September, 1816.

BY ALEXANDER CAMPBELL,

One of the Pastors of the Church of Brush Run, Washington County, Pa.

"The law was given by Moses, but grace and truth came by Jesus Christ."—John 1:17.

"The law and the prophets were until John, since that time the kingdom of God is preached, and every man presseth into it."—Luke 16:16.

PREFACE.

To those who have requested the publication of the following discourse, an apology is necessary. Though the substance of the discourse, as delivered, is contained in the following pages, yet, it is not verbatim the same. Indeed, this could not be the case, as the preacher makes but a very sparing use of notes, and on this occasion, had but a few. In speaking extempore, or in a great measure so, and to a people who may have but one hearing of a discussion such as the following, many expressions that would be superfluous in a written discourse, are in a certain sense necessary. When words are merely pronounced, repetitions are often needful to impress the subject on the mind of the most attentive hearer: but when written, the reader may pause, read again, and thus arrive at the meaning.

Some additions, illustrative of the ideas that were presented in speaking, have been made; but as few as could be supposed necessary. Indeed, the chief difficulty in enforcing the doctrine contained in the following sheets, either in one spoken or written sermon, consists in the most judicious selection of the copious facts and documents contained in the divine word on this subject.

We have to regret that so much appears necessary to be said, in an argumentative way, to the professed Christians of this age, on such a topic. But this is easily accounted for on certain principles. For, in truth, the present-popular exhibition of Christianity is a compound of Judaism, heathen philosophy, and Christianity; which, like the materials in Nebuchadnezzar's image, does not well cement together.

The only correct and safe course, in this perilous age, is to take nothing upon trust, but to examine for ourselves, and "to bring all things to the test." "But if any man will be ignorant, let him be ignorant."

As to the style adopted in this discourse, it is such as we supposed would be adapted to the capacity of those who are chiefly benefited by such discussions. "For their sakes we endeavor to use great plainness of speech."

As the doctrines of the gospel are commonly hid from the wise and prudent, and revealed only to babes, the weak and foolish; for their sakes, the vail of what is falsely called eloquence should be laid aside, and the testimony of God plainly presented to view.

The great question with every man's conscience is, or should be, "What is truth?" Not, have any of the scribes or rulers of the people believed it? Every man's *eternal all,* as well as his present comfort, depends upon what answer he is able to give to the question Pilate of old [John xviii, 38] proposed to Christ, without waiting for a reply. Such a question can only be satisfactorily answered by an impartial appeal to the oracles of truth—the alone standard of Divine truth. To these we appeal. Whatever in this discourse is contrary to them, let it be expunged; what corresponds with them, may the God of truth bless to those to whom he has given an ear to discern and a heart to receive it.

ROMANS VIII, 3.

"For what the law could not do, in that it was weak through the flesh, God, sending His own Son in the likeness of sinful flesh, and for sin, condemned sin in the flesh."

Words are signs of ideas or thoughts. Unless words are understood, ideas or sentiments can neither be communicated nor received. Words that in themselves are quite intelligible may become difficult to understand in different connections and circumstances. One of the most important words in our text is. of easy signification, and yet, in consequence of its diverse usages and epithets, it is sometimes difficult precisely to ascertain what ideas should be attached to it.

It is the term *law.* But by a close investigation of the context, and a general knowledge of the Scriptures, every difficulty of this kind may be easily surmounted.

In order to elucidate and enforce the doctrine contained in this verse, we shall scrupulously observe the following

METHOD.

1. We shall endeavor to ascertain what ideas we are to attach to the phrase *"the law,"* in this and similar portions of the Sacred Scriptures.

2. Point out those things which *the law* could not accomplish.

3. Demonstrate the reason why *the law* failed to accomplish those objects.

4. Illustrate how God has remedied those relative defects of *the law*.

5. In the last place, deduce such conclusions from these premises, as must obviously and necessarily present themselves to every unbiased and reflecting mind.

In discussing the doctrine contained in our text, we are then, in the first place, to endeavor to ascertain what ideas we are to attach to the terms *"the law,"* in this and similar portions of the Sacred Scriptures.

The term *"law,"* denotes in common usage, "a rule of action." It was used by the Jews, until the time of our Saviour, to distinguish the whole revelation made to the Patriarchs and Prophets from the traditions and commandments of the Rabbis or Doctors of the law. Thus the Jews called the Psalms of David, *law.*—John xii, 34. Referring to the 110th Psalm, they say, "We have heard out of the law that Christ abideth forever."

And again, our Saviour calls the Psalms of David *law,* John x, 34. Referring to Psalm lxxxii, 6, he says, "Is it not written in your law, I said ye are gods." Thus when we hear David extolling God's law, we are to understand him as referring to all divine revelation extant in his time.

But when the Old Testament Scriptures were finished and divided according to their contents for the use of synagogues, the Jews styled them the law, the prophets and the psalms.

Luke xxiv, 44, Christ says, "All things written in the law of Moses, in the prophets, and in the psalms concerning me, must be fulfilled."

The addition of the definite article in this instance as well as all others, alters the signification or at least determines it. During the life of Moses, the words *"the law,"* without some explicative addition, were never used. Joshua, Moses' successor, denominates the writings of Moses, "the book of the law;" but never uses the phrase by itself. Nor, indeed, have we any authentic account of this phrase being used without some restrictive definition, until the reign of Abijah, 2d Chron. xiv, 4, at which time it is used to denote the whole legal dispensation by Moses. In this way it is used about thirty times in the Old Testament, and as often with such epithets as show that the whole law of Moses is intended.

When the doctrines of the reign of Heaven began to be preached, and to be contrasted in the New Testament with the Mosaic economy, the phrase *"the law"* became very common, and when used without any distinguishing epithet or restrictive definition, invariably denoted the whole legal or Mosaic dispensation. In this acceptation it occurs about 150 times in the New Testament.

To make myself more intelligible, I would observe that when the terms *"the law"* have such distinguishing properties or restrictive definitions as "the royal law," "the law of faith," "the law of liberty," "the law of Christ," "the law of the spirit of life," &c., it is most obvious the whole Mosaic law or dispensation is not intended. But when we find the phrase "the law," without any such limitations or epithets as "the law was given by Moses," "the law and the prophets were until John," "if ye be led by the Spirit, ye are not under the law," "ye are not under the law, but under grace," &c., we must perceive the whole law of Moses, or legal dispensation, is intended.

I say the *whole* law, or dispensation by Moses; for in modern times the law of Moses is divided and classified under three heads, denominated, the moral, ceremonial, and judicial law. This division of the law being unknown in the apostolic age, and, of course,

never used by the Apostles, can serve no valuable purpose in obtaining a correct knowledge of the doctrine
delivered by the Apostles respecting the law. You
might as well inquire of the Apostles, or consult their
writings to know who the Supralapsarians or Sublap-
sarians are, as to inquire of them what is the moral,
ceremonial or judicial law.

But, like many distinctions handed down to us from
mystical Babylon, they bear the mark on their fore-
head that certifies to us, their origin is not Divine. If
this distinction were harmless, if it did not perplex,
bias and confound, rather than assist the judgment in
determining the sense of the apostolic writing, we
should let it pass unnoticed; but justice to the truth
requires us to make a remark or two on this division of
the law.

The phrase *the moral law,* includes that part of the
law of Moses "written and engraved on two tables
of stone," called the ten commandments. Now the
word *moral,* according to the most approved Lexicog-
raphers, is defined "relating to the practice of men
toward each other, as it may be virtuous or criminal,
good or bad." The French, from whom we have the
term *moral* immediately, and the Romans from whom
we orginally received it, used it agreeably to the above
definition. Of course, then, a *moral* law is a law
which regulates the conduct of men toward each
other.

But will the ten commandments answer this definition? No. For Doctors of Divinity tell us, the first
table of the Decalogue respects our duty to God; the
second our duty to man.

Why then call the ten commandments *"the moral
law,"* seeing but six of them are moral, that is, relating to our conduct towards men? In modern times
we sometimes distinguish between religion and moral-

ity; but while we affirm that religion is one thing, and morality another; and then affirm that the ten commandments are the *moral law*—do we not, in so saying, contradict ourselves? Assuredly the legs of the lame are not equal!

A second objection to denominating the ten precepts "the moral law," presents itself to the reflecting mind, from the consideration that all morality is not contained in them. When it is said that the ten commandments are "the moral law," does not this definite phrase imply that all morality is contained in them; or, what is the same in effect, that all immorality is prohibited in them?

But, is this the fact? Are the immoralities called drunkenness, fornication, polygamy, divorces on trifling accounts, retaliation, &c., prohibited in the ten precepts? This question must be answered in the negative.

If it had been asked, is all immorality prohibited in this saying, "thou shalt love thy neighbor as thyself?" we would readily answer yes; but it is the so-called moral law we are speaking of. We affirm, then, that the above immoralities are not prohibited in the Decalogue, according to the most obvious construction of the words. We are aware that large volumes have been written to show how much is comprehended in the ten precepts. But, methinks, the voluminous works of some learned men on this subject too much resemble the writings of Peter D'Alva, who wrote forty-eight huge folio volumes to explain the mysteries of the conception of the Messiah in the womb of the Virgin Mary! And what shall we think of the genius who discovered that singing hymns and spiritual songs was prohibited, and the office of the Ruling Elder pointed out in the second commandment? That dancing and stage plays were prohibited in the seventh; and supporting the clergy enjoined in the eighth!

According to this latitude of interpretation, a genius may arise and show us that law and gospel are contained in the first commandment, and of course all the others are superfluous.

But this way of enlarging on the Decalogue defeats the division of the law of Moses, which these Doctors have made.

For instance, they tell us that witchcraft is prohibited in the first commandment—incest and sodomy in the seventh.

Now they afterwards place these vices, with the laws respecting them, in their judicial law; if, then, their moral law includes their judicial law, they make a distinction without a difference.

There remains another objection to this division of the law. It sets itself in opposition to the skill of the Apostle, and ultimately deters us from speaking of the ten precepts as he did.

Paul, according to the wisdom given unto him, denominated the ten precepts the "ministration of condemnation and of death;" 2d Cor. iii, 7-14. This we call the moral law. Whether *he* or we are to be esteemed the most able ministers of Christ it remains for you, my friends, to say.

Paul having called the ten precepts the ministration of death, next affirms that it was to be done away— and that it was done away. Now the calling the ten precepts "the moral law," is not only a violation of the use of words; is not only inconsistent in itself and contradictory to truth; but greatly obscures the doctrine taught by the Apostles in the 3d chapter, 2d Cor., and in similar passages, so as to render it almost, if not altogether, unintelligible to us. To use the same language of the moral law as he used in respect to the

minstration of condemnation and death, is shocking to
many devout ears.   When we say the moral law is
done away, the religious world is alarmed;   but when
we declare the ministration of condemnation is done
away they hear us patiently, not knowing what we
mean.   To give new names to ancient things, and
speak of them according to their ancient names, is
perplexing indeed.   Suppose, for example, I would call
the English law which governed these States when
colonies, the constitution of the United States, and
then affirm that the constitution of the United States
is done away, or abolished, who would believe me?
But if the people were informed that what I called
the constitution of these States was the obsolete British law, they would assent to my statement.   Who
would not discover that the giving of a wrong name
was the sole cause of such a misunderstanding?

Hence it is that modern teachers by their innova-
tions concerning law, have perplexed the student of
the Bible, and cause many a fruitless controversy, as
unnecessary as that relating to the mark set on Cain.
It does not militate with this statement to grant that
some of the precepts of the Decalogue have been re-
promulgated by Jesus Christ, any more than the re-
promulgation of some of the British laws does not
prevent us from affirming that the laws under which
the colonies existed are done away to the citizens of
the United States.   But of this more afterwards.

To what has been said it may be added, that the
modern division of the law tends very much to perplex
any person who wishes to understand the Epistles to
the Romans, Galatians and Hebrews;   insomuch that
while the hearer keeps this distinction in mind, he is
continually at a loss to know whether the moral, ceremonial, or judicial law is intended.

Before dismissing this part of the subject we would

observe that there are two principles, commandments or laws that are never included in our observations respecting the law of Moses, nor are they ever in Holy Writ called the law of Moses: These are, "Thou shalt love the Lord thy God with all thy heart, soul, mind and strength; and thy neighbor as thyself." These our Great Prophet teaches us, are the basis of the law of Moses, and of the Prophets: "On these two commandments hang all the law and the prophets." Indeed the Sinai law and all the Jewish law is but a modification of them. These are of universal and immutable obligation.

Angels and men, good and bad, are forever under them. God as our Creator, cannot require less; nor can we, as creatures and fellow-creatures, propose or expect less, as the standard of duty and perfection. These are coeval with angels and men. They are engraven with more or less clearness on every human heart. These are the ground work or basis of the law, written in the heart of heathens, which constitute their conscience, or knowledge of right or wrong.

By these their thoughts mutually accuse or else excuse one another.

By these they shall be judged, or at least, all who have never seen or heard a written law or revelation. But for these principles there had never been either law or gospel.

Let it then be remembered, that in the Scriptures these precepts are considered the basis of all law and prophecy; consequently when we speak of the law of Moses we do not include these commandments, but that whole modification of them sometimes called the legal dispensation.

It must also be observed that the Apostles sometimes speak of the law, when it is obvious that a certain part only is intended. But this so far from clashing with the preceeding observations fully corroborates them. For if the Apostle refers to any particular part of the law, under the general terms, the law, and speaks of the whole dispensation in the same terms without any additional definition, then, doubtless, the phrase the law, denotes the whole legal dispensation, and not any particular law or new distinction to which we may affix the words, the law.

1. We shall not attempt to point out those things which the law could not accomplish.

In the first place, it could not give righteousness and life. Righteousness and eternal life are inseparably connected.

Where the former is not, the latter cannot be enjoyed. Whatever means put us in possession of one puts us in possession of the other.

But this the law could not do. "For if there had been a law given which could have given life, verily, righteousness should have been by the law" (Gal. iii, 21). "If righteousness come by the law, then Christ is dead in vain." These testimonies of the Apostle, with the whole scope of divine truth, teach us that no man is justified by the law, that righteousness and eternal life can not be received through it.

Here we must regret that our translators by an injudicious supplement should have made the Apostle apparently contradict himself. I allude to the supplement in the 10th verse of Rom., 7th chap. From the 7th verse of this chapter, the Apostle narrated his experience as a Jew under the law, and then his experience as a Christian under the gospel, freed from the law. The scope of the 10th verse and its context is to show what the Apostle once thought of the law, and how his mistakes were corrected. If any supplement be necessary in this verse, we apprehend it should be similar to what follows: "And the commandment (which I thought would give me) life, I found (to lead) to death." This doubtless corresponds with the scope of the context, and does not, like the present supplement, clash with Gal. iii, 21.

Indeed the law, so far from being "ordained to give life," was merely "*added* to the promise of life till the seed should come to whom the promise was made." "Moreover the law entered that the offense might abound"—"For by the law was the knowledge of sin." For these reasons we conclude that justification, righteousness and eternal life cannot by any means be obtained by the law.

2. In the second place, the law could not exhibit the malignity or demerit of sin.

It taught those that were under it that certain actions were sinful. To these sinful actions it gave descriptive names—one is called theft, a second murder, a third adultery. It showed that these actions were offensive to God, hurtful to men, and deserved death. But how extensive their malignity and vast their demerit the law could not exhibit.

This remained for later times and other means to develop.

3. In the third place, the law could not be a suitable rule of life to mankind in this imperfect state. It could not be to all mankind, as it was given to and designed only for a part. It was given to the Jewish nation, and to none else.

As the inscription on a letter, identifies to whom it belongs; as the preamble to a proclamation, distinguishes who is addressed; so the preface to the law, points out and determines to whom it was given.

It points out a people brought out of the land of Egypt and released from the house of bondage, as the subjects of it. To extend it farther than its own preface, is to violate the rules of criticism and propriety.

How unjust and improper would it be, to convey the contents of a letter to a person to whom it was not directed—how inconsistent to enjoin the items of a proclamation made by the President of these United States, on the subjects of the French government. As inconsistent would it be to extend the law of Moses beyond the limits of the Jewish nation.

Do we not know with Paul, that what things soever the law saith, it saith to them that are under the law? But even to the Jews it was not the most suitable rule of life. 'Tis universally agreed, that example, as a rule of life, is more influential than precept. Now the whole Mosaic law wanted a model or example of living perfection. The most exemplary characters under the law, had their notable imperfections.

And as long as polygamy, divorces, slavery, revenge, etc., were winked at under that law, so long must the lives of its best subjects be stained with glaring imperfections. But when we illustrate how God has remedied the defects of the law, the ideas presented in this particular shall be more fully confirmed.

But we hasten to the third thing proposed in our method, which is to demonstrate the reason why the law could not accomplish these objects.

The Apostle in our text briefly informs us, that it was owing to human weakness that the law failed to accomplish these things—"In that it was weak through the flesh." The defects of the law are of a relative kind. It is not in itself weak or sinful—some part of it was holy, just and good—other parts of it were elementary, shadowy, representations of good things to come. But that part of it written and engraven on tables of stone, which was holy, just and good, failed in that it was too high, sublime and spiritual to regulate so weak a mortal as fallen man. And even when its oblations and sacrifices were presented, there was something too vast and sublime, for such weak means, such carnal commandments—such beggarly elements—such perishable and insignificant blood, to effect. So that as the Apostle saith, the law made nothing perfect, it merely introduced a better hope. If the law had been faultless, no place should have been found for the gospel. We may then fairly conclude that the spirituality, holiness, justice and goodness of one part of the law, rendered it too high; and the carnal, weak and beggarly elements of another part, rendered it too low; and both together became weak through the flesh. Viewing the law in this light, we can suitably apply the words of the Spirit uttered by Ezk. xx: 25, in relation to its incompetence—"I gave them," says he, "statutes which were not good, and judgments whereby they should not live."

We have now arrived at the fourth head of our discourse, in which we propose to illustrate the means by which God has remedied the relative defects of the law.

All those defects the Eternal Father remedies, by sending His own Son in the likeness of sinful flesh, and for sin, condemns sin in the flesh. "That the whole righteousness which the law required, might be fulfilled in us, who walk not after the flesh but after the Spirit."

The primary deficiency of the law which we noticed, was, that it could not give righteousness and eternal life.

Now, the Son of God, the Only Begotten of the Father, in the likeness of sinful flesh, makes an end of sin, makes reconciliation for iniquity, finishes transgression, brings in an everlasting righteousness, and completes eternal redemption for sinners.

He magnifies the law and makes it honorable. All this he achieves by his obedience unto death. He finished the work which the Father gave him to do; so that in him all believers, all the spiritual seed of Abraham, find righteousness and eternal life; not by legal works or observances, in whole or in part, but through the abundance of grace, and the gift of righteousness, which is by him;—"For the gift of God is eternal life through Jesus Christ our Lord." This righteousness, and its concomitant eternal life, are revealed from faith to faith—the information or report of it comes in the divine word to our ears, and receiving the report of it, or believing the divine testimony concerning it, brings us into the enjoyment of its blessings. Hence it is that Christ is the end of the law for righteousness to every one that believeth. Nor is he on this account the minister of sin—for thus the righteousness, the perfect righteousness of the law, is fulfilled in us who walked not after the flesh, but after the Spirit. Do we then make void the law or destroy the righteousness of it by faith? God forbid: we establish the law.

A second thing which we observed the law could not do, was to give a full exhibition of the demerit of sin. It is acknowledged that the demerit of sin was partially developed in the law, and before the law. Sin was condemned in the deluge, in the confusion of human speech, in turning to ashes the cities of the plain, in the thousands that fell in the wilderness. But these and a thousand similar monuments beside, fall vastly short of giving a full exhibition of sin in its malignant nature and destructive consequences. But a full discovery of its nature and demerits is given us in the person of Jesus Christ. God condemned sin in Him— God spared not His own Son, but delivered Him up. It pleased the Lord to bruise Him, to pour out His soul an offering for sin. When we view the Son of the Eternal suspended on the accursed tree—when we see

Him in the garden, and hear His petitions—when we hear Him exclaim, "My God, my God, why hast Thou forsaken Me?"—in a word, when we see Him expiring in blood and laid in the tomb, we have a monument of the demerit of sin which no law could give, which no temporal calamity could exhibit.

We sometimes in the vanity of our minds, talk lightly of the demerit of sin, and irreverently of the atonement. In this age of novelty, it is said "that the sufferings of Christ were so great as to atone for the sins of worlds on worlds," or at least for the sins of the damned as well as the saved—that "one drop of His blood is sufficient to atone for the sins of the whole world." That is, in other words, the sufferings of Christ so transcended the demerit of the sins of His people as to be sufficient to save áll that shall eternally perish. These assertions are as unreasonable as unscriptural. In our zeal to exalt the merits of the atonement—I say, in the warmth of our passions, and in the fullness of our hearts—let us be cautious lest we impeach the Divine wisdom and prudence. Doubtless, if the merits of His sufferings transcend the demerit of His people's sins, then some of His sufferings were in vain, and some of His merit unrewarded. To avoid this conclusion, some have affirmed that all shall be saved and none perish, contrary to the express word of God. Indeed, the transition from these inconsistent views of the atonement, to what is called Universalism, is short and easy. But I would humbly propose a few inquiries on this subject. Why do the evangelists inform us that Christ died so soon after His suspension on the cross? Why so much marvel expressed that He was so soon dead?—so much sooner than the malefactors that were crucified with Him? It might be presumed His last words solve these difficulties—"It is finished, and He gave up the ghost."

From these and similar premises, it would seem that His life and sufferings were prolonged just so long as was necessary to complete the redemption of His people. We are accustomed on all subjects that admit of it, to distinguish between quantity and quality. In the common concerns of human intercourse sometimes the quality of a thing is acceptable when the quantity is not; at other times the quantity is acceptable when the quality is not. If a thousand slaves were to be redeemed and emancipated by means of gold, the person in whose custody they were could not demand any more precious metal than gold—when one piece of gold was presented to him he might object to the quantity as deficient, though the quality is unobjectionable. In respect of the means of our redemption, it must be allowed that the sufferings of Christ were they. These sufferings, then, were the sufferings of a divine person—such doubtless was their quality. And a life and sufferings of any other quality could avail nothing in effecting redemption for transgressors. If but one of Adam's race should be saved, a life and sufferings of such a quality would have been indispensably requisite to accomplish such a deliverance. Again, if more were to have been saved than what will eventually be saved, the quantity and not the quality of His sufferings would have been augmented. The only sentiment respecting the atonement that will bear the test of Scripture, truth or sober reason, is, that the life and sufferings of Christ in quality, and in length or quantity, were such as sufficed to make reconciliation for all the sins of His chosen race; or for all them in every age or nation that shall believe in Him. There was nothing deficient, nothing superfluous; else he shall never see of the travail of His soul and be satisfied; which would be the reverse of His Father's promise, and His own expectation. When the life and sufferings of Christ are viewed in this light the demerit of sin appears in its true colors—all inconsistencies vanish, and all the testimonies of sacred truth, of Patriarchs, Prophets and Apostles harmoniously correspond. But if we suppose that the sufferings of Christ transcended the demerit of the sins of "His people," then we have no full exhibition of the demerit of sin. Nor are "His people" under any more obligation of love or gratitude to Him than they who eternally perish.

That which remains on this head is to show how the failure of the law in not being a suitable rule of life has been remedied.

We noticed that example is a more powerful teacher than precept. Now Jesus Christ has afforded us an example of human perfection never witnessed before. He gave a living form to every moral and religious precept which they never before possessed. In this respect He was the distinguished Prophet to whom Moses and all the inferior prophets referred. In entering on this prophetic office He taught with a peculiarity unexampled by all His predecessors—"He spake as never man spake."

The highest commendation He gave of Moses was that he wrote of Him, and that he was a faithful servant in Christ's house. From the beginning of his ministry to the end of his life, he claimed the honor of being the only person that could instruct men in the knowledge of God or of His will. He claimed the honor of being the author and finisher of the only perfect form of religion; the Eternal Father attested all his claims and honored all His pretensions. Respecting the ancient rules of life, the law and the prophets, He taught his disciples they had lived their day—he taught them they were given only for a limited time. "The law and the prophets prophesied until John"—then they gave place to a greater Prophet, and a more glorious law. Malachi, the last of the ancient prophets, informed Israel that they should strictly observe Moses' law, until a person should come in the spirit and power of Elias. Jesus taught us that John the Baptist was he, and that the law and prophets terminated at his entrance upon his ministry; for since that time the kingdom of God is preached, and all men press into it. To attest His character, and to convince the church of His being the great Prophet to whom all Christians should exclusively hearken as their teacher; to weaken the attachments of His disciples to Moses and the prophets, it pleased God to send down Moses and Elias from heaven; the one the law-giver, and the other the law-restorer, to resign their prophetic honors at the feet of the Messiah, in presence of select witnesses. "Jesus took with him Peter, James and John into a high mountain, and was transfigured before them, and His face did shine as the sun, and His raiment was white as snow, and behold there appeared Moses and Elias talking with him." Peter, enraptured with these heavenly visitants, proposes erecting three tabernacles—one for Christ, one for Moses, and one for Elias. But while he was thus proposing to associate Christ, the great Prophet, with Moses and Elias, inferior prophets, a bright cloud overshadowed them, and a voice came out of the cloud, an indirect reply to Peter's motion—"This is my beloved Son in whom I am well pleased, *hear ye him.*" Thus when these ancient and venerable prophets were recalled to heaven, Christ alone was left as the great Teacher, to whom, by a commandment from the excellent glory, the throne of the Eternal, we are obliged to hearken. That this transaction was significant of the doctrine above stated must be manifest, when we take into view all circumstances.

Might it not be asked, "Why did not Abel, Abraham, or Enoch appear on this occasion?"   The reason is plain—the disciples of Christ had no hurtful respect for *them*.—Moses and Elias, the reputed oracles of the Jewish nation, were the two, and the only two, in respect of whom this solemn and significant revocation was needful.   The plain language of the whole occurrence was this—Moses and Elias were excellent men— they were now glorified in heaven—they had lived their day—the limited time they were to flourish as teachers of the will of Heaven was now come to an end.   The morning star had risen—nay, was almost set, and the Sun of Righteousness was arising with salutiferous rays.   Let us then walk in the noon-day-light—let us hearken to Jesus as the Prophet and Legislator, Priest and King.   He shall reign over all the ransomed race.   We find all things whatsoever the law could not do are accomplished in him, and by him —that in him all Christians might be perfect and complete—"for the law was given by Moses, but grace and truth came by Jesus Christ."   It now remains, in the last place, to deduce such conclusions from the above premises, as must obviously and necessarily present themselves to every candid and reflecting mind.

1st.   From what has been said, it follows that there is an essential difference between law and gospel—the Old Testament and the New.*

---

* There are not a few professors of Christianity who suppose themselves under equal obligations to obey Moses or any other Prophet, as Christ and his Apostles. They cannot understand why any part of the divine relation should not be obligatory on a Christian to observe; nor can they see any reason why the New Testament should be preferred to the Old; or why they should not be regulated equally by each. They say, "Is it not all the word of God and are not all mankind addressed in it?" True, all the holy Prophets spake as they were moved by the Holy Spirit, and men

No two words are more distinct in their signification then *law* and *gospel*. They are contra-distinguished under various names in the New Testament. The law is denominated "the letter," "the ministration of condemnation;" "the ministration of death;" "the Old Testament or Covenant, and Moses." The gospel is denominated "the Spirit," "the ministration of the Spirit," "the ministration of righteousness," "the New Testament, or Covenant," "the law of liberty and Christ." In respect of existence or duration, the former is denominated "that which is done away"— the latter, "that which remaineth"—the former was faulty, the latter faultless—the former demanded, this bestows righteousness—that gendered bondage, this liberty—that begat bond-slaves, this freemen—the former spake on this wise, "This *do* and thou shalt

---

were the objects of their address. It is, however, equally evident that God at sundry times and in diverse manners spake to men, according to a variety of circumstances, which diversified their condition, capacity, and opportunities. Thus he addressed individuals, and classes of individuals, in a way peculiar to themselves. Witness his addresses to Noah, Abraham, Daniel, Jonah, Paul and Peter. Witness his addresses to the Patriarchs, the Jews and the Christians. Again, men are addressed as magistrates, fathers, masters, husbands, teachers, with their correlates. Now to apply to one individual what is said to all individuals and classes of individuals, would, methinks, appear egregious folly. And would it not be absurd to say, that every man is obliged to practice every duty and religious precept enjoined in the Bible. Might we not as reasonably say, that every man must be at once a Patriarch, a Jew, and a Christain; a magistrate, a subject, a father, a child, a master, a servant, etc., etc. And, certainly, it is as inconsistent to say, that Christians should equally regard and obey the Old and New Testament. All Scripture given by divine inspiration, is profitable for various purposes in the perfection of saints, when rightly divided, and not handled deceitfully. But where the above considerations are disregarded, the word of God

live"—this says, "Say not what *ye* shall do; the word is nigh thee, [that gives life,] the word of faith which we preach: if thou believe in thine heart the gospel, thou shalt be saved." The former waxed old, is abolished, and vanished away—the latter remains, lives, and is everlasting.

2d. In the second place, we learn from what has been said, that "there is no condemnation to them which are in Christ Jesus." The premises from which the Apostles drew this conclusion are the same with those stated to you in this course. "Sin," says the Apostle, "shall not have dominion over you; for ye are not under the law, but under grace." In the 6th and 7th chapters to the Romans, the Apostle taught them that "they were not under the law"—that "they were freed from it"—"dead to it"—"delivered from

---

must inevitably be perverted. Hence it is that many preachers deceive themselves and their hearers by selecting and applying to themselves and their hearers such portions of sacred truth as belong not to them nor their hearers. Even the Apostles could not apply the words of Christ to themselves or their hearers until they were able to answer a previous question—"Lord, sayest thou this unto *us* or unto *all?*" Nor could the eunuch understand the Prophet until he knew whether he spoke of himself or of some other man. Yet many preachers and hearers trouble not themselves about such inquiries. If their text is in the Bible, it is no matter where; and if their hearers be men and women, it is no matter whether Jews or Christians, believers or unbelievers. Often have I seen a preacher and his hearers undergo three or four metamorphoses in an hour. First he is a moral philosopher, inculcating heathen morality; next a Jewish Rabbi, expounding the law; then a teacher of some Christian precept; and lastly, an ambassador of Christ, negotiating between God and man. The congregation undergo the correlate revolutions; first, they are heathens; next, Jews; anon Christians; and lastly, treating with the ambassadors for salvation, on what is called the terms of the gospel. Thus, Proteus-like, they are all things in an hour.

it." In the 8th chapter, 1st verse, he draws the above conclusion. What a pity that modern teachers should have *added* to and *clogged* the words of inspiration by such unauthorized sentences as the following: "Ye are not under the law" *as a covenant of works, but as a rule of life!* Who ever read one word of the "covenant of works" in the Bible, or of the Jewish law being a rule of life to the disciples of Christ? Of these you hear no more from the Bible than of the "Solemn League" or "St. Giles' Day." Yet how conspicuous are these and kindred phrases in the theological discussions of these three last hundred years! But leaving such phrases to those who are better skilled in the use of them, and have more leisure to expound them, we shall briefly notice the reason commonly assigned for proposing the law as a rule of life to Christians. "If Christians are taught," say they, "that they are delivered from the law, under it in no sense—that they are dead to it—will not they be led to live rather a licentious life, live as they list; and will not the non-professing world, hearing that *they* are not under the law of Moses, become more wicked, more immoral and profane?" Such is the chief of all the objections made against the doctrine inculcated respecting the abolition of the Jewish law in respect of Christians, and also as this doctrine respects the Gentile or Heathen world. We shrink not from a fair and full investigation of this subject. Truth being the only allowed object of all our inquiries, and the sole object of every Christian's inquiry, we should patiently hear all objections—coolly and dispassionately hear, examine, and weigh all arguments *pro* and *con*.

That the first part of this objection is very natural, has been very often made, and strongly urged against the doctrine we advocate, we cheerfully acknowledge. As this objection was made against the Apostle's doctrine concerning the law, it affords a strong probability, at least, that our views on this subject correspond with his. We shall then hear how he stated and refuted it. Romans vi, 15. "What then? Shall we sin because we are not under the law, but under grace?" Here he admits the objection, and in his answer incontestably shows that Christians are not under the law in any sense. If they were in any sense, now was the time to say, "We are not under the law in some sense, or under a certain part of it; but in one sense we are under it as a rule of life." We say the Apostle was here called upon, and in a certain sense bound, to say something like what our modern teachers say, if it had been warrantable. But he admits the doctrine and states the objection, leaving the doctrine unequivocally established. He guards the doctrine against a licentious tendency thus—"God forbid!" "How shall we that are dead to sin live any longer therein?" and in the subsequent verses shows the utter impossibility of any servant of God, or true Christian, so abusing the doctrine we have stated. Now whether the ancient way of guarding the New Testament, or gospel, against the charges of Antinomianism or a licentious tendency, or the modern way is best, methinks is easily decided amongst true disciples. Not so easy, however, amongst learned Rabbis and Doctors of the law.

But, query—Is the law of Moses a rule of life to Christians? An advocate of the popular doctrine replies, "Not all of it." Query again—What part of it? "The ten commandments." Are these a rule of life to Christians? "Yes." Should not, then, Christians sanctify the seventh day? "No." Why so? "Because Christ has not enjoined it." Oh! then, the law or ten commandments is not a rule of life to Christians any further than it is enjoined by Christ; so that reading the precepts in Moses' words, or hearing him utter them, does not oblige us to observe them; it is only what Christ says we must observe. So that an advocate for the popular doctrine, when closely pressed, cannot maintain his ground. Let no man say we have proposed and answered the above queries as we please. If any other answers can be given by the advocates themselves than we have given, let them do it. But it is highly problematical whether telling Christians that they are under the law will repress a licentious spirit. True Christians do not need it, as we have seen: "how shall they that are dead to sin live any longer therein?" And dare we tell professing Christians, as such, that the law, as a rule of life, is a condemning law? If not, then what tendency will the mere affirmation that they are under a law as a rule of life which cannot condemn them have to deter them from living as they list. Upon the whole, the *old way* of guarding against immorality and licentiousness amongst Christians will, we apprehend, be found the most consistent and efficacious. And he that has tried the old way and the new, will doubtless say as was said of old, "No man also having drunk old wine, straightway desireth new: for he saith the old is better." And, indeed, every attempt to guard the New Testament, or the gospel, by extrinsic means, against an immoral or licentious tendency, bears too strong a resemblance to the policy of a certain preacher in Norway or Lapland, who told his hearers that "hell was a place of infinite and incessant cold." When asked by an acquaintance from the South of Europe why he perverted the Scriptures, he replied, "if he told his hearers in that cold climate that hell was a place of excessive heat, he verily thought they would take no pains to avoid going there."

But as to the licentious tendency this doctrine we inculcate is supposed to have upon the non-professing or unbelieving world, it appears rather imaginary than real. It must, however, in the first instance be ascertained whether the Gentiles, not professing Christianity, were ever supposed or addressed by the Apostle sent to the Gentiles, as being under the law of Moses. We have under the second head of our discourse particularly demonstrated that the Gentiles were never under the law, either before or after their conversion. To what has been said on this subject we would add a sentence or two. It was prophesied of the Gentiles that they should be without law till Christ came. Isa. xlii. 4, "And the isles shall *wait* for *his* law." The chief glory which exalted the Jews above the Gentiles, which the Jews boasted of to the Gentiles, was that to *them "pertained* the adoption, the covenants, and *the giving of the law."* They exclusively claimed the law as their own. And why will not we let them have it, seeing Hom whose law the Gentiles waited for is come, and has given us a more glorious law. Whatever was excellent in their law our Legislator has re-promulgated. But shall we say that we are under the law as a rule of our Christian life, because some of its sublimest moral and religious precepts have been re-promulgated by Him who would not suffer one tittle of it to pass till he fulfilled it? As well might we affirm that the British law which governed these States, when colonies, is the rule of our political life, because some of the most excellent laws of that code have been re-enacted by our legislators. Paul, the Apostle to the Gentiles, plainly acknowledged in his addresses to them, that they were without law, aliens from the commonwealth of Israel having no hope, &c. And of them he said that "when the Gentiles, who have not the law, do by nature the things contained in the law, these having *not the law,* are a law unto themselves." But, in so saying, does *he* or do *we* excuse their sins or lead them to suppose that they are thereby less ob-

noxious to the wrath to come? By no means. For we
testify that even natural conscience accuses them of
sin or wrong in their thoughts, words and actions according to its knowledge. And consequently "as many
as have sinned without law, shall also perish without
law." In so testifying, do we cherish a licentious
spirit? By no means. For there stand a thousand
monuments in this present world, independent of Jewish law, on which are inscribed these words, "For the
wrath of God is revealed from heaven against all ungodliness and unrighteousness of men." But one thing
demands our observation, that the Apostle sent by
Heaven to preach to the Gentiles, in accusing them of
sins of the deepest dye, and of the most malignant
nature, dishonorable to God and destructive to themselves, never accuses them of any sin which the light
of nature itself would not point out, or natural conscience testify to be wrong. Hence it is that in the
long black catalogue of sins preferred against the
Gentiles, is never to be found the crime of Sabbath-
breaking, or transgressing any of the peculiarities of
Judaism. And now what is the difference between an
ancient Greek and a modern American or European
who disbelieves the gospel? Under what law is the
latter, under which the former was not? Was the
former a sinner and chargeable in the sight of God,
as well as the latter? Yes. Would not natural conscience according to its means of knowing right and
wrong, or the work of the law written in the heart,
condemn the unbelieving Romans as well as the unbelieving Americans? Most assuredly. And what
is the difference? Not that the latter is under any law
that the former was not under, but the means of discerning right and wrong in the latter are far superior
to the former, and consequently their overthrow or
ruin will be more severe. In point of law or obligation

there is no difference between the unbelieving American and the rudest barbarian; though the former is polished with science, morals, &c., like the ancient Greeks and Romans, and the latter remains an uncultivated savage. They will be judged and condemned by the same law which condemned the Roman who died 1900 years ago. And the condemnation of the latter shall be more tolerable than the former, not by a milder law, but because his knowledge of right and wrong was much inferior to the former; and having heard the gospel of salvation and disbelieved it, he adds to his natural corruption and accumulated. guilt the sin of making God a liar, and preferring darkness to light, because he believed not the testimony of God. This is the sole difference in respect of condemnation between the Indian and the most accomplished citizen. From these few remarks it will appear, we trust, obvious to every person who has an ear to distinguish truth from falsehood, that there is no condemnation to them which are in Christ Jesus—that they are under no law that can condemn them—that *he* who was made under the law is become the end of the law for righteousness to them—that being dead to sin, they should live no longer therein—that there is no necessity, but a glaring impropriety in teaching the law as a rule of life to Christians—that all arguments in favor of it are founded on human opinion and a mistaken view of the tendency of the gospel and Christian dispensation —that all objections against the doctrine we have stated as licentious in its tendency are totally groundless. "For the grace of God that bringeth salvation teacheth us that denying ungodliness and worldly lusts, we should live soberly, righteously and godly in this present world. Looking for that blessed hope, the glorious appearing of the great God, even our Saviour Jesus Christ; who gave himself for us that he might redeem us from all iniquity, and purify unto himself a peculiar people, *zealous of good works.*"

3d. In the third place, we conclude from the above premises, that there is no necessity for preaching the law in order to prepare men for receiving the gospel.

This conclusion perfectly corresponds with the commission given by our Lord to the Apostles, and with their practice under that commission. "Go," saith he, "into all the world, and preach the gospel unto every creature." "Teach the disciples to observe all things whatsoever I command you." Thus they were authorized to preach the gospel, not the law, to every creature. Thus they were constituted ministers of the New Testament, not of the Old. Now the sacred history, called the Acts of the Apostles, affords us the most satisfactory information on the method the Apostles preached under this commission; which, with the epistolary part of the New Testament, affords us the only successful, warrantable, and acceptable method of preaching and teaching. In the Acts of the Apostles, we see the Apostles and first preachers paid the most scrupulous regard to the instructions they received from the great Prophet. They go forth into all nations proclaiming the gospel to every creature; but not one word of law-preaching in the whole of it. We have the substance of eight or ten sermons delivered by Paul and Peter to Jews and Gentiles, in the Acts of Apostles, and not one precedent of preaching the law to prepare their hearers, whether Jews or Gentiles, for the reception of the gospel.

This conclusion corresponds, in the next place, with the nature of the kingdom of heaven or Christian church, and with the means by which it is to be built and preserved in the world. The Christian dispensation is called "the ministration of the Spirit," and accordingly everything in the salvation of the church is accomplished by the immediate energy of the Spirit. Jesus Christ taught his disciples that the testimony concerning himself was that only which the Spirit would use in converting such of the human family as should be saved. He was not to speak of himself, but what he knew of Christ. Now he was to convince the world of sin, of righteousness, and of judgment; not by applying the law of Moses, but the facts concerning Christ to the consciences of the people. The spirit accompanying the words which the Apostles preached, would convince the world of sin; not by the ten precepts, but because they believed not on him—of righteousness, because *he* went to the Father—and of judgment, because the prince of this world was judged by him. So that Christ and not law was the Alpha and Omega of their sermons; and this the Spirit made effectual to the salvation of thousands. Three thousand were convinced of sin, of righteousness, and of judgment, in this precise way of hearing of Christ, on the day of Pentecost; and we read of many afterwards. Indeed, we repeat it again, in the whole history of primitive preaching, we have not one example of preaching the law as preparatory to the preaching or reception of the gospel.

This conclusion corresponds, in the third place, with the fitness of things.* That man must be con-

---

*Indeed we have yet to learn what advantage can accrue from preaching the so called "moral law," to prepare sinners for the gospel. In the nature and fitness of things it cannot prepare or dispose the mind to a belief of the gospel. The Apostles teach us that "the law worketh wrath." This is inevitably its effect on every mind which does not believe the gospel. It irritates and excites the natural enmity of the mind against God. A clear exhibition of the divine character in the law, apart from the gospel, tends more to alienate than to reconcile the mind to God. When

vinced of sin by some means, prior to a welcome reception of saving truth, is generally acknowledged. Now, as the gospel dispensation is the most perfect revelation of salvation, it must be supposed that it possesses the best means of accomplishing everything connected with the salvation of its subjects. It must, of course, possess the best means of convincing of sin.

------

a preacher of the law has labored to show his hearers the immaculate holiness, the inflexible justice, the inviolate truth and consuming jealousy of Jehovah, manifested in the fiery law, supposing the gospel kept out of view, he has rather incapacitated and disqualified their minds from crediting the gospel or testimony of the condescension, love, mercy and grace of the Eternal Father to mankind. How opposite is the divine wisdom to the wisdom of many modern scribes and teachers of the law! They preach first the law to natural fallen man, then the gospel. But He who seeth not as man seeth, preached first the gospel to fallen man, and afterwards added the law, because of transgressions, till the seed should come. Eternal life was promised through the seed, and the law added till the seed come.

Nothing can be more inconsistent than the conduct of the law preachers. When they have echoed the thunders of Mount Sinai in the ears of their hearers almost to drive them to despair, and to produce what they call "legal repentance," then they begin to pull down the work of their hands by demonstrating the inefficacy, unprofitableness and danger of legal repentance. Might they not as well at once imitate the Apostles and primitive preachers— preach the gospel, which, when received, produces repentance not to be repented of? Might they not preach Christ crucified, in whom is manifested the wrath and judgment of God against sin; and his condescending love, mercy and grace to the sinner? Might they not, knowing the terror of the Lord, persuade men by the persuasives of the doctrine of reconcilation; rather than to increase their enmity, awaken their suspicions and work wrath in their minds, by an unlawful use of the law? But in order to this, their minds must be revolutionized; they must take up a cross which they at present refuse; and what is difficult indeed, they must unlearn what they have themselves taught others.

This truth, however, does not depend on mere supposition. The fact that the Holy Spirit makes an exclusive use of it in convincing of sin, is a striking demonstration of its superior excellence for that purpose. But independent of these considerations, it must be confessed that the gospel or testimony concerning Christ affords the fullest proof of divine justice and indignation against sin—it presents the clearest view of the demerit of sin, and of all divine perfections terrible to sinners—it exhibits the most alarming picture of human guilt and wretchedness that ever was given, and on these accounts is of all means the most suitable to convince of sin. It was already observed that the eternal Father condemned sin in the person of his Son, more fully than it ever was, or could be condemned in any other way. Suppose, for illustration, a king put to death his only son, in the most painful and ignominious way, for a crime against the government: would not this fact be the best means of convincing his subjects of the evil of crime, and of the king's detestation of it? Would not this fact be better than a thousand lectures upon the excellency of the law and the sanctions of it? But every similitude of this kind falls infinitely short of affording a resemblance of the eternal Father not sparing his Sole Delight when sin was but imputed to him. Having seen that this conclusion corresponds with the commission given by the Redeemer to his Apostles—with their practice under that commission—with the nature of his kingdom, and with the fitness of things, one would suppose that no objection could be preferred against it. But what doctrine of divine truth is it, against which objections, numerous indeed, and strongly urged, and by men who profess to be zealous for the truth, have not been made? Is it the doctrine of sovereign, free, and abundant grace? No. Is it the doctrine of the natural sinfulness and corruption of all men? No, no. Against these, many objections, yea, very many, are urged. We must not suppose, then, that this doctrine we now maintain shall be free from objections. We shall, then, attend to some of those objections which have been made, or which we anticipate may be made against this conclusion.

It may, perhaps, be objected that there are some expressions in the apostolic epistles which imply that the law was necessary to convince of sin, as pre-requisite to a welcome reception of the gospel; such as "by the law *is* the knowledge of sin"—"for without the law sin *was* dead." There is no authority from the original for varying the supplements in these two clauses. If it corresponds with the context or with the analogy of faith, to supply *was* in the last clause, it doubtless corresponds as well in the first clause. But we lay no stress on the one or the other; for before Christ came all knowledge of sin *was* by the law; and "the law entered that the offense might abound." For the law was added to the promise of life, because of transgression, till the seed should come to whom the promise was made. Now we would suppose that when the *seed* is come, and the time expired for which the law was added, it is superfluous to annex it to the gospel, for the same reason it was annexed to the promise made to Abraham. And although it should be allowed that Christians derive knowledge of sin from the law, it does not follow that it is the best means of communicating this knowledge—that Christians are dependent on it for this purpose—nor that it should be preached to unbelievers to prepare them for receiving the gospel.

The seventh chapter to the Romans contains the fullest illustration of the once excellence and utility of the law that is to be found in all the New Testament;

and as this chapter will doubtless be the stronghold of our opponents, we shall make a remark or two on the contents of it.

In the first place, then, let it be remembered that in the fourteenth verse of the preceding chapter, the Apostle boldly affirms that Christians are not under the law. To the conclusion of the sixth chapter he refutes an objection made to his assertion in the fourteenth verse. In the first six verses of the seventh chapter he repeats his assertion, and uses an apt similitude to illustrate it. Having, then, demonstrated that Christians are not under the law, in the seventh verse of the the seventh chapter he states an objection which had been made, or he anticipated would be made, against his doctrine—"If Christians are not under the law, if they are dead to it, if they are delivered from it, is it not a sinful thing?" "Is the law sin, then?" This objection against the nature of the law, the Apostle removes in the next six verses by showing the utility of the law in himself as a Jew under that law; and concludes that the law is holy, just and good. To the end of the chapter the Apostle gives an account of his experience as a Christian freed from the law, and thus manifests the excellency of his new mind or nature by its correspondence to the holiness of the law; so that he most effectually removes the objection made against the law as being sin, and at the same time establishes the fact that Christians *are delivered from it.* Such evidently is the scope of the latter part of the sixth and all of the seventh chapter. We cannot dismiss this chapter without observing, first, that the law or that part of the law which the Apostle here speaks of, is what modern teachers call "the moral law." If so, then Christians are not under it; for the law which the Apostle affirms Christians are delivered from in the sixth verse, in the seventh verse he shows is not sin;

and the law which he shows is not sin, he demonstrates to be holy, just and good. So that here, as well as in the third chapter of his second Epistle to the Corinthians, Christians are expressly said to be delivered from the so-called moral law; and that it is abolished or done away in respect of them. We must remark again that before any thing said in this chapter respecting the utility or excellence of the law can be urged as a precedent for what we condemn—namely, preaching the law as preparatory to the gospel, or a law work as preparatory to genuine conversion, it must be shown that the Apostle gave this account of his experience under the law as preparatory to his conversion. Otherwise no objection can be made from anything in this chapter to the conclusion before stated. But this cannot be; for the account we have of his conversion flatly contradicts such a supposition. Previous to his conversion he was a very devout man in his own way—"touching the righteousness which was in the law he was blameless." See the account he gives of himself, Phil. iii, 4, 5, compared with Rom. vii, 7-12; Acts xxii, 1; xxiii, 1; from which we learn that he was taught according to the most perfect manner of the law, and was a Pharisee of the strictest kind: had clear ideas of sin and righteousness; and, externally considered, was blameless and lived in all good conscience until the day of his conversion. But it was not the law, it was not a new discovery of its spirituality, but a discovery of Christ exalted, that convinced him of sin, of righteousness and of judgment; and instantaneously converted him. So that nothing in his previous life or attainments, nothing of his experience as a Jew, nothing of his knowledge of sin or of righteousness by the law previous to his conversion, can be urged in support of preaching the law or a law work to unbelievers, to prepare their mind for a welcome reception of the truth.

When we shall have mentioned a favorite text of the law preachers, and considered it, we shall have done with objections of this sort. It is Galatians iii, 24. We shall cite from the 23d verse: "Before faith [Christ] came we were kept under the law, shut up unto the faith which should afterwards be revealed. Wherefore the law was our schoolmaster *to bring us* to Christ, that we might be justified by faith. But after that faith [Christ] is come, we are no longer under a schoolmaster." Methinks it looks rather like an insult to the understanding of any person skilled in the use of words, to offer a refutation of the use that is frequently made of the 24th verse. But let the censure rest upon them who render it needful. Every smatterer in Greek knows that the 24th verse might read thus: "The law was our schoolmaster until Christ" came; and this reading unquestionably corresponds with the context. Now is it not most obvious that instead of countenancing law-preaching, this text and context condemn it? The scope of it is to show that whatever use the law served as a schoolmaster previous to Christ, it no longer serves that use. And now that Christ is come we are no longer under it. We see, then, that this conclusion not only corresponds with the commission to the Apostles, with the nature of Christ's Kingdom, with the apostolic preaching, and with the fitness of things: but that no valid objection can be presented against it, from anything in the apostolic epistles.

Some, notwithstanding the Scriptural plainness of this doctrine, may urge their own experience as contrary to it. It would, however, be as safe for Christians to make divine truth a test of their experience, and not their experience a test of divine truth. Some

individuals have been awakened by the appearance of
the aurora borealis, by an earthquake, by a thunder-
storm, by a dream, by sickness, etc. How inconsistent
for one of these to affirm from his own experience, that
others must be awakened in the same way! How in-
compatible with truth for others to preach such occur-
renees as preliminary to saving conversion!

But the difference between ancient and modern conversions is so striking as to merit an observation or
two. Now that the law is commonly preached to prepare men for Christ, it must be expected that modern
conversions will be very systematic, and lingering in
all. While preachers will not condescend to proclaim
the glad tidings until they have driven their hearers almost to despair by the thunders of Mt. Sinai—while
they keep them in anxious suspense for a time, whether
the wounds of conviction are deep enough; whether
their sense of guilt is sufficiently acute; whether their
desires are sufficiently keen; whether their fears are
sufficiently strong; in short, whether the law has had
its full effect upon them: I say, when this is the case,
conversion work must go on slow; and so it is not rare
to find some in a way of being converted for years;
and, indeed, it is generally a work of many months.
It would be well, however, if, after all, it were commonly genuine. Compare these conversions with those
of which we read in the Acts of the Apostles, and
what a contrast! There we read of many converted
in a day, who yesterday were as ignorant of law and
gospel as the modern Hindoos or Burmans. To account
for this we have only to consider and compare the different sorts of preaching and means by which those
were and these are effected.

But some may yet inquire, Are unbelievers under no
law or obligation by which conviction may be communicated to their minds? Or they may ask in other

words, How does the testimony of Christ take hold of them? And why do they welcome the gospel? We have already shown that there is a law written on every human heart, which is the foundation of both law and prophets, under which both angels and men exist, whose obligation is universal and eternal. It is inscribed more or less distinctly on every heathen's heart. It is sometimes called the law of nature, but more correctly called by the Apostle, *conscience*. This natural conscience, or sense of right and wrong, which all men possess in different degrees, according to a variety of circumstances, but all in some degree, is that in them which God addresses. This natural conscience is fitted to hear the voice of God, as exactly as the ear is fitted to hear sounds. This renders the savage inexcusable. For the invisible things of God, even his eternal power and godhead, are manifested to his conscience in the natural world. Now God addresses conscience in those whom he brings to himself in a variety of ways. Sometimes even where his word is come, he speaks by awful events to the consciences of men. In this way he awakens inquiries that lead to the saving truth. Witness the jailor and his house, of whom we read in the Acts of the Apostles. God spake to his conscience by an earthquake, and put an inquiry in his mouth that was answered to his salvation and that of his house. That which fits the savage to hear God's voice in the natural world, fits him or the man of civilization to hear his voice in the gospel, when it is sent to them in power.

Are we to preach this law of nature, then, some will inquire, or are we to show men that they possess this natural conscience, previous to a proclamation of the glad tidings? I would answer this question by proposing another. Am I to tell a man he has an ear, and explain to him the use of it, before I condescend to speak to him? One answer suits both inquiries. We should consider the circumstances of any people before we address them. Do we address Jews? Let us address them as the Apostles did. Persuade them out of their own law that Jesus is the Messiah. Do we address professed Christians? Let us imitate the apostolic addresses in the epistles. Do we preach to barbarians? Let us address them as Paul preached to the Lycaonians—speak to their consciences. Do we preach to polished infidels or idolaters? Let us speak to them as Paul spake to the Athenians—speak to their consciences.

4th. A fourth conclusion which is deducible from the above premises, is that all arguments and motives, drawn from the law or Old Testament, to urge the disciples of Christ to baptize their infants; to pay tithes to their teachers; to observe holy days or religious fasts, as preparatory to the observance of the Lord's supper; to sanctify the seventh day; to enter into national covenants; to establish any form of religion by civil law;—and all reasons and motives borrowed from the Jewish law to excite the disciples of Christ to a compliance with or an initiation of Jewish customs, are inconclusive, repugnant to Christianity, and fall ineffectual to the ground; not being enjoined or countenanced by the authority of Jesus Christ.

5th. In the last place we are taught from all that has been said to venerate in the highest degree the Lord Jesus Christ; to receive Him as the Great Prophet, of whom Moses in the law, and all the prophets did write. To receive him as the Lord our righteousness, and to pay the most punctilious regard to all his precepts and ordinances. "If we continue in his word, then are we his disciples indeed, and we shall know the truth and the truth shall make us free—if the Son shall make us free, we shall be free indeed."

It is remarkable how strong our attachments are to Moses as a teacher: though Moses taught us to look for a greater prophet than he, and to hearken *to him!* It is strange that three surprising incidents in the history of Moses would not arrest our attention and direct us to Christ. With all his moral excellence, unfeigned piety and legislative dignity, he fell short of Canaan. So all who cleave to him will come short of the heavenly rest! His mortal remains, and his only, the Almighty buried in secret; and yet we will not suffer his ashes to rest in peace! He came down from heaven to give place to the Messiah, to lay down his commission at his feet; and we will not accept it! Strange infatuation!

If Moses was faithful in Christ's house as a servant, shall not Christ be faithful as a son over his own house? Let us as his disciples believe all he teaches, and practice all he enjoins in religion and morality; let us walk in all his commandments and ordinances; and inquire individually, What lack I yet? If we are then deficient, let us say with the Jews who disowned him, "We are Moses' disciples, but as for this fellow, we know not whence he is." But let all remember that if he that despises Moses' law died without mercy, of how much sorer punishment, suppose ye, shall he be thought worthy, who despised Christ as a teacher! His commandments are not grievous to his disciples —his yoke is easy, and his burden is light.

Let every one that nameth the name of Christ depart from all iniquity. Let us walk worthy of Him. Let us take heed lest by our conduct we should represent Christ as the minister of sin. Let us not walk after the flesh but the Spirit; and then we shall show that the righteousness of the law is fulfilled in us. Then shall no occasion be given to the adversary to speak reproachfully. And if any should still urge the stale charge of Antinomianism, or affirm that we live in sin that grace might abound, did evil that good might come, or made void the law through faith, let us put to silence the ignorance of foolish men, by adorning the doctrine we profess with a blameless conduct. Let us not merely rebut such insinuations with a "God forbid!" but evince, how shall we that are dead to sin, live any longer therein.

May he that hath the key of David, who openeth and no man shutteth, and shutteth and none can open, open your hearts to receive the truth in the love of it, and incline you to walk in the light of it, and then ye shall know that the ways thereof are pleasantness, and all the paths thereof are peace! *Amen.*

TO THE CHURCH SCATTERED
THROUGHOUT AMERICA.

BY BARTON W. STONE.

Barton W. Stone was born near Port Tobacco, Md., December 24, 1772. Died at Hannibal, Mo., November 9, 1844.

My dear Brethren:

Your edification in Christ Jesus, your fellowship in the Spirit, your union with all saints, and your prosperity in the Lord, have long been the wish and prayer of my heart, and labor of my life. In the prosecution of these Divine objects, I see, on a retrospect, my many imperfections; I blush at the remembrance, and pray my Lord, and beseech my brethren to forgive. Knowing that the time of my departure is near, I wish to write a few things to you, which may be profitable after my decease, and which may speak when I am dead.

About the beginning of this century my mind was uncommonly exercised on the subject of religion. I then evidently saw what I yet see, that the sects in which the religious community was divided, were antiscriptural, and insuperable mountains in the way of the progress of truth. With others in the same spirit, I set myself against this evil, and determined before God to exert my feeble powers to remove it from the religion of heaven, and promote Christian union, both by my example and by my endeavors in the cause of truth. The odds were fearful, a handful

149

against the formidable array of long-established
parties. In Israel's God we trusted, and *"forward"*
was our motto. Beyond our most sanguine anticipa-
tions the cause of union prospered. One thing as-
tounded us; the clergy of all the sects, who should be
foremost in every good work, were our bitterest opposers. We had to combat for every inch of ground
we possessed, and for every fortress we gained.

In this mind have I continued to this day; and yet
feel the same spirit to labor in the good cause, but
the flesh is too weak to sustain the burden, after a
warfare of nearly half a century.

My dear brethren, we have advanced and become a
great people. Now is the time of danger, now there
is need of humility, watchfulness and prayer. We
begin to be respected as a people, and begin already to
vie with others in numbers. A Joab is sent by the
higher powers through the length and breadth of the
land to number Israel. O that the fate of Israel of old
may not be ours! If it proceeds from pride, and if
God has regard for us, we may expect a diminution
in our ranks. Instead of thanksgiving and praise to
God, because he has so wonderfully prospered our
labors in uniting so many thousands, it is to be feared
that pride may yet succeed, and spoil all our works.
Israel were often seduced from the true worship of
God to the idolatry and communion of the nations
among which they dwelt, and this always took place
in the days of their prosperity. So we may be so
captivated by the doctrines, forms, popularity and re-
spectability of the sects around us that we may try to

accommodate the truth of God to their prejudices, in order to gain their favor, and eventually to enlist them on our side, and join in our mighty union. Such union is no better, if as good, as that of the Romanists, who are exceedingly zealous for union. A union of ten pious, uncompromising persons in the truth, is better than ten thousand of the contrary character. Truth must never be sacrificed for the union of numbers. Truth preached and lived in the spirit will cut its way through all opposition.

But what is truth? The Bible, and the Bible alone— not opinions which men have formed of the Bible, whether comprised in a confession of faith, or in a Christian system, or in thirty-nine articles, or in a discipline. Our union first commenced on this ground, and sectarianism first received its deadly wound from this weapon, and by no other will it die the death, if its death is to be effected by moral means. If we begin to magnify our opinions, and make them tests of fellowship, we depart from the foundation laid in Zion, and shall be under the necessity of becoming a sect by forming a book of opinions as our creed, and demanding a subscription to it as the basis of union. This must be a progressive work; it can not be effected at once. There is too much light in the world at present for its growth. "Here a little and there a little," must precede its introduction. My dear brethren, watch and pray, lest you fall into temptation and mar the work of God. Stand fast in the liberty wherewith Christ has made you free, and be not entangled again with the yoke of bondage.

On this foundation I have been immovably fixed for
many years, and shall remain for the few days I may
live. Some of my own brethren may think I do not
advocate Christianity. It may be so; for I confess
myself a fallible creature, and therefore I warn my
brethren not to receive anything I have said or written
as truth, unless sustained by the infallible Word. They
who think I am not advocating Christianity may be
wrong, for they also are fallible, and must not be
trusted without careful examination by the Word.

I well remember that when my mind was opened at
first to see the truth as stated above, I said that if all
the world should depart from it, I never would. When
all my fellow-laborers had departed from it, and left
me alone, I still felt and repeated the same words, and
still repeat them.

A factionist I never can nor will be. Should I
stand in the way of the present reformation in the
opinion of any, it will not be long. Let them publicly
withdraw from me their fellowship. To cast me out
of the Church they can not, without they cast out all
those who receive the Bible alone, and who are anti-
sectarians.

The sects have their churches, like the States of
Greece, closely concatenated, though sometimes the
chain is broken. Are we beginning to imitate them?
Do we begin to yield the power and right of the
churches to the clergy? It may be a harmless thing
in the present generation; but posterity may writhe
under the galling chain. What means so much written
on organization? The first link is loose—unfastened

—and that link is love. Without this the churches may be chained together by human device; but this is not the organization of the head of the Church. We may devise plans of organization, but they will all prove fallacious. Human bonds may bind human beings, who have not the spirit; but spiritual bonds cannot bind together such persons.

The great secret of church government and organization has been almost overlooked. It is the indwelling of the Holy Spirit in each believer and member of the Church. "The fruits of the Spirit are love, joy, peace, longsuffering, gentleness, goodness, meekness, fidelity, and temperance; against such there is no law." No law of Heaven nor of earth will condemn them. "There is no condemnation to them that are in Christ, who walk not after the flesh, but after the Spirit," the Spirit which dwells in them. Such a church as is composed of such members, is easily governed by the law of Christ, and they need no other. But those of the opposite character, who have not the Spirit, and who walk after the flesh, are not subject to this law, nor indeed can be. "The works of the flesh are adultery, fornication, uncleanness, lasciviousness, idolatry, witchcraft, hatred, variance, emulations, wrath, strife, seditions, heresies, envyings, murders, drunkenness revilings, and such like"—such shall not inherit the kingdom of God. We greatly lack the Spirit; where that abides there is order and good government. Where that is not, there is confusion, and every evil work; there is theory for better organization—for a more perfect system of church government. The simple rules given by Christ will not answer the purpose to govern the carnal and worldly professors of religion. Let us be filled with the Spirit and walk in the Spirit, and the simple government of Christ will be all sufficient.

Should it be inquired, what is that government for the church, ordained by Jesus Christ? that shall be the subject of some future number.

THE CHURCH.

The first Church of Christ established on earth after his resurrection is found in the first chapter of the Acts of the Apostles, which church was composed of one hundred and twenty members only. "The number of the names together were about a hundred and twenty." These names were those of the eleven apostles. "These all continued with one accord in prayer and supplication, with the women and Mary the mother of Jesus, and with his brethren." Among them were Barsabas, or Barnabas, and Matthias, who was afterward chosen an apostle to fill the place of Judas Iscariot. Of all this number we find not one infant; and what is said of this church excludes the idea of an infant being a member of it. For it is said, "These *all* continued with one accord, in prayer and supplication." Infants can not feel that accord, nor engage in prayer and supplication, all acknowledge. Besides, this church of one hundred and twenty chose an apostle by casting lots or votes. This could not be the work of infants.

Again, "they were all filled with the Holy Ghost,

and began to speak with other tongues, as the Spirit gave them utterance." It may be said, that those filled with the Holy Ghost were the apostles alone. But the Scripture says, "they were *all* filled with the Holy Ghost;" and this was the fulfillment of Joel's prophecy, "Your sons and your daughters shall prophesy, and your young men shall see visions, and your old men shall dream dreams. And on my servants and on my handmaidens I will pour out in those days of my Spirit; and they shall prophesy." If infants had been of this number, and prophesied with the men and women, the miracle would have been more extraordinary and convincing than that which appeared among the adults. But no mention is made of it, and no one contends or believes that it was a fact.

The result of Peter's preaching on that occasion was glorious. "Many were pierced to the heart, and cried out, what shall we do?" Infants did not thus act. "Then they that gladly received his word were baptized (no infants yet), and the same day there were added unto them about three thousand souls; and they continued steadfastly in the apostles' doctrine and fellowship, and in breaking of bread, and in prayers."

We see no place for infants yet, for such worship can not be performed by them. Could it be proved that infants were in this church, it would afford an irrefragible argument that they should eat the Lord's Supper, and thus would be settled the doubt of pedobaptists. All that follows in Acts 2:42 to the end equally excludes the idea that infants were members of this church. The last sentence is incontrovertible.

"And the Lord added to the church daily the saved."
Acts 5 : 14, "And believers were the more added to the
Lord, multitudes both of men and women."

In favor of infant church membership, it is argued,
by Divine appointment they were members of the old
church, by what authority are they excluded from that
in the New Institution?.

Answer: Suppose under the old constitution of
Kentucky females were admitted to the same privileges
in government as the men—they had equal right to
vote at the polls, and to hold and exercise all the offices
of the government as the males. In process of years
the constitution was altered, and these rights were
indirectly taken from the females. The qualifications
of voters to fill the offices in government were, that
every male of twenty-one years and over had a right
to vote for officers in government; and that every male
over twenty-five years old had a right to fill offices by
the election of his compatriots. The women might
argue, we once had the right to choose representatives
in the government, and to be chosen as such. By
what authority are we excluded from these privileges
under the new constitution? It nowhere says that
females shall no longer enjoy these privileges.

I grant, the constitution nowhere says in direct
terms that women are excluded from the privileges;
but indirectly it does exclude them—for the qualifications for these privileges as stated in the constitution,
are inapplicable to females. We may say that infants
were allowed the privileges of church-membership under the old institution; but in the new, they are in-

directly excluded, not possessing the qualifications required to be in those who are admitted to be members of the church.

The whole Jewish nation were members of the old church, and pleaded before John the baptizer their right to all church privileges. John did not admit their plea to be valid. If the old and new churches are the same, how could the three thousand believing Jews be added to the church? Could they be added to that of which they had always been members? We think not.

A part of the inhabitants of Kentucky might still adhere to the old constitution, which admitted females to an equal share in government with the males; but they are evidently not recognized as citizens of the commonwealth, but as traitors in opposition to it. So the Jews, a part of the world, still adhere to their old constitution, which admits of infant church-membership. But they are not acknowledged citizens of Christ's Church, but aliens and traitors in opposition to it. So in part are to be viewed all those who adopt the old constitution of the Jews, or blend it with the new, without Divine authority. This is a subject of importance, and should be calmly considered, and not hastily passed over through prejudice or prepossession.

UNITY.

During the days of the apostles, the Christians lived in union and harmony among themselves; not altogether in a union of opinion, for this is unattainable, if desirable in the present imperfect state of man;

but they lived in a union of spirit. They were of one heart and of one soul.

This union is portrayed by the pen of an inspired apostle, in Eph. 4: 5, 6. 1st. He says there is one body under the direction of one head, one law-giver. They are one with the Father and the Son Jesus Christ. The present state of the church shows many bodies, many heads and many law-givers. Can they all be the Church of Christ? Impossible, if judged according to the Scriptures.

2nd. "There is one Spirit." This Spirit dwells in the one body. "Ye are the temple of the Holy Spirit." This body is the habitation of God through the Spirit —the Spirit of God—the Spirit of Christ which dwelleth in them, the same Spirit by which God will quicken their mortal bodies, or raise them from the dead. Rom. 8. The fruits of the indwelling Spirit are love, joy, peace, etc. (Gal. 5.) Every member of the body possesses this Spirit and bears the same fruits.

3d. "They are all called to one hope." This, the object of their hope, is set forth in the Gospel, as, glory, honor, immortality and eternal life, with all the blessings of Heaven, promised in the New Covenant.

4th. "One Lord." Though there be lords many, with us there is but one Lord Jesus Christ, by whom are all things, and we by him. He is Lord of all in heaven and in earth. To his orders and commands all Christians are obedient. To his government they all submit.

5th. "One faith." Though there be faiths many, yet with us there is but one faith, the faith of Jesus

Christ, the faith once delivered to the saints, the faith
which the apostles preached, and to which they urged
obedience for salvation. The New Testament is the
one faith of Christians.

6th. "One baptism." This is the baptism which
the apostles were commissioned by the Saviour to administer to all believers, and is one part of obedience
to the one faith, through which salvation is promised.

7th. "One God and Father of all." For though
there be gods many, with us "Christians" there is but
one God, the Father, of whom are all things, etc.

Here is a confession of faith, one in which Christians
were once united according to the will of God. Every
article of it is essential to our salvation. On this must
the church settle again, before she becomes united,
and before the world can be saved.

Can any Christians of any sect object to unite on
this Divine confession of faith? Do not all acknowledge there is but one body, of which Christ is the
head? Do not all acknowledge that the Spirit of the
Son dwells in this one body, and that each member
drinks into this one Spirit, and bears the fruits of the
Spirit,—love, joy, peace, etc.? Do not all Christians
have the same hope set before them,—glory, honor,
etc.? Do they not all claim the same faith, the New
Testament? True, they have and may have different
opinions of many truths of this faith; yet if with these
opinions, they show that they are members of the one
body, and have the one Spirit, and bear the fruits of
the Spirit, that they are inspired with the hope of immortality to be holy as God is holy, who will reject

them? Let them have their opinions, seeing they do not influence the heart to evil practices. "Him that is weak in the faith receive ye, without regard to diversity of opinions." To unite upon opinions is like building a house upon the sand—it will fall.

Do not Christians own the one Lord Jesus Christ the Son of God, sent to be the Saviour of the world? Different opinions are formed and entertained with respect to his person; but do not all true Christians show their love to him by keeping his commands? Do they not unreservedly trust in him, believing firmly that he is able to save them? Speculation and controversy on this point have done incalculable mischief in the Christian world.

Do not all profess the one God and Father of all? Surely there can be but one faith on this subject, however jarring may be the speculations of men.

Which of all these sects can say, we are in this union? I ask each, are you the body of Christ? Then you alone have the one Spirit. All the other bodies of the sects are not the body of Christ, and have not his Spirit dwelling in them, and therefore are none of his. If any one sect claims to be the body of Christ, then unchristianize all the other sects. Can all the sects collectively make the one body? Then all the sects have the one Spirit dwelling in them, and consequently have the fruits of the Spirit—love, joy, peace, etc. Can it be possible then that they are all one, and yet divided into contending factions? Can they all have the one Spirit and bear the fruits of it, and yet instead of peace, love, etc., bear the fruits of hatred, discord and strife? *"Judaeas appella credat, non ego."*

These human-constituted bodies must be dissolved before they become the one body of Christ, and drink into the one Spirit. They must cast away their various faiths, and receive the one faith of Christ. They must relinquish their vain philosophy respecting the Father and the Son, and learn the truth from the Great Teacher.

My brethren of the various denominations, hear the exhortation of an old man, now past the age allotted to mortals, who must soon quit the busy scenes of this life. You all see and the pious of every name deplore the miserable state of Christianity as now presented to view. It is high time to awake out of sleep, and no longer indulge in dreams of better days, while we are inactive to hasten them on. You need not conviction of the vanity of expecting a union of the sects as such; you must pronounce the idea chimerical and absurd. It must be effected on God's own plan, and it will be effected, or the prayer of Jesus remain unanswered. Some of you say it will be effected in the millennium. No, it must be effected before, that the world may be brought to believe and be saved. When Christ shall come the second time, it will be to judge, not to save the world.

While Protestants are wrangling and dividing, it is food to the Papists, who eagerly watch and wish for our destruction. By our conduct we are healing the deadly wound of the beast, who is pouring, *now* pouring his vassals in thousands on our peaceful

shores. They are decoying our citizens' children to
their high schools and instilling into the tender minds
their pernicious, anti-Christian doctrines. Many of
the dignitaries of the established church of England
are engaged to effect a union with the old mother.
This is natural. Our divisions and strifes are fast
paving the way for Papal despotism, for Papal rule,
and for the Papal inquisition. Our divisions are driv-
ing thousands to scepticism, and hardening the world
of the ungodly to their utter gain. Our divisions are
drinking up the spirits of the godly, destroying the
influence of Christianity, and barring the way to
heaven.

This, my brethren, you will acknowledge; and yet,
how—oh, how can you be inactive? How can you
any longer labor to establish a party, and not summon
all your powers to promote the union of Christians?
"Self must be humbled, pride abased, else they destroy
our souls." I fear that real Christians in every party
are in the minority and the opposite character among
them will, of course, oppose. But we must come out
from among them, and be separate—leave all for the
kingdom of heaven's sake.

You know, my brethren, this event must take place
sooner or later, and the sooner the better. But you
ask, "what shall we do? I daily pray for the union of
Christians, and am waiting for God to effect it." Do
you wait for God to work a miracle to convince you
of a plain duty? Do you wait for him to force his
people to do right? In vain you pray, in vain you
wait, while you remain idle and inactive in the great
work.

MOSES AND CHRIST. .

Redemption—a Type.

BY WALTER SCOTT.

Walter Scott was born October 31, 1796, in Moffat, Scotland. Came to America in 1818. Died at Mayslick, Ky., April 23, 1861.

"A prophet shall the Lord your God raise up unto you, from among your brethren, like unto me: to him shall you hearken; and it shall come to pass that the soul that will not hearken to the voice of that prophet shall be cut off from among the people." (Deut. 18.)

These are the words of a great man, who, professing to speak by the Spirit of God, here offers himself as a type of the promised Messiah.

It was not, then, to keep Israel in the vicinity of their own land—the promised land—that God placed them in Egypt, where they were enslaved, oppressed and corrupted in their state, morals and religion; neither was it merely to place them in their own land that he brought them out of Egypt. Both their descent into and their exodus out of that kingdom were typical, and had a higher significance. The exit of Israel was designed of God to shadow forth and throw into bolder relief the major fact or feature in the future Messianic order of things, namely, *"Redemption."* Their civil and religious deliverance from Pharaoh and idolatry, is therefore but a type on the lower level of thought, analogous in its general feature, however, to that re-

163

demption from death and sin by the Messiah which the Christian religion offers to our faith on the higher scale of spiritual perception.

The following are the general lineaments of the illustrious type—the kingdom of ancient Israel, whose miraculous rescue forms one of the most renowned facts in the world's history, and makes the Jews by far the most famous and interesting nation of antiquity.

THE TYPE.

1. The Redeemer, Moses.
2. The Redeemed, Israel unorganized.
3. The Rescue, or Transition in the cloud and sea.
4. Their Civil and Religious Organization.
5. Their Wilderness state.
6. Their hope of Canaan.

The reader will perceive by these particulars that the Typical Redemption was first *inorganic,* then *transitional,* and finally *organic.* Israel was at last nationalized on a great charter of civil and religious rights and privileges; and, as an independent nation, gifted with laws and ordinances of their own.

THE ANTITYPE.

1. The Redeemer, Messiah.
2. The Redeemed, Christians unorganized.
3. Their Transition or rescue by water and Spirit.
4. Their Civil and Religious Organization.
5. Their state in the world.
6. Their hope of Heaven.

Such are the salient points of similitude between the two systems—the typical and the anti-typical—the Mosaic and Messianic redemption, long after sung in heaven, to harps of gold, by holy martyrs, as the Song of Moses and the Lamb.

"It was comparatively an easy thing," says one, "for the Jewish worshiper to understand how, from time to time, he stood related to a visible sanctuary and an earthly inheritance, or go through the process of an appointed purification by means of water and the blood of slain victims applied to the body—much more easy than for the Christian to apprehend his relation to a heavenly sanctuary, and realize the cleansing of the conscience from all guilt by the inward application of the sacrifice of Christ and the renewing of the Holy Spirit."

It is much easier for us to verify in our meditations the temporal and visible redemption of ancient Israel from Pharaoh and false religion by Moses the man of God, than our own spiritual and invisible redemption from sin and death by Jesus the Son of God. But should even the type fail to give to our cogitations on the eternal redemption that definiteness which was designed, one truth remains, viz: that as certainly as the rescue from Egypt, though difficult at first, was achieved at last, so certainly will our rescue from sin and death, though difficult at first, be achieved at last; and the heavenly Canaan, despite our weakness, be given to the faithful of all ages and nations.

From the fall of man,—from the day God adjudicated him to death, yet promised him a Deliverer,—

every successive revelation made by him to man, was, we may safely aver, an advance from the lower toward the higher strata of thought touching the great **Redemption**. Though at the deluge the population of the globe and the great globe itself perished; though the few souls who survived that catastrophe seemed, amid its horrors, doomed to inevitable destruction, and when rescued looked like the last remnant of a perishing humanity; though at that crisis all things seemed to be thrown back fifteen centuries into a state of less hopefulness than at the fall itself, yet they were not. Adam, for want of faith, had lost all; but at the era of the deluge Noah was found to be a righteous man, who, Abdiel-like—

"Among the faithless faithful only he," "built an ark by faith to the saving of his house by which he condemned the world and became an heir of the righteousness which is by faith." (Heb. xi.) Thus the race of man commenced its second career in the world under the hopeful auspices of a man of faith. And so from Adam to Noah was one important advance toward the great Redemption. It was the elimination of faith, and its glorification among men as the great religious principle, without which it is impossible to please God.

But again, when afterward God laid hold of the seed of Abraham to deliver them from the tyranny and Idolatry of Egypt, and organize them as a distinct nation, with a mild government, and manners and customs of their own, he made another advance-step toward the Messianic order of things, and with sufficient clearness intimated by the typical kingdom the final organization of the men of faith.

Having eliminated the great typical thought indicated by the rescue of Israel from Pharaoh, Idolatry and Egypt—namely, *"Redemption,"* let us, *currente calamo,* trace the several features in the type by which it assimilated itself to the antitype and thereby prefigured the kingdom of Christ.

A certain personage, a Pantheist, rejected, in my presence, our religion, because it was, he said, founded on the pernicious doctrine of punishing the innocent for the guilty.

It was answered that most people chose to view that matter in the light rather of a grand personage greatly and heroically offering himself in a desperate case in behalf of the unfortunate. The gentleman evidently viewed the death of the Messiah under the delusive idea that all good and great actions necessarily turn on the maxims of ordinary morality; but history proves that the great mutations and ameliorations in society have turned rather on the axis of an extraordinary *heroism.* In both religion and politics, science and the arts, this held good. Adam, Noah, and Moses, Nimrod, Cyrus, Alexander, Cæsar, Napoleon, were heroes; Socrates, Aristotle, Plato and Pythagoras were heroes; Newton, Bacon, Watt, Franklin, and Morse were all heroes—all self-sacrificing men. Messiah, then, was a hero—a hero from heaven, to achieve what none but a hero from heaven could achieve, namely, the emancipation from Satan, sin and death of the race of man. Would the honor and glory and fame of rescuing a world have been more worthily and more wisely awarded to the guilty than to the innocent? The Scriptures are in excellent keeping with themselves. The race that was destroyed by a power *ab extra,* shall by an *ab extra* power be rescued. If hell ruined us, heaven has redeemed us. It would be as safe to except to the heroism of certain Greeks and Romans in the ancient world, or to David and Judas Machabeus, Wallace, Washington, Tell, Hampden, Henry or Kosciusko, as to that of the glorious Messiah, the Lord Jesus Christ.

The state of this world makes room for magnanimity to display itself. The redemption of the race was the grand occasion, and Christ, the Son of God, met it with all greatness of heart. The moral code of Pantheism makes no room for this. Would it be decorous that heaven should have less magnanimity than earth? That when heroes go thither they should find none so great as themselves? Magnanimity is not limited to earth.

1. *The Rescue.*—In the typical rescue—the redemption of ancient Israel—there was a grand heroism evinced. To present himself at the court of Egypt and prefer before her king claims to two millions of his subjects, was sublime in the man who did it. Moses was a hero-redeemer; and the fact presignified that in the substantive and Messianic order of things, there would be heroism. Let us, then, meditate upon Moses as a *hero,* and afterward upon God's Son heroically exchanging heaven for earth, riches for poverty, the crown for the cross, life for death, and we shall per-

haps obtain a glimpse of his glory, his love and his heroism.

2. *Israel Unorganized.*—Enslaved in Egypt to Pharaoh and false religion, Israel was a striking type of mankind enslaved to sin, Satan and death. What but the heroism of Moses, illuminated and made sun-bright by the resplendent miracles which God empowered him to perform, could possibly have roused from their deathlike slumbers in Egypt, and prepared for an exodus from that country, so great a mass of flesh and blood—so vast a people? Yet the whole was but a shadow—a type of that substantive heroism whereby the whole world will be aroused to a sense of its enslavement, not merely to tyranny and idolatry, but also to the wicked one himself.

3. *The Transition.*—The passage of Israel from Egypt to the wilderness, through "the cloud and sea," is a proper figure of the transit of the regenerated portion of mankind passing, by water and Spirit, or faith and baptism, from the world to the church. In art, in science, in all system—material, political and religious—the transitional is greatly important. Here in the type and antitype it forms a part both of the spiritual and the temporal salvation. Birth, baptism, the telegraph, the steam-engine, the academy, algebra, and the dark ages in history, etc., etc., all belong to the transitional.

4. *Israel Nationalized.*—On the fiftieth day from eating the passover, Israel was assembled by authority around the base of Mount Sinai, and on that day received the organic law—the two tables or ten com-

mandments. Antitypical to this the disciples of the Messiah were assembled by authority in Jerusalem, where, fifty days after the last passover, they received the organic law of the "Spirit of Life," and were nationalized as the kingdom of God and his Messiah. In this order of things, Christ takes the place of the Jewish ceremonial, and the Holy Spirit the place of the law.

5. *Their Wilderness State.*—Touching Israel in the wilderness, we can-not conceive how so great and wise a man, as was their hero, should, except by divine authority have led them into such a desert—a land made terrible by "fiery flying serpents, and scorpions and drought;" a desert of sand and shrubs, of pits and the shadow of death, of rocks and hoary mountains, where desolation herself held her solitary reign. But "the man of God" knew by whose authority all things were done; therefore were they fed by miracle. The Most High gave them angels' food; he fed them with manna and gave them water from the rock; their raiment waxed not old, neither did their sandals wear out, or their feet swell for forty years. As an eagle stirreth up her nest, fluttereth over her young, spreadeth abroad her wings, so the Lord alone did lead them, and there was no strange God with them. Deut. 32.

But the antitypical people, Christians, are vastly more numerous than ever were the typical, and now form the grandest nations upon earth. Yet, in the wilderness of this world, where all the enginery of the old serpent is in full play, God feeds them. Or if he "suffers us to hunger," it is that he "may humble" us, that he may "prove" us, and make us "know our own heart;" and that "man shall not live by bread alone, but by every word that proceedeth out of the mouth of God."

"Behold what manner of love the Father hath bestowed upon us, that we should be called the sons of God. Therefore, the world knoweth us not, even as it knew him not. Beloved, now are we the sons of God, and it doth not yet appear what we shall be, but we know that when he shall appear we shall be like him, for we shall see him as he is. And every one who hath this hope in him purifieth himself even as he is pure."—1 John, 3. The church is in her wilderness, state, and is misapprehended and unknown by the world.

But God not only fed Israel, but gave them drink from the rock . The people thirsted for water, and in their terrible destitution were ready to stone Moses, the man of God. But Jehovah, equal to every emergency, came to the rescue, and directed his most venerable servant, with the elders of Israel, to go unto the rock Horeb. The command was that he should "smite the rock," and the promise, that it should "give forth water" for the people to drink. All the elements of this scene are great and sublime. Horeb, white with years, elevates his hoary head to mid-heaven in the front of the thousands of Israel, who lay encamped around his base. Moses, with the elders, has taken his position, and stands with the rod of God in his hand, ready to smite at the signal given. "I will stand before thee on the rock." The eyes of the impatient and thirsty Israelites are eagerly fixed on Moses; while he, from his giddy eminence on the rock, sees far and wide below him the tents of Jacob stretching away in the distance.

At early morn the sacred cloud, at a distance not to be measured by the eye, inclined, we may suppose, toward Mount Horeb, and shading the tribes below, was gazed on by all with eager expectation. After a tedious but solemn interval the center became the point of incidence and the cloud was seen to lower itself with awe-inspiring grandeur, till at last, in the form of a reversed pyramid, it reached the nadir of descent—the highest summit of the venerable Horeb! The glory of the Universe stood before Moses on the rock.

This was the signal to smite. He did so; and suddenly, as if a sea had been tapped, the waters gushed forth as a torrent and ran "as a stream in the desert." The cloud enveloped the mountain, and "thou, O God, didst send a plentiful rain, whereby thou didst confirm thine inheritance when it was weary."—Ps. 68, 9. "That rock," says the apostle, "was Christ."—1 Cor. 10. That is, I suppose, the rock with the divinity on it was a type of Christ with the divinity in him, whence we draw living water, water from the rock to refresh us when we are weary.

6. *Their Rest in Canaan.*—We have glanced at Israel in their inorganic, transitional and organic states. But the type is double. It was in their organic state they sojourned in the wilderness, in this state

they passed through Jordan, and in this state they entered into Canaan. It is as organic elements of the church that Christians sojourn on earth; it is as such they pass the Jordan of death; and it is as such they ascend to the true Canaan.

The typical inheritance was a land of brooks of water and fountains and depths that spring out of the valleys and hills—a land of wheat and barley, of fig trees and vines, of pomegranates and olives, and milk and honey, and wine and oil—a land blessed of the Lord, fresh with the dews of heaven and fat with corn and wine—the glory of all lands, wherein Israel did eat meat to the full. Yet "the rest that remaineth for the people of God" is but poorly typified even by such a land. In our march through the wilderness of this world, till we reach the Jordan of death, we too are fed with manna, and refreshed with living water from the Rock. Our vestments and sandals of peace and righteousness, like the garments and sandals of Israel, according to the flesh wax not old; and our faith and heart, like their eyes turned to Jehovah in the cloud, ever turn to Jehovah in the flesh, who is to us a pillar of cloud to shade us by day, and a pillar of fire to give us light by night.

We traverse the frozen North, the burning Sahara of rosy Africa, the flowering pampas of the shining South and West; we roam the isles and archipelagoes of all seas; ascend all rivers, climb all mountains, and dare the war of all the elements; yet our "feet swell not." Our souls are missionary; the energies of Yahveh Jesus, the Spirit of God is in us; the world is ours, hinder us not; we must possess it; we will take it. Though unknown and greatly afflicted, we seasonably renew our strength at the fountain of life; we soar the world around; we "mount up as on the wings of eagles; we run and are not weary; we walk and are not faint." Is. 40.

Touching the people of God in the present wicked world, to see that they are appointed to tribulation, we have but to look at Israel in the wilderness. "The world knoweth us not." Yet "there remaineth a rest for the people of God."

To create a great and famous nation, and make it an involuntary type of another nation; to constitute the redemption of the former, the sensible type of the redemption of the latter; hold it in his hand for fifteen centuries and cast it away in the presence of all the world when the substantive nation appeared, are, of all the doings of God in this world, among the most remarkable and sublime.

But the words "redemption," "redeemer," and "redeemed," indicating the world's salvation, must needs be defined and understood; and it required all the potency of these celebrated and tremendous deeds—all the salvation that God granted to Israel, and all the plauges which he inflicted on Pharaoh—to impart to our obtuse thoughts a lively and well-defined apprehension of the meaning and certainty of the great redemption. Christians will at last be rescued from sin, death, and the grave, as certainly as Israel was rescued from Egypt, Pharaoh, and false religion.

Moses was not merely a redeemer, but a prince who

ruled those whom he redeemed, and in this quality was a type of the Messiah.

On the supposition that the Creator had set himself to rescue fallen man and re-established his own authority on the earth, we would naturally suppose that his attributes of creation and sovereignty would again be called into requisition, and developed in the origination and organization of a people to be called by his name as his family, nation, or kingdom. History meets our conjectures here, and recognizes ancient Israel as that kingdom.

Again, as there really subsists between the Old and the New Testament the typical relation claimed, then we naturally conjecture that the substantive or Messianic kingdom will be clearly anticipated in the shadowy department of these oracles, and set forth there both in its inner and outer forms, by some promient and illustrious type that will greatly aid and define our conceptions of this kingdom in some important particulars. Accordingly we find that to be historically true, which we would naturally expect on the assumption of the literal fact. The things spoken by Moses were spoken "for a testimony" or type of the things afterward to be "spoken by Christ;" or the nation of Israel organized with a mild government and the typical religion, is a figure of the future Messianic people organized with just government and the Christian religion. The kingdom of Israel was composite, and had its civil as well as its religious department; the former ruled by Moses and the latter by Aaron.

However varied, there are but two classes of sovereign power, namely:

The inner and the outer, or
The spiritual and the political.

The political is outward and secular, taking cognizance only of actions; the spiritual is inner and religious, taking cognizance also of thoughts. Israel was nationalized with these two classes of sovereign power, being personally and politically responsible to Moses, their civil ruler; and in their consciences subject to Aaron, as Gods' High Priest, the head of the religious department.

The Jews hold to the perpetual obligation of their law. Now that system of things or the kingdom of Israel was necessarily one of two terms, both of which could not possibly be true; that is, it either was that grand kingdom promised to the Fathers in the Holy Scriptures, which was to take cognizance of the "reins and heart," or it was not. If it was, then Aaron, as the High Priest of God, had the power of adjudicating on "the thoughts and intents of the heart." But we know that he possessed no such power; and in this consisted the principal defect of his order. The inner government is divine, and nothing short of divinity can possibly administer it, and nothing but a conviction of God's omniscience can form its basis. It is from his appointment to this inner authority and rule—this perfect kind of government, that we know that Jesus our Lord is divine. He says of one of the churches, "I will punish her children with death, and all the churches shall know that I am he that trieth the reins and heart." On account of the imperfection of the Levitical order, therefore, the inner government passed from Levi to Judah, or from Aaron to Christ. The worshiper under Christ must not only do no evil, but he must not think it. Our High Priest speaks thus, "Why do evil thoughts arise in your heart?" The first prayer put up to Christ, our great High Priest, after his ascent to heaven, had reference to his omniscience; "Thou, O Lord, who knoweth the hearts of all men, show which of these twain thou wilt choose."

If then the kingdom of Israel was not that order of things promised to the Fathers, as we see it could not on account of the defectiveness of its hierarchical order be, we ask what was it? Internally and externally in Aaron as in Moses, it was a type of the outer and inner government of the Messiah's empire.

Israel in the wilderness was not organized religiously till a year after they were organized civilly. But as certainly as outward action implies inward thought, so certainly do these two forms of government imply each other. For as the outer or political is for peace, so the inner or spiritual is for salvation. Where there is no outer government there can be no peace, and where there is no inner, there can be no salvation. Where there is neither peace nor salvation, where men obey neither magistrates nor mediators, the state is in anarchy; now "any kind of government is better than no government;" and the Jews falling into this anarchy after the coming of Christ, were cast away.

The inner government of God's kingdom passed into the hands of Christ.

The powers of Israel, their throne and altar, their crown and miter, their croisier and scepter, their king and priest, reproducing themselves from age to age, had but echoed along the centuries from Moses to Christ their own defectiveness and the inexorable necessity of placing the two forms of government in the hands of Christ and his saints, as prophecy indicated.

One will say, "we have seen the consciences of God's people pass into the hands of Messiah, but when did the outer government pass into the hands of his saints —after the ascension of Christ,, his disciples were citizens of the Roman empire as before, and since?" I answer, God ofttimes redeems his promises as we do our notes, by installments. Israel was organized civilly before they were organized religiously; in Christianity this order is reversed. We have received the inner government first; but the time will come "when the saints," as Daniel says, "shall possess the government," and all "power, authority and rule" be recovered to God by his Son and his saints.

God says to Israel, "I have taken you to be my servants; you shall not sell the land forever, for the land is mine, and ye are *strangers* and *sojourners* with me" (Lev. 25).

When, therefore, we look at Moses and Aaron as the servants of God, and the kingdom of Israel as in a state of vassalage or involuntary servitude to God; when we see them all internally and externally as types of the future Messianic order of things, we see them in a proper point of view.

As certainly then as Moses ministered the civil law, and Aaron the ceremonial in Israel, so certainly in the Milennium will Christ minister, as he does now, the inner government and his saints the outer over all the earth! All shall be right in the church, all right in the state, and the kingdom of this world organized with mild and beneficent government, and the true religion shall shine forth as the kingdoms of our Lord and his Messiah forever and ever. Good government and the true religion make a Millennium.

I have said this type is double. By this I mean that while in its inorganic, transitional and organic states, it prefigured our religion in these three states, it also as an organism journeying in the wilderness under Moses, toward Jordan and the Holy Land, typified the Christian Church passing through the wilderness of this world under Christ, toward the Jordan of death and the heavenly Canaan that lies beyond.

> "O'er all those wide extended fields
> Shines one eternal day;
> There God, the Sun, forever shines,
> And scatters night away."

To rescue from the iron grasp of a tyrant two millions of human beings, to take them by great signs and wonders from their ancient abodes, and lead them through the sea into a wilderness where they could be fed and sustained in all things only by miracles; to nationalize them there with a mild government and the true religion, and keep them in the desert forty years, till he had taught them new manners and customs, new laws and civil institutions, and by judgments purged out from among them all the rebels, were the greatest of all God's doings in the ancient world.

Well might Moses appeal to them for the grandeur of the whole and say:

"Ask now of the days that are past which were before thee; since God created man upon the earth; and ask from one side of heaven to the other, whether there has been anything as this great thing is, or hath been heard like it? Did ever people hear the voice of God speaking out of the midst of the fire, as thou hast heard, and live? Or hath God essayed to go and take a nation from the midst of another nation by temptations, by signs, and by wonders, and by wars, and by a mighty hand, and by a stretched-out arm, and by great terrors, according to all that the Lord your God did for you in Egypt before your eyes? Unto thee it was showed that thou mightest know that Jehovah he is God; there is none else beside him" (Deut. 4).

As, then, our first set of types, Adam, the flood and Melchisedek, presignified respectively the following:

(1)   Regenerative Headship,
(2)   Transition,
(3)   Organization,

So Israel after the flesh, in their exodus from Egypt, prefigured the same. And in this display of his omniscience the Most High was but laying deep in his divinity the foundation of our faith and of his own

government among men; for the typical kingdom of
Israel, in its great redemption from Egypt, is not
merely a sign, like Adam, the flood and Melchisedec,
but a design, a bright outline of the Messianic kingdom
in its fullness. It was not, as in their case, three distinct types making but one outline; but one grand
type passing from bondage to liberty, from slavery to
a great salvation, and thereby describing the future
spiritual kingdom of Messiah as passing by baptism
from slavery to liberty, from the world to the church
through its several phases, as follows:

1. The Inorganic.
2. The Transitional.
3. The Organic.

It is said by Lord Bacon that "things are double."
They are certainly so in this instance, the type being
for the eye of the body, and the antitype for the eye
of the mind; the former for observation, the latter for
reflection; the visible for sense, the invisible for faith.

The typical system of the Bible is a fundamental
portion of the Bible, and was evidently elaborated and
wrought out by its author in order to secure future
ages against the numerous impostures which darken
and affect the history of the world. Any code of
religion offering itself for the faith of mankind, if it
bears not the stamp of God's omniscience and the
typical co-relation, cannot be of the Scriptures. But
Christianity being the very complement of its typology,
must be the true religion.

How, but by inspiration, could Moses possibly fore-
know and foreshow, at the distance of fifteen centuries,

that the Messiah, like himself, would be a hero-Redeemer—a law-giver at that? The fortuitous here would be encumbered with greater difficulties than the designed—the incidental with more than the miraculous.

Prophecy is the history of the world, casting its shadow before.

ADDRESS TO THE DISCIPLES.

BY JOHN SMITH.

John (Raccoon) Smith was born in Sullivan County, Tenn., October 15, 1784. Died at Mexico, Mo., February 28, 1868.

The following from the "Life of John Smith" by J. A. Williams will serve to explain the causes that brought out the "Address to the Brethren":

His travels as an evangelist now (1832) began; and, with the same zeal that had inspired him in 1828, he went abroad, far and near, laboring unceasingly to reform, to unite, and to convert. His voice was heard along the valley of the Big Sandy in the east, and upon the banks of the Green River in the west. He proclaimed the unsearchable riches of Christ in the counties upon the Ohio, and constituted churches along the borders of Tennessee.

He soon discovered that while the disposition to affiliate with all true Christians, on the Bible alone, was very general among his brethren, yet their prejudice against B. W. Stone, growing out of their ignorance of his doctrine, was, in some other places also, a formidable barrier to union. Some, too, in their opposition to all measures of expediency in matters of religion, in their pious distrust of human wisdom, or their scrupulous devotion to the letter of the New Testament, demanded a special precept for the action of the elders and brethren about Georgetown in setting apart the two evangelists, and pledging them a compensation for their services. Such men now refused their co-operation, and otherwise discouraged the execution of the plan adopted. "But we are fully able, and fully determined," said Stone, "to assist these evangelists to support their dependent families, should all others forsake us."

For the benefit of those Reformers who honestly doubted the wisdom or propriety of the affiliation which he had helped to bring about, and which he was now laboring to extend and confirm throughout the State, Smith prepared and published an

183

address, in which he endeavored to meet and remove their objections.

Concerning his address, John Rogers, his co-laborer, remarks: "The simplicity, the candor, the charity, the piety, the dignity and noble independence which this communication exhibits, are characteristic of the man who wrote it, and, what is better, of the religion which he professes. And I am much mistaken if it does not contain a fair and clear statement, as far as it goes, of the principles and practices of the Christian brethren in these regions, and not only here, but generally in the West. I do, therefore, confidently hope that it will be greatly useful in promoting the good work of union and co-operation among those who have acknowledged and submitted to the one Lord, one faith, and one baptism, the one God and Father of all, who is over all, and with all, and in all.

It becomes my duty to lay before our brethren and the public the principle from which I acted, when, with many Reformers, so-called, and many of those called Christians, we met together, broke the loaf, and united in all the acts of social worship. It will be recollected that all our remarks relative to the Christian brethren are confined to those with whom we have associated about Lexington, Georgetown, Paris, Millersburgh, and Carlisle. When the Christians and the Reforming brethren united, as above named, we calculated at the time that the captious, cold-hearted, sectarian professor, and the friends of religious systems formed by human device, would misrepresent and slander us. But we do not mind all this. It is no more than we expect from such characters; and we hope we shall always be able to bear reviling like Christians, and not revile again. We do not publish this address with the hope of satisfying or silencing our opposers; but hearing that some of our warm-hearted, pious, reforming brethren, having heard many reports, and not being correctly informed on this subject, have become uneasy, fearing that the good cause of Reformation may be injured by the course which we have taken in relation to the Christian brethren, we therefore feel it to be a duty which we owe to our brethren, and to the cause which we profess, to lay before them and the public, candidly and plainly, the principle from which we have acted, relative to this matter, which is as follows:

When we fell in company with the Christian teachers, we conversed freely and friendly together. With some one or other of them we have conversed on all the supposed points of difference between them and the Reformers, and all the erroneous sentiments which I had heard laid to their charge, such as the following:

1. That they deny the Atonement. On this point I found the truth to be, in substance, about this: that they do not deny the Atonement, but they do deny the explanation which some give of it. At the same time they declare that pardon and salvation here are obtained through faith in the sacrifice and blood of Jesus Christ. They expect, and pray for, all spiritual blessings through the same medium, and hope to overcome at the last, and obtain eternal salvation, by the blood of the Lamb, and by the Word of his testimony. This, substantially, if not verbatim, one of their principal teachers said to me; and this, I believe, they are all willing to say, so far as I have been conversant with them.

When I have conversed with them about the various

speculations upon the character of Christ, or the *modus existendi* of the Divine Being, they have said that, by the misrepresentations and violent opposition of their enemies, they had been sometimes driven into speculations on that subject. They also say they are not willing, but desirous, that all speculations on that subject may cease forever; and that all should speak of the Saviour of sinners in the language of the inspired writers, and render unto him such honor as did the primitive Christians. So say I; and let Unitarianism, Trinitarianism, and all other human isms, return from whence they came, and no more divide the affections, prevent nor destroy the union, of Christians forever. Amen, and Amen!

2. I have also conversed freely with the Christian teachers upon the subject of receiving the unimmersed in to the church, and of communing with them at the Lord's table. They have said that they have had, and still have, in some degree, their difficulties on this subject. In their first outset they were all pedobaptists. Having determined to take the word of God alone for their guide, some of them soon became convinced that immersion was the only Gospel baptism; and they submitted to it accordingly. They went on teaching others to do likewise; the result has been that all, with very few exceptions, belonging to their congregations in this section of country, have submitted to immersion. They have not, for several years past, received any as members of their body without immersion. And, with regard to the propriety of communing at the Lord's table with the unimmersed, they

are determined to say no more about it, there being no apostolic precept nor example ·to· enforce it. But whatever degree of forbearance they may think proper to exercise toward the unimmersed as best suited to the present state of things, they are determined, by a proper course of teaching, and practicing the apostolic Gospel, to bring all, as fast as they can, to unite around the cross of Christ—submitting to the one Lord, one faith, one immersion, and thus form one body upon the one foundation, according to the apostolic order of things.

Here I must say, that when the Christian brethren have spread the Lord's table in my presence, they did not invite* the unimmersed to participate. When the Apostle said, "Let a man examine himself, and so let him eat," he did not say this to the unimmersed, or those who were not in the kingdom, but to the church of God at Corinth, the members of which had heard, believed, and had been immersed. (Acts 18:8). In a word, I believe that the Christian teachers with whom I have had intercourse teach as plainly, and as purely, what the primitive teachers taught, and require as precisely what they required, in order to the admission of members into the congregation of Christ, as any people with whom I am acquainted.

I have not written this for the sake of the Christian brethren, but for the sake of some of our Reforming brethren, who seem to be alarmed, fearing that I and

* Nor debar them.—B. W. Stone and J. T. Johnson, Editors *Christian Messenger.*

some other Reforming teachers have injured the good cause in which we have been engaged by sanctioning all the speculations and errors which have been laid to the charge of the people called Christians, whether justly or unjustly. That our Reforming brethren may be enabled to judge and determine upon the propriety or impropriety of our conduct, when we and the Christian brethren united in all the acts of social worship, we have thought it proper to lay before them what we understand to be the views and the practice of the Christian teachers, in the several important particulars named above.

If, in doing this, we have in any particular been mistaken, or have misrepresented them, we can assure them that we have not done it designedly; they will, therefore, have the goodness to correct the error, and pardon me. On the other hand, if the above named views of the Christian brethren be correct, I would then ask any brother, what law of Christ is violated when we break the loaf together? Or when we meet with those on the King's highway, who have been immersed upon a profession of their faith in the Lord Jesus Christ, and are walking in his commandments, by what rule found in the New Testament could we reject them, or refuse to break bread with them?

3. It may be asked, if the people called *Christians,* who have ceased to speculate upon the character of Christ, have given up their Unitarian opinions? And may it not as well be asked, have they who speculate upon the character of Christ before they became Reformers given up their Trinitarian opinions? To

both these questions I would answer, I do not know, neither do I care. We should always allow to others that which we claim for ourselves—*the right of private judgment.*

If either Christians or Reformers have erroneous opinions, they never can injure any person, provided we all have prudence enough to keep them to ourselves. Neither will they injure us, if we continue to believe the Gospel facts, and obey the law of the King. If all who profess to be teachers of the Christian religion would keep their opinions to themselves, teach the Gospel facts, and urge the people to obey them, the world would soon be delivered from the wretched, distracting, and destructive influences of mystical preaching.

4. Again, it is asked, when you break bread with those called Christians about Georgetown, etc., do you not sanction all the sectarian speculations of all those who are called by the same name throughout the United States? No. The Christian churches are not bound together by written, human laws, like many others; and even if they were, I should not believe that I had sanctioned any sectarian peculiarity which might be among them, because I find nothing either in Scripture or reason to make me believe so. If such an idea had been taught in the New Testament, surely the Reformers never would have acted as they have done, and are still doing. For example: after many of us became Reformers, we continued to break bread with many of those who continued to plead for all their old sectarian pecularities and human traditions—even in

our own congregation—without even so much **as**
dreaming that we were sanctioning all or any of their
unscriptural peculiarities, or those of the Associations
with which we were in correspondence. You will say
that all these had come into the kingdom by faith and
immersion. Granted; and so had those Christians with
whom we broke bread, so far as we know.

Once more. It is well known that brother G. Gates,
as yet, stands formally connected with the Elkhorn
Association; and that all the Reformers cheerfully
commune with him, as they ought to do, at the Lord's
table, not thinking, for one moment, that in so doing
they sanction all the peculiarities which belong to that
body, and all the other Associations with which they
stand formally connected. Similar cases might be
multiplied, but we deem it unnecessary.

When our brethren shall have seen this, we hope
they will be satisfied that we have not laid aside our
former speculations, and taken up those of any other
people. They can not think that we wish to amalga-
mate the immersed and the unimmersed in the congregation of Christ. We do not find such amalgamation
in the ancient congregation of Christ. Therefore,
whilst contending for the ancient order of things, we
can not contend for this.

5. We are pleased with the name Christian, and **do**
desire to see it divested of every sectarian idea, and
everything else but that which distinguished the
primitive Christians from all other people, in faith
and practice, as the humble followers of the meek **and**
lowly Redeemer. And we do believe that the Christian

brethren about Georgetown, etc., would be as much gratified to see this as we would be ourselves.

The. friends of the Reformation may easily injure their own cause by giving to it a sectarian character; against which we should always be specially guarded. And in order to avoid this, and all other departures from the Apostolic order of things, we can not, **we** will not, knowingly sanction any tradition, speculation, or amalgamation unknown to the primitive Christian congregations. On the other hand, we are determined, by the favor of God, to the utmost of our ability, to teach what the primitive disciples taught; and in admitting persons into the congregation of Christ, **we** will require what they required, and nothing more. We will urge the practice of all the Apostolic commands and examples given to the primitive Christians, and thus labor for the unity of the disciples of Christ upon this one foundation. And whenever we find others—whatever they may have been called by their enemies—laboring for the same object, aiming at the same thing, we are bound joyfully to receive them, treat them as Christians, and co-operate with them.

We have now laid before our brethren, candidly and plainly, the principle upon which we have acted, relative to the union spoken of between the Christians and Reformers about Georgetown, etc., which, **we** think, is perfectly consistent with that from which we have acted for several years past. But if we have done anything which the Gospel or the law of Christ will not justify, we would be glad to know it, as we do desire, above all things, to know the whole truth, and to practice it; and as we think that the best of us, either as individuals, or as congregations, are not fully reformed, but reforming.

JOHN SMITH.

SERMON ON HUMILITY.

By William Hayden.

Wm. Hayden was born in Westmoreland County, Pa., June 30, 1799. Died at Chagrin Falls, O., April 7, 1863.

"And there was a strife also among them, which of them should be accounted the greatest" (Luke 22:24).

False ambition has, perhaps, been productive of more evil to the human race than any other cause. It is nothing else than supreme selfishness. It sometimes assumes very specious names and appearances. When it strives for the mastery in the political world, it styles itself patriotism. Then you hear the demagogue eloquently pleading the interests of the "dear people," the honor of his country, while denouncing his competitors as enemies to both. When it seeks for pre-eminence in the church, it shows itself in zeal for orthodoxy, for long-established usages. Or, perchance, it grows dissatisfied with all these, and would throw society into a ferment and proclaim "reform," "progress with the spirit of the age," placing itself at the head of parties, armies, and nations, or if disappointed in this, turning misanthrope, finds fault with everything and complains of the ingratitude of mankind. In the church, the individual no longer able to endure or fellowship the corruption and hypocrisy of brethren, leaves the church and concludes he can best serve his God, *i. e.,* his own pride and envy, alone.

193

Such persons are very zealous Christians so long as they can be put forward and have things in their own way. If an individual is suspected of possessing more of the confidence and esteem of the brethren than himself, he can never hear without pain such brother commended; but to ease his mind with as good a grace as may be, he will admit there are some good qualities in the brother, but he has certain faults, which ought to be known in order to form a just estimate of his character.

Doubtless many deceive themselves into a notion that their motives are pure, that it is the glory of God and the interest of his cause they have at heart, when pride, envy and jealousy lie at the bottom of all they say and do. Even the pure in heart will have enough to do to keep themselves pure. The religion and morals of paganism were quite consistent with, nay, encouraged and patronized this love of pre-eminence, insomuch that "a strife for the mastery" in all their games and pursuits, in peace and war, was most manifest. Their historians and poets, their painters and sculptors, published and extolled, celebrated and gave a sort of immortality to the successful aspirant, which in turn inflamed the ardor and fired the ambition of others. The consequences were that pride and all the warring passions of their nature were let loose and stimulated to the utmost; the very gods were, indeed, supposed to be delighted with the contest, insomuch that envy, rage, malevolence, with all their consequences, filled the world.

The world could not possibly be reformed without

a religion essentially different, which should cut off
the very root of all those principles of action and institute others which should implant, cherish, and cultivate to perfection the opposite of the lust of the flesh,
and the lust of the eye, and the pride or ambition of
the world.

Christianity is the only system of religion and morals
that can bless the human race.   Instead of pride, humility; instead of envy, esteem for others; instead of
hatred and revenge, gentleness, brotherly kindness,
and benevolence.   The gospel reveals to us the true
state and condition of mankind, *all* guilty before God.
With all their boasted attainments, discoveries, and
improvements, their wisdom, learning, arts, pleasures,
and religion, *all wrong,* ignorant, false, vain, destructive to man, offensive to God, without God, without
hope, lost.   At the same time, the compassion of the
everlasting God, his truth, justice, and mercy revealed
in the sacrificing for our sins his only begotton Son,
the humbling, repenting and submitting of ourselves
to him, the infallible assurance of forgiveness, of resurrection and eternal life, and the eternal condemnation
of all who neglect the gospel, the whole sustained by
miracles, signs, wonders, and prophecies, addressed to
the senses and reason of mankind, calling for immediate submission.   Such a proclamation honestly
heeded could not fail to reform the human race.   Nothing else could do it.   Hence the gospel, and nothing
but the gospel, is "the power of God to the salvation
of all who *really* believe it."   'Tis this, and only this,
that makes man to know himself, his origin, destiny,

nature, relation, wants, wounds, sorrows, and remedies. The value his Maker sets upon him, the vanity
of the world and all its ambitions and pomp, how
empty and foolish its pleasures, how good and gracious
is the Lord, how kind and gentle the Saviour, how dignified, majestic, powerful, rich, and glorious, till, his
heart delighted, and his soul enraptured with the love
and philanthropy of the God and Father of our Lord
Jesus Christ, he is reconciled in feeling, and obeys from
the heart the gospel; being then free from sin, he is
a child of God, an heir of glory; his spirit is full of
joy, abounding in all compassion to man, his fellow.

True Christianity makes true Christians, corrupt
Christianity makes at best imperfect Christians. In
the latter case, however sincere, partyism and all its
attendant evils will more or less prevail; in the former,
union, humility, love, peace, and good-will, and all
moral excellence must be the fruit.

The first thing Christ said in his Sermon on the
Mount was, "Blessed are the poor in spirit, for theirs
is the kingdom of heaven." Instead of extolling pride,
ambition, and turbulence, which have filled the earth
with carnage, crimes, and tears, he condemns them all,
and inculcates those principles which, however despised by heroes, poets, orators, statesmen, are the only
principles that can promote "Glory to God in the highest, peace on earth, and good will among men."

But alas! How slow to learn, how slow to practice
the pure religion, the holy gospel of the Redeemer!
And the disciples making their boasts of the Bible
alone, how *far* from appreciating, honoring, and ex-

hibiting pure Christianity. Have we not seen envy
and strife, insubordination, jealousy, rivalry, and reck-
lessness? "Which of us shall be accounted the greatest?" I am not sure that this demon has not pursued
at times persons of all stations, the most obscure and
private disciples, deacons, overseers, preachers, exhort-
ers, editors. "My sacred honor" is too often mistaken
for the honor of Christ and his cause. It is true,
while we are clothed with mortality we shall be liable
to faults and imperfections of character. We see such
things everywhere, even in "the twelve," before they
received power from on high. It is also to be lamented
that men of the world choose rather to look at the imperfections of Christians than at the perfections of
Christianity and its glorious Author. But we can not
prevent it; they will not look at the religion of Christ,
but through its advocates; and therefore the Saviour
said, "Let your light so shine before men, that others
seeing your good works shall glorify your Father
which is in Heaven." And an apostle said, "So is the
will of Good that with *well doing* you put to silence
the ignorance of foolish men." And in no other way
can we open the way to the human heart. Therefore,
how pertinent all the exhortations of the apostles to
purity, humility, peace, and love.

I would not be understood, however, to say there
is no ambition to be cherished by the gospel, or that
there is no true greatness to be aimed at by the Christian. Far from it. But the ambition and greatness
here is free from envy, and is compatible with the most
pure and sincere esteem for all, even those who excel

us. Christ said whoever wishes to be great must be servant. Now, suppose a brother superior for talent, education, or property. That brother is not haughty nor overbearing, but gentle, kind, condescending, full of liberality, and all goodness; affects no superiority in apparel, style, or manners; seeks not applause; rather diffident than assuming; delighting in the happiness of others; taking pleasure in doing all he can to happify all around him, in his family, neighborhood, the church, and the world abroad. Who can envy him? A man whose only superiority consists in goodness can not be envied by any man, saint, or sinner, scarcely by a hypocrite.

Goodness, supreme goodness, no man can hate. No matter how much worth, talent, learning, or fame be connected with it, if these be subordinate to goodness, and directed by wisdom, they will command the admiration and affection of the human heart. Therefore, it is that we love God. Therefore, it is that certain men will have an influence in society beyond others and are not envied but beloved.

So, also, the good man can not envy any one. He can not envy the rich brother while himself is poor, if the rich one is governed by goodness. And if the rich, or learned, or talented, be he not a good man, though he be famed and admired, and have an influence beyond what moral worth gives him, still his fame and influence must have an end, and his pride will have a fall; consequently, he is not to be envied.

The greatest man in the world, then, is he who is most like the Saviour of men; who lays all his honors,

gifts, or attainments at the feet of Jesus, and gives
him all the glory. It is he who abounds in all goodness, purity, and godly fear. It is he whose soul is
moved at the wretchedness of mankind, and is only
concerned to see men redeemed and God glorified
through Jesus Christ. It is he who has the least taste,
and is least attracted by things admired and pursued
by the giddy, gay, ungodly world of mankind, while
he glories in the Lord.

CHRIST'S CONVERSATION WITH NICO-DEMUS.

BY M. E. LARD.

Moses E. Lard was born in Bedford County, Tenn., October 29, 1818. Died at Lexington, Ky., June 17, 1880.

"Except a man be born of water and of the Spirit, he can not enter into the kingdom of God."—John 3 : 5.

It is difficult, if not impossible, in the judgment of most professors, to overestimate the importance of the new birth; and when we reflect on the position assigned it by the Saviour, this judgment must be felt to be correct. Without it no man can enter the kingdom of God. Into that kingdom he may desire to enter, may pray to enter, may even think he has entered; but into it he can never go without being born again. This determines its value.

Now, in whatever the new birth may consist, whatever processes may be necessary to complete it, no matter how many, nor what its component parts, of one thing I am satisfied: its solution must be sought mainly in a well-conducted analysis of the conversation with Nicodemus. If, on examination, this conversation does not suggest its explanation, I shall despair of ever attaining one. Confirmation from other portions of Holy Writ this explanation may

200

receive, but a solution the new birth itself will not receive. The conversation with Nicodemus is the very soil in which the pearl lies buried.

At once, then, I come to consider the great doctrinal statement in that conversation which involves the whole subject. It runs thus: *"Except a man be born of water and of the Spirit, he can not enter into the kingdom of God."* This statement I regard as presenting us with a complete view of the new birth, as informing us in what it consists, as comprehending, in other words, the two grand *facts* which constitute it. In the declaration, "Except a man be born again he can not see the kingdom of God," the Saviour merely propounds the doctrine of the new birth generally, in a statement of the necessity of it; whereas, in the more elaborate statement, "Except a man be born of water and of the Spirit, he can not enter into the kingdom of God," he states definitely in what it consists, reiterating the necessity of it. The former statement propounds the doctrine, the latter statement explains it.

Now, unless it should turn out that the Saviour has made provision equally for the salvation of those within and those without the kingdom of God, then the necessity of the new birth becomes absolute and overwhelming. If the blessing of remission of sins be limited to those within the kingdom, then neither flight of fancy nor fertility of imagination can exaggerate the importance of being born again. Should it so happen, moreover, that the Saviour has, in the declaration now in hand, afforded us the means of knowing what it is to be born again; if he has put it beyond our power to plead unavoidable ignorance in regard to it, pity, Lord, pity the willful blindness of countless thousands who now call themselves the children of God!

The great statement of which I am now treating naturally divides itself into two clauses, each clause comprehending an integral part of the new birth, and the two parts exhausting it. These clauses are, respectively: *Born of water, born of the Spirit.* I shall now attempt to unfold their meaning at length, and in the order in which they occur.

The first question to be settled, and a most important one, is: In what sense are we to construe the expression *born of water,* in a literal or in a figurative sense? This question will, perhaps, be best answered by resolving the expression into the two simple members which compose it, and by examining each of them separately. These members are *born of* and *water.* To some this division may seem unnecessarily minute. I do not think it so. By thus breaking down the clause into these two simple verbal members, its subjects come singly into view, by which means each can be subjected to a more severe, because a more distinct, examination.

Upon the import of the expression "born of," which all allow to be metaphorical, there exists, I believe, no diversity of opinion, provided only we can settle definitely the import of the term water. Are we, then, to construe this term in its ordinary and literal acceptation or in a figurative sense? In the latter sense, respond many. Let us now examine the hypothesis implied in this response, which, being concisely expressed in the form of a proposition, is this: *The term water is figurative.*

But this proposition is only asserted; it is not proved. Before, therefore, it can justly challenge our assent, it must be supported by relevant and satisfactory testimony. This testimony we have a right to demand, yet it has never been adduced, though the proposition has often been reasserted. In proving the proposition, we should expect to see a course pursued something like the following: We should expect an accurate analysis of the new birth, in which its constituent parts would all be clearly pointed out; we should expect an orderly enumeration of these parts, *each being complete without water;* we should expect at least a few apt remarks on the grounds and propriety of using the term water in a figurative sense; we should expect to be shown, with remarkable clearness, what thing the term, in its figurative sense, is intended to denote—precisely what it expresses; we should expect to be shown that this thing, thus expressed, actually constituted one of the previously enumerated parts of the new birth; and, finally, we should expect the whole argument to be strongly summed up, and the results shown to correspond minutely with the great elementary doctrines of salvation as set forth by Christ and His apostles. But have these reasonable expectations been gratified? They have not.

Here, then, I might, on grounds strictly just, rest for the present the discussion of this proposition. I

shall, however, proceed to test its accuracy still further, though, in logical fairness, under no obligation
to do so.

The term water is figurative. This is a tough saying. Innumerable have been the efforts which have
been made to sustain it; yet not the semblance of success has ever crowned one of them. On all lies the
stain of iniquity. What, I am curious to know, has
ever put it into any head of man to say of the term,
it is figurative? The answer is not difficult. The literal meaning of the term stands against those who have
so said; stands against their tenets, and shuts them out
of the kingdom of God. Hence, *to accommodate them*
it must be figurative. This, and no other, is the answer.

But is the term figurative? Then is it so for sufficient reasons, which being assigned, would account
for the fact; and these reasons are discoverable. For
if no such reasons exist, then is the term figurative
without a reason, which, in the case of a term used
by the Saviour, is inadmissible; and unless discoverable,
though the reasons may exist, the effect is the same
with us as though they had no existence. It is presumed, then, that these reasons, unless purely imaginary, will be found in some one or more of the following items:

1. The nature of the case, of the new birth;
2. The laws regulating the use of figurative language; or,
3. The sense resulting from a figurative construction.

First, then, as to the nature of the case. This I

conceive to be the ground on which chiefly, if not
alone, the figurative construction of the term water
is to be defended. For if the nature of the case be
such that this term can not be, in a literal acceptation,
predicated of it, even in part, then is the figurative
construction the alternative we must accept. Are we,
then, obliged, by a necessity inherent in the nature of
the case, to construe the term water figuratively? If
not, then must we construe it ordinarily and literally?
Now, if any such inherent necessity exist, it must be
owing to the fact that the new birth is, in all its parts
and circumstances, complete without water; for, if not
thus complete, then we need the term water to express
the fact. But before we can infer anything from the
nature of the case, we must, of course, know what the
case itself is. Here, now, we encounter a serious
difficulty. For, until the import of the term water
is settled, the meaning of the new birth remains doubtful. This is one of the terms employed by the Saviour
to describe the new birth. Until, therefore, we settle
its meaning, we remain ignorant to this extent of what
the new birth is. Hence, from the nature of this thing
we can infer nothing.

But should it be alleged that we can know, independently of the import of the term water, in what
the new birth consists, and therefore in what acceptation the term is to be taken, I ask how? There are
but two possible ways. Either we must be able to
know it in and of ourselves, and independently of the
Word of God, or from passages of Scripture which
contain no allusion to water. No one who is not will-

ing to be the dupe of his own fancy, will assert that he can know anything of the matter in the first-named way. Neither can he know anything of it in the second, for the only passage in the New Testament, which describes the new birth fully, contains the term water. Hence, till we know what this term means, we shall never know what the new birth is.

Second. As to the laws regulating the use of figurative language. Most words, as is well known to the reader, are capable of being used in two acceptations: a literal or ordinary, and figurative; some even in three: literal, ordinary, and figurative. In many instances it happens that the ordinary import and the literal are the same, as is the case with the term water; in some, again, the ordinary and the figurative agree, while the literal often differs from both. Hence, in construing a passage, the first thing in order is to ascertain, by the aid of some safe rule, the acceptation in which its terms are to be taken. This rule is, with one consent, allowed to be mainly the sense intended by the writer. But this, though the chief, is not the only means frequently at hand for determining this point. The manner in which a term is introduced often enables us to decide it. When a term is attended by the words *like, so as,* with many others, which serve to introduce comparisons and other figures, we at once pronounce the term, so attended, figurative. But where this is not the case, and where the sense does not imperatively demand it, it is both arbitrary and dangerous to construe a term figuratively.

Now, is the term water, in the clause in hand, attended by any verbal sign indicative of a figurative use? Certainly not. Here, then, the inference is conclusive against a figurative construction. But does not the sense of the passage require it to be so construed? True, it is so asserted; but this is precisely the thing which I deny, and which I do not intend shall be taken for granted. But the assertion can not be true; for, on the contrary, it is only when the term is construed literally that the clause makes any sense at all. Construe it figuratively, and you forever hide every vestige of meaning in the clause. Indeed, the real question here at issue is not whether the term is or is not figurative, but whether it has a literal, or absolutely no meaning. The question is not what meaning are men willing to receive, but what is the meaning they *must receive,* or reject all meaning. Too many, I well know, are not willing to receive the literal meaning; and this is their sole reason for preferring a figurative one. But this is not to make the will of God, but the preference of man, our rule of action.

But let us concede for a moment that the term water is figurative. To what class, then, of figurative words does it belong? Indisputably it is a metaphor; for to this class belong all those words which are used figuratively with no verbal sign to denote the fact. Now, a word is used metaphorically when it is taken from denoting what it ordinarily means to become, for the present, the name of something which it does not ordinarily mean. Still, in all cases, it becomes the name of some *real thing,* never of *nothing.* A word, moreover, is used metaphorically because the thing which it usually denotes resembles, in more or less respects, the thing which it is used metaphorically to denote, and because it is wished to suggest that resemblance. Of metaphors there are two classes, determined by the manner in which we discover the meaning of the metaphoric word. To the first class belong all those words which, on being simply heard in their connection, instantly, without any extrinsic aid, suggest to the mind their meaning. To the second all those words which, on being simply heard, do not instantly suggest their meaning, so deeply is it hid, but have it brought out by some added explanation.

The following may serve as instances of the two classes:

1. The Saviour said of Herod: "Go and tell that fox, behold I cast out demons, and I do cures to-day and to-morrow, and the third day I shall be perfected." Here we as instantly collect His meaning as if he had said, Go and tell that *cunning king.*

2. "He that believes in me, as the Scripture has said, out of him shall flow *rivers of living water.*" Here the mind is held in complete suspense, unable to penetrate the mystery in which the term water involves the sentence, until it is added: "But this spoke he of the Spirit which they that believe on him should receive."

Now, to which of these two classes—and there are no others—does the term water, now in question, belong? Not to the latter; for no explanatory clause is added. Neither to the former; for, on being pro-

nounced, it suggests, on the figurative hypothesis, just
no meaning at all. Hence, again from these premises
nothing can be inferred in support of the preceding
proposition, but, rather, it is felt to be false.

Third. The sense resulting from a figurative construction.. This brings me to notice the most objectionable feature in this whole theory; for, not only
has the term water been treated as figurative, without
a single reason, but, where it has been assigned any
meaning at all, it has been a most fanciful one. Surely,
my hearers need not be informed that figurative language has meaning no less than literal; nor that an
idea is wholly unaffected by the kind of language in
which it is conveyed. A thought remains the same
whether communicated in literal or in figurative language. But, clearly, he who asserts a word to be
figurative, must know what it means; otherwise, if
conscientious, he would not venture the assertion.
Hence, clearly, must they who assert that the term
water is figurative know what it means? But have
they pointed that meaning out? Never; this they
dare not attempt.

True, we are told that water is an emblem—an emblem, too, of purification. But the term water, now in
hand, is held to be figurative; hence, of course, there
is here no water. It is excluded by the very nature
of the case; therefore, since there is here no water,
there is here no emblem; and since no emblem, nothing emblemized, and hence no purification. Thus this
groundless conceit vanishes.

But is the term water figurative? Granted, for a

moment. Still, it has meaning. Let, now, this meaning be determined—definitely determined. Next, let the term water be displaced from the clause in hand, but its meaning retained in some fit word. Then let us read: "Except a man be born of [*the thing which the term water denotes, no matter what it is*] and the Spirit, he can not enter into the kingdom of God." From this there is absolutely no escape. Settle what the term water stands for. Then, of that thing unless a man be born, against him the kingdom of God is forever shut. True, we thus get rid of the water; but whether we thereby ease the way into the kingdom of God may well be doubted. Still, two things are left, of both of which we must be born. This increases difficulties, not diminishes them; hence, better retain the water. Then only are we true to reason, true to Christ.

Since, then, it is only asserted, not proved, that the term water is figurative; since there is no inherent necessity in the nature of the case for this construction; since the laws of figurative language do not demand it; and since, from such construction, either no sense at all results, or one which does not better the case—since all these things are true, I hence conclude that the term water is construed correctly only when taken in its literal and ordinary acceptation. Hence, when the Saviour says, "Except a man be born of water," he means simply and literally water.

What, now, is it to be born of water? On this question I need not dwell long. To be born of, as already conceded, is figurative. Literally, it denotes the event which brings us into natural life; figuratively, then, it must denote an event like it. The two events must resemble each other as type resembles impression, or, if not so exactly, still closely. First, then, we have water given; second, in this a man is buried; third, out of it he emerges. Is not this being born of water? If the reason or the-eye may be appealed to in any case to settle either the meaning of a word, or determine the analogy of facts, the question is answered. *This is being born of water.* But this is precisely what takes place in immersion; hence, I conclude that, to be born of water and be immersed are merely two different names—that figurative, this literal—for one and the same act.

A corroborative item or two, and I am done with the first part of my subject. Water is never present in any act connected with the kingdom of Christ, except one. But in that act it is always present, and never absent. That act is immersion. But in the expression, "born of water," *water is present;* hence, it must be in immersion, since it can be in nothing else. Again, it seems that to be born of water and be immersed are identical.

Christ is called the first-born from the dead. This is the statement of a fact, and in it occurs the word born. The fact is Christ's rising from the dead; hence, to arise out of the grave is to be born from the dead. But a man is dead to sin, is buried in the water, and rises out of it. If, now that rising can be called being born from the dead, then is this rising being born of water. If, in argument, analogy be worth anything, it is decisive here.

If the expression, "born of water," does not signify immersion, its meaning is not determinate. Then no living man can say whether he is in, or not in, the kingdom of God. But Christ has not left us in doubt on so vital a point; hence, the expression must be determinate, and signifies immersion.

I here terminate my examination of the clause "born of water." The result is submitted to the candid and thoughtful hearer only, but to him with no fear as to the end.

I now proceed to inquire into the meaning of the second division of my subject, namely, "Born of the Spirit." Important as has been the discussion of the preceding division, the discussion of this will be generally felt to be still more so, and I by no means wish to diminish the just interest which may be felt in it.

I shall set out with the assumption, new, perhaps, to many, that the Saviour, after stating in what the new birth consists, then proceeds to explain so much of it as is embraced in the clause "born of the Spirit." One thing, at least, will be conceded, that what is here embraced was least likely to be understood, and, therefore, stood most in need of explanation. Upon the import of the clause "born of water" the great Teacher said nothing. Of this Nicodemus needed no explanation. As soon as he learned from the Saviour that he spoke not of a literal re-birth, instantly the meaning of the clause would flash into his mind. He would intuitively take the term water literally; this done, and the meaning of "born of" would be at once perceived. But not so with the phrase "born of the Spirit." Of necessity all would be dark here. Of being born of the Spirit, or of being begotten by it, he had no means of information. To him the subject was absolutely new. Not one incident of universal history could shed a ray of light on it. In his case, therefore, an explanation was especially necessary. Hence the assumption that we have one.

With what is here last said corresponds, as I deem, the next verse, namely, "That which is born of the flesh is flesh; and that which is born of the Spirit is spirit." Hardly can this verse be held to be free from difficulty; not that its difficulty is insuperable, but only that it is not free from it. In the expression, "that which is born of the flesh is flesh," we have the statement of a simple well-known matter of fact. In this statement every word is to be taken literally; nor can any one acquainted with the fact stated misunderstand the terms in which it is expressed. Flesh produces flesh literally, or the one is the offspring of the other. This we know to be so. But the difficulty lies not here. It is in the expression "that which is born of the Spirit is spirit," or more strictly, perhaps, in the parallelism which we draw between the two expressions. In the expression last cited the word born is not to be taken literally; for in regeneration no personal spirit is produced; that is, the Holy Spirit does not produce the human spirit in the sense in which flesh produces flesh. In regeneration the human spirit is only *changed,* not *produced.* Hence, in the second expression, the word born is not to be taken literally but figuratively, as denoting, in general terms, simply a change. Now the difficulty, as I conceive, lies here: In drawing the parallel we make Spirit stand to spirit as flesh stands to flesh, in each case the one producing the other. Clearly this is wrong. Certainly flesh produces flesh; but Spirit only changes spirit. Here there is no product, at least no product of substantive spirit. Hence, in the first expression, the word born is to be taken literally, but in the second figuratively. This causes, unless carefully noticed, confusion, and in this we feel the difficulty. But how, it may be asked, do I know this, or from what do I learn it? I answer, from the very nature of the case. In regeneration the human spirit already exists; it is, hence, not produced. Consequently the difference in the subjects determines a difference in the terms.

But on the supposition that the Saviour is now explaining so much of the new birth as relates to the Spirit, this is precisely what we should expect Him to say. The word born denotes a change. The Holy Spirit is the agent who effects this change. The human spirit is the subject in which it takes place. That which is born of Spirit—the Holy Spirit—is spirit, the human spirit. The Holy Spirit begets the human; that is, effects the change which takes place in it. The whole process embraces four items, indicated in the four following questions: 1. Who effects the change? 2. What is changed? 3. How is the change effected? 4. In what does it consist when effected? These four questions exhaust the subject. Two of them have now been answered—the Holy Spirit effects the change, the human spirit is changed. Only two, therefore, remain to be answered. Of these the Saviour, in the following verses, answers only the third, namely, how is the change effected? The fourth is not answered by him in the interview with Nicodemus, but is answered elsewhere in the New Testament, as will be shown in the course of this sermon.

Here it is proper to determine another point before proceeding further. Should we read *born* of the Spirit, or *begotten* by it? This depends altogether on the view we are taking of the matter in hand. If we are viewing regeneration as completed, completed in both its parts, completed in water, completed in spirit, then it is proper to say born of the Spirit; otherwise it obviously is not. Whenever the two parts of the process are viewed separately, then, clearly, we should say begotten by the Spirit, not born. The Holy Spirit begets the human, or, more strictly, begets a change in it, prepares it for entrance into the kingdom of God. In this preparation the Holy Spirit, as agent, merely acts on the human spirit, changing it. The human spirit is not conceived of as coming out of, or proceeding from, the Holy Spirit. Hence begotten, not born, is the proper word. Again: being begotten by the Spirit is the first part of the whole process of being born again. It consequently antecedes the other part, being born of water, and is hence more correctly expressed by begotten than born. Further, as the word born applies to the last act in natural generation, so likewise it applies to the last act in regeneration. This act, in regeneration, is coming out of the water. Hence, to it we should apply born, to the other begotten. Accordingly the verse in hand would, perhaps, be more correctly rendered. *That which is begotten by the flesh is flesh, and that which is begotten by the Spirit is spirit.* This much must be correct, more than this might not be; it is hence best to say this much, no more. Certainly, in the fifth verse, we should render the original by born, thus: "Except a man be born of water and of the Spirit, he can not enter into the kingdom of God." Here begotten is wholly inadmissible, since we can not be begotten by water, but must be born of it. Again, it is not by being begotten simply that we enter into the kingdom of God; it is by being born. In the fifth verse the word denotes the act which translates us into the kingdom. It is hence the act of being born, not of being begotten. In the subsequent verses, however, where the word occurs, it is best to render it begotten. I shall accordingly do so, as already in the sixth.

It will be remembered that we are now speaking on the assumption that after the fifth verse, the Saviour proceeds to explain how we are begotten by the Spirit. With this assumption agrees the seventh verse more naturally than with any other. The verse reads: "Marvel not that I said to thee, ye must be born again." When I am speaking to a man, and it is obvious to my eye that he does not understand me, and I say to him: Wonder not that I should speak to you thus, for what, most naturally, does my remark prepare him? For an illustration or an explanation? If I have already explained myself, clearly it prepares him for an illustration. But if not, then an explanation is expected. Now, in the case in hand, the Savior had submitted no explanation. Most naturally, then, it seems, would his remark induce the expectation of one. I hence still assume that the following verse contains one.

The verse reads thus: *"The wind bloweth where it listeth, and thou hearest the sound thereof, but canst not tell whence it cometh, and whither it goeth; so is every one that is born of the Spirit."*

No passage in the New Testament has been so variously and so inconsistently construed as this. Hardly any two men understand it alike. Hence it is cited to prove anything or nothing, as may happen to suit the tenets of him who uses it. Generally, by the parties of the day, it is held as containing an *illustration* of the mystery of being begotten by the Spirit. This, I conceive to be the radical misconception which has utterly obscured the sense of this fine passage. Without one solitary verbal mark, in the original, indicative of an illustration, or the slightest ground on which to conclude that one was ever meant, has the verse been assumed to be illustrative, and rendered accordingly. A more unaccountable departure from some of the best established laws of exegesis than its rendering, in some respects, exhibits, I have not met with. And long since, I doubt not, would the present

rendering have been utterly discarded, had it not con-
tributed to foster a deep-seated error on the subject
now in hand. To any one who is bold enough to think
for himself it is clear that the verse, as it now reads,
has simply no appreciable meaning whatever. I shall
hence, with no sort of scruple, use whatever means
may be at command to free it from darkness.

First, then, in regard to the word which, in our
common version, is rendered *"wind."* This word
occurs in the Greek New Testament three hundred
and eighty-six times. In three hundred and eighty-
four of these it is rendered into English either by the
term *Spirit,* or by its equivalent, *ghost.* Once, in the
Book of Revelation, it is rendered "life," where, beyond doubt, it should have been rendered "a spirit."
But in not a single case in the New Testament, except
the verse in hand, is it rendered "wind." Now, in
translating, one great rule to be observed is this: To
translate the same original word *uniformly* by the
same equivalent English word, unless the sense forbids it. No translation is deemed good which violates this rule, none very faulty which does not. Now,
since the word in hand, out of three hundred and
eighty-six instances, is, in three hundred and eighty-
four of them, uniformly rendered by the word *Spirit,*
or by a word of the same meaning, the presumption
in favor of a similar rendering, in the two remaining
instances, is as three hundred and eighty-four to two.
And when it is remembered that the sense does not
forbid this rendering, this presumption becomes an
imperious necessity. For these reasons, therefore, I

render the original by the word spirit, understanding thereby, *the Holy Spirit.*

The leading word thus rendered, and the whole verse, is literally translated thus: *The Spirit breathes where it sees fit, and you hear its voice, but know not whence it comes and where it goes; in this way is every one who is begotten by the Spirit.*

On this passage three questions arise, namely: What act of the Spirit does the word breathe express? Is it true that we of this day know not whence the Spirit comes, and where it goes? And is the sense of the last clause of the verse complete?

1. What act of the Spirit does the word breathe express? Be it what it may, one thing is clear, in the act something is heard. This word, then, suggests a probable answer to the question. Only when the Spirit *speaks,* do we *hear* it. Speaking, then, is most likely the act which the word breathe metaphorically expresses. With this, moreover, agrees the word *voice.* The original of this word is a generic term, expressing sound generally; but, when applied to persons, it always denotes the voice heard in speaking. But, in the present case, it applies to the Holy Spirit, a person. Hence, it is legitimate to infer that it denotes the voice of the Spirit heard in speaking. But this voice is never heard, except through prophets and apostles. It is only when in man that the Spirit speaks to him; hence, the act is an act of speaking, and the voice heard, the voice of inspired men. Through these men the Spirit speaks, and, speaking thus, we hear its voice.

2. Is it true of us in the present day that we know not whence the Spirit comes, and where it goes, or is the clause applicable to us? I reply: The clause is not applicable to us of this day, for the reason that, in no intelligible sense, can it be said of us that we know not the whence and the whither of the Spirit. Indisputably it comes from God, and is sent into the saints. But this, though true of us, was not true of Nicodemus. We have light on the point, which he had not. Of him, therefore, the clause was true, but not of us. As yet, the Saviour had taught nothing respecting the Spirit; the apostles had taught nothing, and the New Testament was not written. That, therefore, was true of Nicodemus at the time, which is inapplicable to us, and which ceased to be true of him, if he lived, as soon as the Spirit was sent. Hence, in construing the verse, we must construe it as all applicable to him, but as applicable to us only with the clause in hand omitted. In one view only can the clause be deemed applicable to us of the present day. If the Spirit be conceived of as roaming up and down on the face of the earth, in some occult manner unmentioned in the Bible, and unintelligible to man, then may we construe the clause of ourselves. In any other view it must be held as applying only to Nicodemus, and only when applied to him has it any determinate meaning. The view of the clause here maintained frees the verse from at least half the confusion which lies on it. It is presented as necessary, and as barely disputable, and

certainly relieves a passage of Scripture of no small difficulty.

3. Is the sense of the last clause of the verse complete, namely, *in this way is every one who is begotten by the Spirit?* That it is not, is intuitively felt by every reader. Involuntarily, we ask, in what way?. The question implies the incompleteness of the sense; for, were the sense complete, no impulse would be felt to ask the question. Now, in order to render the sense full, and to leave no question remaining, we have to use, in translating, one word more than is in the original. Are we at liberty to do this? Certainly it is often done; but should it be done here? I believe it should, and my reasons for so believing are concisely these: First, as already said, the sense is incomplete without the word. There is, therefore, a necessity for it. Indeed, without it the verse is an eternal enigma. Second, to supply a word not only completes the sense, but gives a sense in strict accordance with what we know to be elsewhere taught. In a doubtful case these two reasons for a particular conclusion, with none against it, may be generally accepted as decisive. I, hence, decide in favor of the word. Supplying it, and the clause reads thus: *In this way is begotten every one who is begotten by the Spirit.*

It will be remembered that, in commencing the investigation of the second part of my subject, I assumed that an explanation of *how* we are begotten by the Spirit was contained in the following verses. I am now ready to show that this assumption was well taken. In order to do this, I shall omit the clause herein held to be inapplicable to us; merely that I may present, in closer union, the really dependent clauses of the verse. Omitting, as here said, and the whole verse reads thus: *The Spirit breathes where it sees fit, and you hear its voice; in this way is begotten every one who is begotten by the Spirit?* How, then, is a person begotten by the Spirit? *By hearing its voice.* Of the truth of this I feel profoundly convinced, whether the preceding premises necessitate it or not.

In confirmation, however, of the conclusion, I cite the two following Scriptures:

1. "Of His (the Father's) own will begat he us *with the word of truth."* But the word of truth is what we hear from the Spirit. Now, by this, James affirms we are begotten. The preceding conclusion, therefore, is true. That to be begotten by the Father and by the Spirit is one and the same begetting, is here taken for granted.

2. "Being begotten again, not of corruptible seed, but of incorruptible, *by the word of God."* Here Peter declares, in so many words, that we are begotten by the word of God. This word is from the Spirit, and is what we hear. Hence, by hearing, we are begotten again.

4. But when begotten, in what does the change consist? The following contains the answer: *"Every one who believes that Jesus is the Christ, has been begotten of God"* (1 John 5:1).

From this passage one of two conclusions indisputably results: Either to be begotten of God is to believe, or this includes that, since every believer is begotten. It is here held that to be begotten and to believe are identical. Hence, when a person is begotten, the change consists in believing that Jesus is the Christ. Here, then, I end the second part of my subject.

Finally, from all the foregoing premises and reasonings, I conclude that to be "born of water" is simply to be immersed; and to be begotten by the Spirit to believe in Jesus Christ. Few conclusions of men will ever rest on safer grounds, or be better entitled to confidence.

And now to show, in conclusion, that when Christ says, "He that believes and is immersed shall be saved," He only asserts, at the close of his earthly career, what he had at its commencement asserted to Nicodemus in different language, I submit the following:

He that believes, and is immersed, is saved, and is, therefore, in the kingdom of God. Hence, he that believes, and is immersed, is born of water and of the Spirit, for, otherwise, he can not enter the kingdom of God. The only way to escape the force of this pithy argument is to deny that he who is saved is in the kingdom of God. If a man can not be saved, and be at the same time out of the kingdom, the argument is final.

A DISCOURSE ON ASSURANCE.

BY A. WILFORD HALL.

Dr. A. Wilford Hall was born August 18, 1819, near Bath, N. Y.

Beloved Friends:—We shall read as the basis of our discourse the 22d verse of the tenth chapter of Paul's Letter to the Hebrews: "Let us draw near with a true heart, in *full assurance of faith,* having our hearts sprinkled from an evil conscience and our bodies washed with pure water."

No one question, perhaps, more deeply interests the professed followers of Christ than this: "How can a person, in this life, be *fully assured* that God, for Christ's sake, has forgiven his sins?" To the answer of this question our present discourse shall be mainly devoted.

There are three distinct views of this subject entertained by the different denominations in Christendom, one class maintaining that no person can be certain of pardon in this life; that if we are forgiven, the Almighty, in His wisdom, locks up the fact in the secret counsels of His own will, leaving us the subjects of doubt and fear so long as we remain on earth. Under this view of the subject, no person could, in the language of the text, draw near to God "in *full assurance* of faith," their assurance being but partial, and not *"full."* The second class maintains that every

224

pardoned man absolutely knows the fact, that he has "full assurance" that God has blotted out his iniquities, and that he knows it because he has received a direct communication from heaven, attesting the fact by an impression made upon his heart, and that he can not be mistaken, because he *feels* his sins forgiven, and, therefore, *knows* it. Such men prefer the full assurance of *feeling* to the "full assurance of *faith,*" and do even ridicule the idea of a man rejoicing in the full assurance of pardon, with no other basis for his assurance than "faith which comes by hearing and hearing by the word of God."

The third class maintains what we are about to prove, namely, that unfeigned faith in the word of God and obedience to the stipulated conditions of pardon are all-sufficient to give a man *full assurance* that he is pardoned, justified and saved, independent of any other witness, directly from heaven or from any other source. Nay, we affirm still more—that from the simple testimony of the living oracles we may positively *know* our sins forgiven, and this is all the second class referred to claims to be necessary. They tell us that, according to our theory of assurance, a man can have nothing but bare *belief,* and can, therefore, never *know* his sins forgiven, and consequently can never, in this life, at least, enjoy the full consolation of those who have the witness of the Spirit upon their souls, by which they *know* their sins forgiven. Neither will they hesitate to grant, if it is possible for a man to know his sins pardoned by simple belief in testimony, that this is all we need; for what can we ask

more than to *know* the fact? With the permission
of this attentive audience, we shall endeavor to show
that to believe a thing with all the heart is to *know* it
—not physically, but morally.

For the sake of illustrating these two kinds of
knowledge, moral and physical, we would introduce
a case or two. For instance, we know there is such a
city as New Orleans, *morally,* but we do not know it
physically, from the fact that we never saw it. We
know, *physically*, that there is such a city as Cincinnati, because we have seen it, and do not, therefore,
as in the other case, depend exclusively upon the testimony of others. This is a fair distinction between
moral and physical knowledge. We know, morally,
that which we learn from the testimony of others; but
we know, physically, anything we learn through the
direct evidence of one or more of our five senses. Yet,
notwithstanding the distinction here made, we are as
certain of what we know *morally* as *physically*. Take,
for example, the case to which we have just alluded.
I am just as sure that there is a city called New Orleans, as that there is one called Cincinnati. Let each
one of the audience now test the matter for himself.
Are there not towns or cities which you have never
seen, that you are just as sure exist as you are of the
existence of your county seat, which you visit, perchance, every month?

But you ask me to prove, first, that what I learn
solely from the testimony of others, independent of
the direct testimony of any of my senses, is *knowledge*
in any sense whatever; and not to take for granted

the very point upon which the whole controversy turns. This, we are gratified to inform you, we are prepared to do. And perhaps this is as suitable a place to introduce the testimony as any other. First, then, we shall appeal to the apostle Peter. "Therefore, let all the house of Israel *know assuredly,* that God hath made that same Jesus whom ye have crucified both Lord and Christ" (Acts 2: 36). We ask, in what way did the Jews know that Jesus had been coronated at the right hand of God? They certainly did not *see, hear,* nor *feel* Him. We answer, then, confidently, that they knew it in no other way, and by no other means, than by the oral testimony of the apostles on that occasion. Hence, they *knew it, morally.* They knew, physically, that the apostle Peter stood before them, for they *saw* and *heard* him; but as they had the direct evidence of none of their senses attesting the fact of Christ's coronation, they could have known it only in a moral sense, which is equivalent to believing it with all the heart.

We shall next hear the apostle Paul. "We *know* that if our earthly house of this tabernacle were dissolved, we have a building of God, an house not made with hands, eternal in the heavens" (II. Cor. 5: 1). Did the brethren at Corinth *know,* physically, by the direct evidence of their senses, that they had a building of God in heaven? They certainly had not been there to see it. The fact is, they knew it, *morally,* by the testimony of the Lord, through His apostles; or, in other words, they believed this doctrine with all their hearts, which amounts to the same thing.

Our third witness shall be the apostle John. "We *know* that when he appears we shall be like him, for we shall see him as he is" (I. John 3:3). This could only have been *known* by the teaching of the apostles, who spake under the influence of the prophetic Spirit, and not by the direct evidence of any of our senses, and hence is *moral,* and not *physical,* knowledge. Upon these testimonies—which are but a small specimen of what could be adduced—we rest the proof of this part of the subject.

The Lord, in His wisdom, saw fit to base Christianity, as connected with the happiness of man, upon the loftiest and most dignified principle of our nature; and as the things for which we hope are spiritual, and not merely animal, hence He saw proper to base our assurance upon the principle of *faith,* or *moral knowledge,* which the mere animal can not possess. Those who refer to their *feelings,* which are but the legitimate offspring of animal excitement, as proof of their acceptance with God, and the pardon of sin, put themselves down to a level with the beast that perisheth, by basing their assurance upon "what they know naturally (or physically) as brute beasts" (Jude 10), and thus discard in toto the principle of faith as the basis of the Christian hope. The apostle says, "We walk by *faith,* and not by *sight*" (II. Cor. 5:7); or, as John Wesley observes, "not by *sense, sight* being put for *all the senses.*" This is correct. Hence, when a person says, "I know my sins are forgiven, because I *feel* it," it is evident that his religion is all animal, based upon a principle common to all the animal tribes.

But you ask, "Is it not the design of Christianity to make men feel well?" I answer yes; but their good feeling must be the result of their assurance of pardon, and not their assurance the result of their good feeling. The popular theology of the age, to use a homemade remark, has got the cart before the horse. Ask that enthusiastic person who has just "got through" why he feels so well, and he will answer in an ecstasy of joy, "Because I *know* my sins are all forgiven." But ask him him how he *knows* his sins are forgiven, and he will reply, "Because I *feel* so well!" Thus he feels well because he knows he is forgiven, and knows he is forgiven because he feels well!

This kind of circular logic is something like the Catholic priest who, when assailed by a Protestant, proved the infallibility of the Catholic Church by the Bible, and, when attacked by the skeptic, proved the Bible to be true by the infallibility of the church. This thing of making our feelings the proof of our conversation, and our conversation at the same time the cause of our good feelings, is what Paul calls "measuring themselves *by themselves*" (II. Cor. 10: 12), and adds that such individuals *"are not wise."* We think the same. But ask a wise man, an enlightened convert to Christianity, why he is so happy, and why he appears to be so overwhelmed with joy, and he will answer, "Because God, for Christ's sake, has forgiven my sins." But how do you *know* your sins are forgiven? "Because God hath sworn by two *immutable* things, *in which it is impossible for him to lie,* that we might have s*trong consolation* who have fled for refuge to lay hold on the hope set before us." (Heb. 6: 18.) He would tell you that he has *"full assurance of faith,* having his heart sprinkled from an evil conscience and his body washed with pure water," and that he *knew, morally,* as certain as that there is a God, or that Christ died for our sins, that he was justified, pardoned and saved, because God had pledged His immutable oath, and he, having fulfilled the conditions on his part, God did not, because he could not, forfeit His word. But how about your good feelings? I enjoy them as the result of my *faith,* which gives me the "full assurance" of my acceptance. The historian informs us, the jailer, after having his "body washed with pure water," "rejoiced (how?), *believing* in God." (Acts 16: 34.) And the apostle Peter says, *"believing,* we *rejoice* with *joy unspeakable."* (I. Pet. 1: 8.) Now, if *"joy unspeakable"* be the result of simply *"believing,"* as the inspired apostle here testifies, what more is necessary, and what more could be desired, even by those who maintain *feeling* as the ground of their assurance? But to show conclusively that Christianity recognizes no other principle, as the basis of our assurance and consolation, than faith, we quote the apostle Paul. "Now the God of hope fill you with ALL *joy* and *peace* IN BELIEVING." (Rom. 15: 13.) What is there left for any other principle to effect? But you ask, why are all our consolation, joy, peace and assurance of pardon the result of faith? Because the *word* which we *believe* contains the unspeakable promise of pardon, which we enjoy, through a compliance with its stipulated terms. This word—so far from being a dead letter, as many teach—is *"quick* and *powerful,"* "living and abiding forever." The Saviour says, "These things I have *spoken* unto you, that your *joy* might be *full."*. (John 15:11.)

True, you say, the *word,* when spoken by the Saviour, could produce *full joy;* but can this be said of the word when written? John answers, "These things *write we* unto you, that your *joy* may be *full."* (I. John 1:4.) But you ask if the apostle had the same words to write that the Saviour spoke? Let the Saviour answer in His prayer. "I have given them the *words* which thou hast given me, and they have received them and have known surely that I came out from thee." (John 17:8.) Thus, we have another reason why we can derive all *joy* and *peace* from believing the word, from the fact that if the apostles could *"know surely"* that Christ was the Messiah by the evidence of His words, we may certainly know from the same words that our sins have been forgiven. But you say, true, the word, when spoken by the Saviour, might have that influence, but not when written; for then it becomes a dead letter; and, certain it is, that we can know nothing from the testimony of that which has no life. But let us see. "These things have I *written* unto you * * * that ye may *know* that ye have eternal life." (I. John 5:13.) Why write to them that they might *know* it, if they could know it in any other way? But you say, true, we may know a thing by *written* testimony to some extent; but can we know the *certainty* of a thing through that medium? Luke answers, "Forasmuch as many have taken in hand to set forth in order a declaration of those things which are *most surely believed* among us, it seemed good to me also, having had perfect under- standing of all things from the very first, to *write* unto thee, in order, most excellent Theophilus, *that thou mightest* KNOW the CERTAINTY of those things." (Luke 1:1-4.) Ah, then, we can positively *"know the certainty"* of a thing just by written testimony; and this is all we want in order to be *fully assured* of any fact, even the pardon of sin.

But then, says one, I want some better testimony than the mere word, to prove that my sins are for- given. I wonder how those preachers, who talk in this way, would like it, should they state a fact to which they were an eye and ear witness, and I say to them: Gentlemen, I want some better testimony than your *mere word* that what you state is true! I should be turned out of the synagogue, sure as fate, did I speak of their word as they do of the word of the Almighty! Yet they pretend to believe the Bible! The truth is, however, that men who will speak thus of the living oracles, do not believe with all the heart that the Bible is a revelation from God. Nay, I as- sert still further, that any man, pretending to be a Christian, who can ask or even desire any other wit- ness to prove his sins forgiven than the word of the Lord, is a skeptic at heart, and at the same time strongly tinctured with hypocrisy, for pretending to believe what in his very heart he is not willing to credit! When men call upon God to send down the Holy Spirit to bear witness to their hearts that they are born

of God, methinks that if the Almighty should reply,
He would give them a similar answer to that which
Abraham gave the rich man. You have Christ and
the apostles, and you would do well to give heed to
their testimony; for if you will not believe what they
have taught, you would not be persuaded, though one
arose from the dead; neither would you believe, though
the Spirit should descend again from heaven in bodily
shape and teach the way of the Lord; for even then he
could not teach more than *all the truth;* and this he
taught through the apostles. "He shall guide you
into *all truth,*" says the Saviour; and as what He then
taught, and left upon record in the New Testament,
is just as true now as it was then, consequently just
as much to be believed, it follows, as certain as that
like causes produce like effects, if you will not believe
what He has already taught, you would not believe
Him should He come down from heaven again and
teach the same thing. Where, then, the propriety of
offering up to the Father of lights such an unreasonable and skeptical prayer? It is the same in effect
as saying, "Almighty Father, it is true, Thou hast informed us in Thy word, if we will comply with the
terms of reconciliation, which are there distinctly laid
down, that our sins and iniquities shall be remembered
no more. We have complied with these terms, but we
want some better evidence than Thy bare word to prove
that we are pardoned. Therefore, O Lord, send down
Thy Spirit into our skeptical souls, and make us to
know our sins forgiven; for Thy written word, which
Thou hast already spoken to the children of men, we

do not believe, and therefore we ask Thee, O Lord, in great mercy, to overlook our infidelity, and send us better testimony." Wonder what such men would have said, had they been in the place of the man sick of palsy, when Christ addressed him, "Son, be of good cheer, *thy sins be forgiven thee*". (Matt. 9:2.) They doubtless would have replied, "Lord, we know Thou hast power to forgive sins, but still we want some better testimony than Thy *bare word!*" When the Saviour commanded this same individual to take up his bed and *walk*, how did he know that he was "immediately made *whole*"? Answer: By his *feelings,* because this was a *physical* and not a *moral* effect, and hence could be known only by physical testimony. But in the other case there was no physical effect produced; it was wholly moral, and hence could be known only by moral testimony.

I have often heard a certain class of preachers use an argument something like this, to prove that a man can know his sins forgiven by his feelings: "If I had a pain in my head, and would assert the fact to this audience, they are bound to believe me, because my word stands unimpeached. But you ask how I know I have a pain in my head? I answer, by my feelings. Is not this satisfactory evidence? Very well; if you would believe my word in this, let us try another case. I assert that my sins are forgiven. You ask how I know? I answer, by my feelings. You are bound to receive my testimony in this, for it is just as good authority as in the other case."

This one argument embodies nine-tenths of all the

sophistry and mysticism of this perverted age, relative to conversion and the evidence of pardon; and let this one sophism be fairly analyzed and set aside, and the system of modern revivalism *has lost its only prop.* Let this be distinctly borne in mind. We now state, what we have before intimated, that things of a physical nature we know only by physical means. For example: When we are sick, we know it by our feelings. When *thirsty, hungry, sleepy, cold,* or *warm,* we know it by our *feelings,* from the bare fact that the proposition to be proved in each of these cases is physical, and hence the proof must be of the same kind; or, in other words, the proposition and proof in all cases must be *homogeneous.* Now, it is impossible, in the very nature of the case, to prove a physical proposition by moral testimony, and *vice versa.* Take a case, for example: You wish to prove to me that my head aches. Now, what effect will moral testimony have upon my mind? Just none at all. You might bring forward twelve of the best men in this place, whose word has never been disputed, and should they all testify under the most solemn oath that I had a pain in my head, if I did not *feel* it, their testimony would not have the least tendency to convince me of the fact. All the moral testimony on earth would not be sufficient to prove this one physical fact, so long as there was the testimony of one physical witness against it. But let one of those witnesses take that staff and give me a *physical* argument by way of a pretty severe blow on the head, and such evidence would have a tendency to produce conviction in my mind that I had the headache.

But again: My father, who lives in a distant part of the State, has just deceased, leaving me an estate of ten thousand dollars; but I know nothing about it. A messenger has arrived to let me know the fact. Now this, to me, is a moral proposition, though to him it is physical, as he saw the old man breathe his last, and had the privilege of reading his will. But how is he to convince me that these are facts? Can he do so by any physical operation he may perform upon me? Let him strike me, drag me from the stand, throw me out of doors, or do what he will to me, and has he convinced me of that fact under consideration? By no means. I am just as ignorant of the matter as I was before. Remember, that to me it is a *moral* proposition, and can consequently be sustained only by *moral* testimony. Nothing that could be applied to any of my senses, unless it speaks either by words or signs to my understanding, would give me the most distant idea of the subject. Hence he must either speak or write it, in order to give me the desired information.

The great mistake upon this subject is in supposing that sin is a *material* of some kind, clinging to the vitals of the sinner, and that forgiveness consists in some kind of an internal physical renovation. At least, the way the subject is presented to the public, according to the popular doctrines of the day, we would necessarily be led to think that such was the fact. But let it be distinctly understood that sin is a *moral evil,* and forgiveness in no case consists in an internal operation so far as the sinner is concerned, but is in every case a mental operation of the individual who forgives. For instance: The convict upon the gallows is about to swing. The governor, as an embodiment of the will of the people, resolves to forgive him, and does so. But does the poor convict, just then, feel an internal operation. Nay, verily, he still stands trembling upon the threshold of death, expecting in a few minutes to drop into eternity. Forgiveness, then, does not take place in the sinner, or else this poor, trembling convict would have known it. But a messenger is instantly dispatched to the gallows. The sheriff, with the proper authority in his hand, informs the convict that he is a pardoned man. Joy now lights up his countenance, and just in proportion to the strength of his faith in the testimony presented, will be his joyful feelings as the result of pardon. But you ask, was there not an important change which took place in the bosom of that convict? Certainly there was; but this change was not the act of forgiveness—for that took place in the mind of the governor some time before the convict knew it—but the change was effected by the evidence which the convict received from the governor's hand that he was pardoned. So the sinner is pardoned, not in his own bosom, but in the court of heaven, in the mind of Jehovah; and the evidence he has of this fact in the word of God gives him *"full assurance of faith,"* and *"believing,* he *rejoices* with joy unspeakable and *full* of *glory."* He does not, however, have to wait, as in the similitude, after he is pardoned, for a witness to come down from the court of heaven to notify him of the fact; for the very law which lays down the terms of pardon to rebel man, also contains the promise of forgiveness as soon as the sinner complies. Neither are these stipulations without the proper marks of authority. The Almighty, it appears, as if to forestall every objection and obviate every difficulty, that there might be no necessity to look for "better testimony," has attached to these conditions of pardon the adorable signatures of the Father, Son and Holy Spirit. Is this all? Nay; underneath we behold the great RED SEAL of the blood of Christ, and, as if to confirm and ratify the whole, Jehovah Himself stoops from His majestic throne, and records a most *solemn oath,* by two *immutable things,* in which it is impossible for Him to lie, that the promise of pardon to the man who complied with the conditions thereof might be just as *immutable* as Himself.

"If thy brother *trespass* against thee, *forgive him.*" This is a positive command of our Saviour. Well, a brother has trespassed upon my rights. I tell him his fault between me and him alone. He repents, and asks my forgiveness. I say to him, Brother, in the name of the Lord, I most freely forgive you. He is, then, of course, forgiven. But how does he *know it?* Answer: By my word, and by it alone. Now, says the apostle, "As Christ forgave you, so also do ye." Can we not, then, by the "bare word" of Christ, know our sins forgiven, if we can rest satisfied of the same thing upon the testimony of a mere man? Yes; for, says the apostle John, "If we receive the *witness of men,* the *witness of God is greater."* (I. John 5:9.)

But suppose, after I have pledged my word to my brother that he is forgiven, he puts his hand on his breast and says, with a deep sigh, "I feel such a strange load about my heart; I fear I am not forgiven!" Would not this be *prima facie* evidence that he had no confidence in my word? And how must the Almighty look down from heaven upon professed Christians, and even ministers, who treat *His* word in the same way?

How common it is to hear men preach that the words of Satan, whispered into the ear of our Mother Eve, possessed power enough to ruin mankind, and at the same time will deny that the words of Christ contain power enough to save them! Strange, indeed, that the devil has more power than the Almighty! Others affirm that the "gospel is the *power of God* unto salvation," and yet will act just as inconsistently as the other class, by contending that, notwithstanding the gospel has power enough to save men, yet, after this is done, it has not sufficient power to give them the full assurance that they are saved! They need another witness directly from heaven before this fact can be established!

But the worst evil attending this system of modern revivalism—or that system which makes *feeling* the test of pardon and acceptance with God, instead of faith in the written Word—is the unstable and unsettled condition of its converts. Those who have feeling as the basis of their religion are fluctuating as the tide. While their feelings are excited by a protracted meeting, their hopes are bright. But when the im-

mediate excitement of the meeting dies away, and
they are at home combating with the cares and per-
plexities of life, their good feelings begin to subside
and their religion begins to go down with them. This
is natural; for good feelings being the foundation of
their assurance, as soon as the foundation gives way,
the whole superstructure reared thereon must fall.
Hence, when this dark and gloomy state of feeling
begins to come on, and the very basis of their assurance of pardon begins to give way, it is natural for
them to entertain many doubts and fearful forebod-
ings as regards the genuineness of their conversion.
Then, it is, you will hear them begin to sing the
words most appropriate to their desponding state of
mind—

> "Dear Lord, if indeed I am thine,
>   If thou art my sun and my song,
> Say, why do I *languish* and *pine*,
>   And why are my *winters* so long?
> Oh, drive these *dark clouds* from my sky;
>   Thy *soul-cheering presence* restore;
> Lord, take me to thee up on high,
>   Where *winters* and *clouds* are no more."

But why these "dark clouds" and "long winters"?
Because good feeling, which was the only assurance
they had that their sins were pardoned, has left them,
and they now look upon themselves as deceived; and
many, by this natural tendency of that system of things,
are led to abandon and curse all religion as a scheme
of sheer deception and priestcraft.

Others having, perhaps, a larger organ of veneration, are not willing to give it up yet, notwithstanding their assurance of acceptance with God has all left them, and accordingly, they attend the first protracted meeting in the neighborhood, and by the means of great animal excitement, succeed in "getting through" a second time. They now declare that their sins are all blotted out, and that they never knew what religion was before. This is acknowledging that they actually were deceived the first time; for they thought they were converted when they were not. And how do they know that they may not be deceived this time also? for their religion this time came in precisely the same way that it did the other.

But the meeting passes off and the excitement again dies away, and in a few weeks you hear those doubly-converted Christians, with their heads bowed down like a bullrush, singing that same old, gloomy, dark, cold, cloudy, wintry, skeptical song, "Dear Lord, if indeed I am thine."

Not so, however, with the man whose trust is in God and the *word of His grace.* He has deliberately and understandingly bowed to the terms of pardon, as taught by the inspired ambassadors of Christ, and can now claim the pardon of sins and adoption into the family of God, by the highest authority in heaven and earth. He defies all creation to dispute his claim; for he appeals for proof to the *infallibility* of the Spirit, the *veracity* of Christ, and the *immutability* of God. How sure, then, is the foundation upon which we build. It is a *terra firma* which will stand the fiery ordeal when the earth shall reel to and fro, the elements melt with fervent heat, and the heavens shall flee away and be no more. Truly does the poet remark—

> "How *firm a foundation,* you saints of the Lord,
> Is laid for your faith in his *excellent word.*"

I rejoice for such a high rock, and for such a strong tower, in which to hide securely from the lashing of the billows and peltings of the storms of life. In the midst of all the conflicts and vicissitudes that flesh is heir to, this hope stands by us and bears up our sinking spirits; and though the mildewing hand of poverty should lie heavily upon us, and the scourge of sickness invade this trembling house of clay, yet "the Scriptures assure us that the *Lord will provide.*" With this *"full assurance of faith"* in the Word of the immutable promise, no fear shall find a dwelling place within this bosom; and though Satan should bring down upon us the fury of the storm, and hurl thickly about us the arrows of death, yet the God of Jacob "will never leave us nor forsake us." And when the heavens shall be rolled together as a scroll, and the earth be renovated by fire, this confidence in the all-sufficiency of the Word of the immutable God will bear us up far above the melting elements, to stand with our immortalized and glorified persons—

> "Where bliss is known without alloy,
> And beauty blooms without decay;
> Where thoughts of grief, in cloudless joy,
> Shall melt like morning mist away."

Amen and Amen.

THE LOVE OF GOD.

By William Baxter.

Wm. Baxter was born in Leeds, Yorkshire, England, July 6, 1820. Came to America in 1828. Died at New Lisbon, O., 1880.

"For God so loved the world that he gave his only begotten Son, that whosoever believeth in him should not perish, but have everlasting life" (John 3: 16).

Never were words more deeply fraught with meaning than those which the Saviour uttered in the hearing of the learned rabbi of Israel, words of deep import to you, to me, to the whole family of man. They make known the most benign attribute of the divine Father; present before us its loftiest exhibition and declare to dying men its blissful result. That tribute is the love of God; the exhibition of it, the death of his Son; the result, the eternal salvation of all those who, by holy obedience, manifest their trust in the Lamb of God that taketh away the sin of the world.

The angels who beheld the marvels of creative power when God called our world into being, saw not, until the fourth day, the regal sun, the queenly moon, the starry host. Nor did hoary patriarch, mitred priest or inspired prophet ever behold such glories as met the gaze of the fishermen of Galilee when Jesus appeared to them on the holy mount, as he appears to the immortals now. For four thousand years God had been giving the world proofs of his love; but how deep, how tender, how exhaustless that love the world never knew until the Saviour's words to Nicodemus were fulfilled.

In contemplating the love and compassion of God, there is danger of a trust and confidence that borders upon presumption; while too great attention to the severe attributes—such as justice and holiness—may lead to doubt, and even despair. Viewed in connection, the beauty and harmony of the whole is to be seen. As in the deluge, while there is anger and justice, so there is an ark, a dove, and olive leaf, the smoke of sacrifice ascending, and, over all, the rainbow hues of love and peace; the fierce, surging waters, like the frown of God—the rainbow, like his smile of love.

Thus, we may contemplate the power of God as displayed in creating and sustaining this vast universe; behold it in the fierce tornado and the wild commotion of the ocean storm; see it reflected in the glare of the forked lightning, as it darts across the darkened heavens; hear it proclaimed by the muttering thunder, as if he were speaking in tones of wrath to a guilty world; and we shall find there is nothing in all this calculated to awaken any other feeling save that of terror and trembling awe.

When we remember that God fills all things—that he is everywhere present—that thought is calculated to arouse our fears, and rivet upon our minds the conviction that we can not go where he is not; we feel that God is above, beneath, around us; with us in

the crowded city and the solitary desert; in the pursuit
of pleasure, and the hurry of business; in the bustle of
noonday and the silence of midnight; in the hall of
revelry and the temple devoted to his service; with us
at home and abroad, in and around our daily paths;
and, with the minstrel king, we are led to exclaim,
"Whither shall I go from thy Spirit, or whither shall
I flee from thy presence? If I ascend into the heavens,
thou art there. If I make my bed in hell, thou art
there. If I take the wings of the morning, and
dwell in the uttermost parts of the sea, even there thy
hand shall lead me, and thy right hand shall hold me."
And the boldest will tremble when he remembers that
he is in the presence of the Ever-present One.

If we remember that God knows all things, from
the thoughts of the loftiest intelligence that burns
near his throne to the instinct of the most insignificant
creature that he has made; that he looks on us not as
man looks, but his piercing eye sees through all our
disguises and concealments, penetrates the flimsy veil
of hypocrisy, discerns the very thought and intents of
the heart, we quail before the searching glance of the
all-seeing One, to whom the secrets of all hearts are
known, and who will disclose them before the assembled universe, for our approval or condemnation,
in the judgment of the great day.

We call to mind the declaration of Holy Writ, that
justice and judgment are the habitation of Jehovah's
throne, and his righteous laws, which we have so
often broken, rise up and condemn us. A fearful day
of retribution in the future threatens, and our guilty

souls find no refuge, no hiding-place in the storm from the justice of God.

We turn to his holiness, the stainless purity of his character; we look at the defilement which sin has brought upon us; we feel that, like the leper, we should place our hands upon our mouths and cry, "Unclean! unclean!" His purity, contrasted with our sin, his holiness with the corruption which we feel in our own nature, leaves us no foundation for hope in the holiness of God. Had God manifested no other attributes of his nature than these, the condition of man would have been hapless in the extreme; hope would have long since died in the human heart, and our race would have toiled on in despair, from the cradle to the grave; but it is recorded on the sacred page that "God is love," that "God so loved the world," and these glad words drive away all our fears; they bid us draw near with filial confidence, and from full hearts cry, "Father! Father!"

As the loveliest and sublimest objects in nature, under certain circumstances, rather alarm than delight us, so some of the attributes of God, contemplated singly, fill the soul with dread; but, when viewed in relation to each other, they glow in the hues of loveliness alone. Thus, if we wander at nightfall in the depths of the forest, there is naught around us to give delight; the night wind sweeps through the overspreading branches like a wail of woe, and strange shapes are dimly seen through the gloom; a horror of great darkness fills the mind with vague and undefined terror, and we long to escape from the fearful place. But, lo! the moon rises in queenly splendor, and pours her mild radiance over the scene; the dew-drops glisten upon the leaves like diamonds set in emeralds, the wind's sad sigh now becomes a lofty hymn, and the scene, late so desolate and drear, as if by enchantment, is changed to one of surpassing loveliness. How awful, in the midnight gloom, is the thunder of Niagara! How awe-inspiring the fierce rush of its fearful leap into the gulf below! The soul is hushed in its solemn presence, while fancy shapes its rising mists into unearthly forms. But day comes on apace, and all its terrors depart; like pure crystal seems the torrent now; the sunbeams irradiate the falling spray, and the late dreadful cataract wears a rainbow, like a crown of glory, on its brow. And thus it is, when the heart is depressed by the thought that God is all-seeing, ever-present, holy, just and true; then the thought comes that he is full of compassion and tender love, and, like the moonbeams to the darkened forest, or the sweet sunlight to the cataract, so is the light of love to those attributes that once inspired terror alone. The power of the Almighty, under the guidance of love, will be exerted for the protection of the object, of that love; his presence, which made us tremble, will become, of all things, the most desirable; his universal knowledge will make him acquainted with all our wants and all our woes; holiness will grow brighter in the light of love; the severity of justice will be softened; for in the great exhibition of love which God has made in the death of his Son, justice and mercy truly have met, righteousness and peace have embraced each other.

God has ever loved our race. From the time that his mandate called our first parent from the dust, his kind care and tender love have been extended over us. The sentence of exile from Eden had scarcely been pronounced when God made known his love to man by giving the gracious promise, that one born of woman, like a mighty conqueror, should bruise the head of the arch enemy and win for man a brighter Eden than Adam lost. God manifested his love by permitting man to approach him through the medium of sacrifice; by his speaking, through angels, to Abraham, Isaac and Jacob; by the rites and ceremonies of the Mosaic institution; by sending prophet after prophet, and teacher after teacher, to instruct our race and draw it back to himself. But all these exhibitions of love failed to recall lost man from his wanderings. He treated his messengers with scorn, and, by his perversity, forfeited all claim to his merciful forbearance; yet God forsook him not, but gave him the strongest possible proof of his love, to win him from sin and sorrow to happiness, to holiness, and heaven. Love consists not in word, but in deed. Men prove their love by their actions, as did the Roman Decias, who, in order to secure victory on the side of his country, in accordance with the prediction uttered by the oracle, drew his robe around him, and, rushing into the thickest ranks of the opposing host, yielded himself a willing victim, that Rome might be free; or, as Winkelried, who gladly threw himself on the Austrian spears to open the way for liberty to

Switzerland; or, as Leonidas, who, with the noble three hundred, met the rushing myriads of the Persian despot, and bravely died, that Greece might not wear the yoke. Thus God, stooping to the usages of men, to prove his love for our race, gave his only begotten Son, that whosoever believeth in him should not perish, but have everlasting life.

But let us examine the meaning of the saying, "Gave his Son." Does it mean that God sent his Son as an ambassador, attended by shining legions of angels, to treat with our revolted race, and bring them back to their allegiance? No; he came in lowly guise; no stately palace received him; no princely couch sustained his infant head! no national rejoicing hailed his birth; an obscure village is the place where the Son of the Highest makes his appearance; and he is cradled where the horned oxen fed.

But was the obscurity of his birth and the coldness of his reception, the privations and dangers of his infantile years, all that was meant by God giving his Son? Ah, no; for, though when he first appeared among men he stooped from heaven to earth, this vast descent came far short of exhausting its meaning, and we must seek it in his future history.

Behold him, in the desert, undergoing fierce trial. The adversary of our race assails him on every point, while demons and angels look with deep anxiety for the issue of this superhuman conflict. He triumphs, but it is only to encounter new trials; for, though he were maker of all things, yet did he suffer need, and, on one occasion, we hear the homeless wanderer exclaim:

"The foxes have holes, and the birds of the air have nests; but the Son of Man hath not where to lay his head." Contrast his friendless destitution with the glory he had laid aside, on our behalf, and then ask, Is not this a wonderful display of our Father's love?

But let us follow his eventful life, through priestly hate and pharisaic invective—a life stigmatized as evil, though spent in doing good—to that scene of sorrow which transpired in Gethsemane Garden on the night of his dark betrayal. He had just eaten the last supper with the twelve; he had seen Judas depart; and well did he know the foul purpose which filled his traitorous bosom. The echoes of the hymn which closed the feast had died away, and, with his disciples, he sought the retirement of the garden, whose calm solitude had often invited to solemn contemplation and earnest prayer.

"Tarry ye here, while I go and pray yonder," he says, and soon he is alone. The work he came to perform is nearly accomplished, but, as the closing scene draws near, his nature seems to shrink from the dread encounter; deep sorrow, like a mountain weight, presses on his heart, and his soul becomes exceedingly sorrowful, even unto death. He prostrates himself on the cold, damp earth, and, in the most touching tones, he makes his petition to the Father. He pours out his soul to God in strong cries and tears, but no other deliverer can be found, and he treads the wine-press alone.

He rises and seeks his disciples; but they had forgotten their sorrows in sleep. He leaves them, and again prays in anguish of spirit. He even asks the third time, and, while prostrate in the dreadful agony of that fearful hour—such was the burden of our guilt, so intense the pain and mental agony which he endured, that his sweat was as great drops of blood falling down to the ground—and the meek sufferer, in that hour of mortal anguish, cries: "Father, if it be possible, let this cup pass from me, nevertheless, not my will, but thine, be done."

We now begin to perceive the meaning of the words, "God so loved the world that he gave his only begotten Son," as we gaze on the sorrowful scene which transpired near the hour of midnight in that garden's shade. Oh! it was a frightful and a gloomy hour. Angels, doubtless, were near, weeping, too, if angels ever wept, and gazing with intense interest upon the sight, and wondering when this scene of sorrow, this scene of love, would end. Demons, too, looked on with scowling hate, or rejoiced in the apparent defeat of the great Champion of our race; while man, alone of all created intelligences, for whom, too, all this was transpiring, was unobservant and unmoved. It might be thought that the scene might, with propriety, close here; that a sufficient proof of the love of God had been given; that it was enough that his Son had descended to earth in humility; that he had dwelt amid scenes of sorrow and privation; that, under the load of our guilt, while we had no tears for our own crimes, they had caused the bloody drops of agony to fall from the body of God's beloved Son. But, no; God has another exhibition of love, than which himself could give no greater. Without the shedding of blood, there could be no remission. Man must die, or the Son of the Hightest must bleed. God gives the just for the unjust, and the spotless Lamb of God is slain for us.

We now come to the grand climax of the love of our heavenly Father, in which all the rich fullness of his affection is displayed; and, if man be not convinced of his love by this crowning act, he must forever remain in utter and hopeless skepticism. This is heaven's last argument; for, when God gives his Son to die, there is no greater gift in the treasury of the skies to demonstrate his great, his exceeding love to man.

It is a solemn, and often a fearful thing, to die. There is something in death's approach which makes the best and bravest tremble; the severing of all earthly ties; the cold, clammy sweat, the failing breath, the struggle of the spirit for life, and the unspeakable anguish which often attends the closing scene, makes us shrink instinctively from the dying strife. Some, however, who have fallen on the battle plain, in their country's cause, have been known to die exultantly, in the moment of victory exclaiming: "'Tis sweet, oh, 'tis sweet for my country to die!" The Christian martyr has been seen to yield up his life amid devouring flames, in proof of his attachment to his Lord and Master. Nay, many, very many, have triumphed on the bed of pain and languishing, and, upborne by a living faith, have looked upon death with an unfaltering gaze. But, when death comes attended with open shame and ignominy, when the infuriated mob pours out its reproaches on the object of its hate, and clamors furiously for his blood; when no tear is shed for the sufferer; when his eye looks around for a single look of pity, and sees it not; when his ear listens for one kind word to soothe his last agony, and hears it not; then, indeed, is death terrible. And yet to such a death did God give his Son. He gave him freely for us all, that he might taste death for every man. He met it in its most repulsive form—partook of the death appointed for the vilest malefactors, in token that the benefits of his death might be enjoyed by the vilest of our race. Betrayed by a false friend; seized by rude foes in the garden, hallowed by his prayers; deserted by his disciples, he is confronted by those who have long thirsted for his blood.

It is night; yet with indecent haste, they begin the trial. False witnesses fail to fasten any crime upon him. The Roman govenor declares, "I find no fault in him." Yet, when all the vile arts of flattery, intimidation and perjury fail, for confessing the truth, that he is the Son of God, he is condemned to die. It is day—high day—and now the scene of shame, the scene of sorrow, begins. The multitude, excited by their leaders, demand his execution; and, in answer to their bloodthirsty clamors, the victim is led forth. His body, lacerated with cruel stripes, seems one gushing wound; yet that bleeding body and thorn-pierced brow awaken no pity in the breasts of his relentless persecutors. Ten thousand eyes glare fiercely upon him—ten thousand voices rend the heavens with the shout of "Crucify him! crucify him!" as with fiendish exultation, they behold him delivered to their will. And now the living tide presses to the city gate; the priest, the scribe, the publican, the Pharisee, soldiers and civilians, rich and poor, all are in that throng, all animated by the same thirst for blood, all joining in bitter execrations, all striving to fill, with unmingled bitterness, the cup of agony he is called upon to drink; and yet no malediction falls from the lips of that meek sufferer; no bright-armed legions are called from the skies, to spread destruction through that ungodly throng; but, as a sheep led to the slaughter, with painful step and slow, he urges his way up the rugged steep of Calvary. The goal of his earthly course is reached; his unresisting form is nailed to the accursed tree; the cross is upraised, and the spotless victim hangs on high; and for a season the powers of darkness seem to triumph. The turbaned priest mocks him in his bitter agony; the Pharisee smiles in scorn; the rabble revile and insult the dying victim.

> "Still from his lip no curse hath come,
> His lofty eye hath looked no doom,
> No earthquake's burst, no angel brand
> Curses the black, blaspheming band."

No; but from those pale lips, quivering with anguish, issue the kind, compassionate words: "Father, forgive them"; and thus, in agony, he hung, bleeding, suffering, dying; he bowed his head, cried, "It is finished," and died for us; and it is in this scene that we must look for the full import of the words, "God so loved the world that he gave his only begotten Son."

But why all this divine compassion, all this love, and

all this woe? The answer is: "That whosoever believeth in him should not perish, but have everlasting life." Not that all our race will be saved because Jesus died; not that the unbelieving and disobedient will be forced to the heaven they have striven to avoid; not that the proud scoffer and despiser of God's Son will be saved by that blood he now spurns and tramples upon; but that whosoever believeth may come to Christ and live. But does a mere acceptance of the truth set forth in the text save? No; the sinner must trust in the Crucified One; must love Him who laid down His life for his sake; must prove his love and trust by obeying His commandments; for the faith that leads not to love and all holy obedience, is not the faith of the gospel. But what is meant by the phrase "not perish"? Does it mean "shall not die"? Surely not, for believers and unbelievers alike taste of death, and are laid in the narrow mansion appointed for all the living. The perishing, from which the believer is to be rescued, is more than the death of the body. It is the despair, the remorse, the unutterable woe, the bitter pang of the second death, which all shall know who despise the gift of God's great love, and, by their unbelief and consequent disobedience, exclude themselves forever from the paradise above. The believer in the Son of God, however, has more to expect than a mere escape from the woes consequent upon disobedience; for it is not only declared "that he shall not perish," but the gracious promise is added, "that he shall have everlasting life"—a life not of endless duration only, but a life of eternal blessedness in the presence of Him who makes heaven glorious and the angels glad. The society of the prophets, the apostles, the martyrs, and all the pure in heart; a place near the crystal stream that flows from beneath the throne; the fruit and the shade of the tree of life; exemption from sickness, sorrow and tears; the harp of praise, the crown of glory, the palm of victory, everlasting joys, eternal songs, all the heart can wish—nay, more than the loftiest thought can conceive of blessedness, are all included in the promise of everlasting life—the inheritance of the believer in Jesus.

A word to those who have not availed themselves of the merciful provisions of the gospel of peace, and we have done. You have seen the wonderful display of love which God has made, and all this was done for you. You have seen the Lamb of God bleeding, groaning, agonizing, dying, not to save friends, but to secure happiness for his foes. Will God permit you to slight all this love, and all this sorrow, and yet hold you guiltless? Will you steel your hearts against all that God has done and Christ has suffered? Amid all those manifestations of tender compassion, will you force your way down to ruin, and madly seek that perdition from which the Redeemer died to save you? Will you still trample under foot his loving kindness and tender mercy, and expose yourself to all the unspeakable horrors of death eternal? Stop, I entreat you! Be persuaded by your soul's peril, by the Saviour's blood and tears. If you shrink from the responsibilities of a follower of Christ, think, for a moment, of the fearful responsibilities of his enemies.

If you shrink at the difficulty of obedience, think of the danger of disobedience. If the weight of the cross appall you, think, oh, think of the brightness of the unfading, the immortal crown! God loves you; can you doubt it, when you look upon the cross and its bleeding victim? Christ loves you; can you doubt it when, for you—

> "He left his starry crown,
>   And laid his robes aside;
> On wings of love came down,
>   And wept, and bled, and died"?

Can you doubt it when, through his gospel, he is ever crying: "Come unto me"? Can you stay away when he says: "He that cometh unto me, I will in no wise cast out"? Turn, then, from all your sins away, "for the wages of sin is death." Turn to the Saviour, believe in him, love him, obey him; "for the gift of God is eternal life through Jesus Christ our Lord."

THE CHURCH—ITS IDENTITY.

By Benjamin Franklin.

Benjamin Franklin was born February 1, 1812, in what is now Belmont County, O. Died at Anderson, Ind., October 22, 1878.

"But we think it right to hear from you what you think: for, as it respects this sect, we know that it is everywhere spoken against." Acts 28:22. (Anderson's Translation.)

The Lord says, in Matt. 16:18, referring to the confession Peter had made: "On this rock I will build my Church." My work in this discourse will be to define and identify the community styled by the Saviour "my Church." This is evidently the same community styled "this sect" in my text. The former is the Lord's way of speaking of the body in view, and the latter the way men, not in the community, and not understanding it or its position, but owing it no ill-will, spoke of it. This language comes from "the chief men of the Jews," as we learn from verse seventeen. That which our Lord calls "my Church," they call "this sect." Those "chief men of the Jews" regarded the body, or church, merely as a "sect," or faction, and certainly a very unpopular one, as it was "everywhere spoken against."

This word "sect" is never used in a good sense in the New Testament; nor is the original word from which it comes. *Hairesis,* the original word from which we have "sect," occurs nine times in the New

Testament, and is translated "sect" five times, and "heresies" four times. We read of damnable *heresies* (2 Pet. 2:1), and find *heresies* put down with "the works of the flesh" (Gal. 5:20); and find the statement added, verse twenty-one, "that those who practice such things (as heresies) shall not inherit the kingdom of God." Heresy is ranked with "lewdness, uncleanness, wantonness, idolatry, sorcery," etc. In the speech of Tertullus, accusing Paul (Acts 24:5), he charges him with being a ringleader of the "sect" of the Nazarenes. Verse fourteen, same chapter, we find Paul's reply, in which he says: "After the way which they call sect, so do I worship the God of my fathers." He does not admit that the body with which he was identified was a sect, but that it was *called a sect*. We can not, therefore, speak of a "Christian sect," or call the church a sect, without as great an impropriety as to speak of a *Christian* heresy, or call the church a *heresy*.

There is a community called, in the New Testament, "the kingdom of God" (John 3:3); "the church of the living God" (1 Tim. 3:15); "one body" (Eph. 4:4). To be in this body, church, or kingdom, is the same as to be "in Christ." It is to be in a justified state, or pardoned state. To enter into it, is to enter into a state of justification or pardon. In entering into that body, we come to the blood of Christ, which cleanses from all sin; to the Spirit and to the life of Christ, all of which are in the body. If we enjoy pardon, the benefits of the blood of Christ, the Holy Spirit, the life of Christ, we must be in the body. God and Christ dwell in the church, which is the temple of God and the "pillar and support of the truth." To dwell with God and Christ, enjoy the cleansing of the blood of Christ, the remission of sins, the impartation of the spirit of God, and the new life, we must be in Christ, or in his body—the church. To be out of the church is to be separated from God, Christ, the Holy Spirit, the blood of Christ, the life of Christ, and justification. It becomes a matter of momentous importance, then, to know that we are in Christ, or in the church.

It is not enough to know that we are in a *church,* but we must know that we are in "the church of the living God," "the kingdom of God," or "body of Christ." There is not a promise in any other institution or community but this. The Lord has one church, and we must not mistake something else for that church. How can we know that we are members of the church unless we know what the church is? If we do not know what the church is, we do not know whether we are in the church or not, whether we are in Christ or not, whether we are justified or not. If we intend to enjoy God, Christ, the Holy Spirit, the blood of Christ, and, in one word, the salvation of God in the kingdom or church, we must be in that kingdom. To be in the kingdom or church, we must know what it is. How shall we, then, identify the church or kingdom of Christ? I lay down the following points for consideration:

I.   A body, or community, not built on the foundation which God laid, is not the community which the Lord calls "my church."

II.   A community not founded and established in the right place, is not the church of Christ.

III.   A community not founded at the right time is not the kingdom of Christ.

IV.   No church can be the true church not founded by the proper persons, Christ and the apostles.

V.   A kingdom with any other law than the one given by the Head of the church, is not the kingdom of Christ.

VI.   Any community labeled with a foreign name, or a name not found to designate the body of Christ, in the New Testament, is not the kingdom of God.

A failure at any one of these points is fatal to the claims of any body professing to be the body of Christ. It is due to the greater portion of the religious bodies of our day, called "churches," to state distinctly that they do not claim to be the kingdom of God, or the body of Christ.   Excepting a few, the balance only claim to be *branches* of the body, or church of Christ. Where a church does not claim to be "the church," but simply *a branch* of the church, the members are only members of a branch, and the officers are only officers of a branch, and not members and officers of the body of Christ.   These branches, and officers in them, are as separate and distinct from the kingdom of Christ and the officers in it, as Great Britain and Russia, and the officers of these respective governments.   One of these *branch* communities does not respect the acts of another, or in any way regard them.

These different *branch* communities are distinct, separate, and independent kingdoms, with different laws, officers, names, foundations, times, and places of origin. They are not built on the same foundation, did not originate at the same time and place, have not the same law and officers, nor the same ecclesiastical organization, and are, to all intents and purposes, independent and distinct communities. If one of them dies, there is no grief or lamentation among the others, in view of the loss, nor an effort *to save another branch of the same church from dying.* They are all willing it should die. They have not one particle of sympathy for it. If a new party attempts to rise, the parties in existence, instead of thanking God that another orthodox church has been born, taking it by the hand and raising it up to manhood and rejoicing in its appearance, turn their batteries on it from every quarter, denouncing it as a "damnable heresy," and do their utmost to destroy it. When they fail, and find that it will live in spite of all their denunciations and efforts to kill it, they turn round and recognize it as another "orthodox denomination." Not a new religious party ever came into existence on the face of the globe that was not denounced as a *heresy* when it first made its appearance, and that was not fought and opposed while it was young and weak. But when a party becomes strong, influential, and popular, it becomes an *orthodox branch of the church!* Thus, all the parties now called "orthodox branches" were once styled "heresies;" and that, too, when they were better than they are now; but when they could fight their way, and live, in spite of the old ones, they ceased to *be heresies,* and became *good orthodox branches!*

I. We have said, that no party, or community not built on the foundation which the Lord laid in Zion, is "the Church of the living God." What, then, is the foundation of the true Church? The Lord inquired of the apostles, "Who say you that I am?" Peter replied: "Thou art the Christ, the Son of the living God." The Saviour proceeded: "On this rock I will build my Church." On which rock? On this grand statement, which flesh and blood had not revealed, but which the Father in heaven had revealed, and which he compares to a rock—that "Jesus is the Christ, the Son of the living God"—"on this," says he, "I will found my Church." This is the great proposition of the Divine government. In it all the minor propositions are included. In it centers, and on it rests, the entire revelation from God to man. If this grand proposition concerning Jesus, that "he is the Christ, the Son of the living God," is true, the entire Scriptures are true; for this being true, he knew all things, and his numerous quotations from Moses, the Psalms, and the Prophets, as *the word of God,* and *the language of the Spirit of God,* is an indorsement of all these writings. His calling the apostles, sending them and qualifying them, as well as endowing them with supernatural power, gave them an endorsement that no man can in honor evade. This grand proposition is the foundation of the Church, the faith, all true piety, and the hope of heaven. It is not a proposition concerning a theory, a speculation, or subtlety, but a proposition concerning *a person,* who was dead and is alive, and lives forever and ever. This proposition is of such momentous magnitude, if true, that we will be lost forever if we do receive it. The Almighty Father will cast us off forever, as if we had rejected himself in person, if we reject this fundamental proposition concerning his Son. The moment we receive this proposition, we bind ourselves to receive all that Jesus taught, do all he commanded, and furthermore, we have a right to hope for all he has promised.

How many churches have we in this generation that are built on this foundation, or that will receive a person on this foundation? I regret to know that many of them openly declare this *not suf-ficient.* They maintain that we must have something more. In doing this, they do not honor our most gracious and adorable Lord, but dishonor him. Is there one church in the world that ignores all articles of religion, written out by *uninspired men,* in receiving the sinner, and that receives him on the confession that "Jesus is the Christ, the Son of the living God?" There is one Church that does this. This Church is built on this great truth, and receives every person that comes on this foundation-truth, to the initiating rite of the New Institution; and it will receive him on nothing else. Those received on this foundation, and united in one body, are on the rock—the sure foundation. Those built on any other foundation, or not on this foundation, can not claim to be the Church of the living God, the body or kingdom of Christ. The Romish Church is not built on *the truth* that "Jesus is the Christ the Son of the living God"—the rock—but on "the lie" that Peter is *the rock*.

The central idea, or foundation-thought, in the Episcopal Church, is its form of church government. Its very name originated in this peculiar form of government. This is a side foundation, or another foundation, and not the one which the Lord laid. Not being built on the true foundation—the one which God laid—it is not the building of God, not the temple of God.

The fundamental, or central idea in Methodism, or in the Methodist body, is method. It took its name from the idea of *method*. It is founded on the idea of *method*. There is nothing religious, spiritual, or celestial in *method*. There are as many methods of doing evil as of doing good. Still, this is the central idea of the largest Protestant party in the world. This is not only *another*, but almost *no foundation*. No wonder that a people should be dividing every few years, with a central idea so feeble in its attractive powers. The Presbyterian body has for its central, or fundamental idea, the *Presbyterial form* of Church government, or the idea of governing by a *presbytery*. This is, so far as it is a foundation at all, *another foundation*, and not the one which God laid. The body, or building on it, is not on the true foundation, and not the building of God. The central idea in the Baptist body is *baptism*. The body takes its name from the initiatory rite of the kingdom, and not from the head over all, blessed forever and ever. It is founded on *an ordinance,* and not on *the truth* concerning him who authorized the ordinance. This is another foundation. So on, the whole round of sectarian establishments. Not one of them is founded on the true foundation—the truth—concerning Jesus, that "he is the Christ, the Son of the living God." Not one of them has confidence enough in our Lord to make *the truth* concerning him its central idea, its foundation. Not one of them is willing to indentify itself with our Lord, commit itself to him as its teacher, leader, and head, and binding itself to his holy law, declare itself for him, and all he taught.

II. A community not founded or established in the *right place* is not the true Church. I am rejoiced that I need no special effort to show the place where the true Church was founded. All agree that *in Jerusalem* was the place. The Lord said it behooved the Messiah to suffer, and to rise from the dead on the third day; and that repentance and remission of sins should be preached in his name to all nations, *beginning in Jerusalem.* It would be easy to refer to the prophets, and to many portions of the New Testament, and show, beyond all reasonable doubt, that the true Church was founded in Jerusalem. But, as all parties admit this, I shall not occupy my limited space in arraying the proof.

If my hearers desire to know whether the body with which they stand identified is the true Church, let them inquire *where it was founded.* If it was founded in Jerusalem, it may be the true Church; but if it was not founded in Jerusalem, it is most conclusive evi-

dence that *it is not the true Church.* No matter how
many good people there are in it, nor how many good
things are taught and done in it, it is not the true
Church. One clear difference between a counterfeit
and genuine note detects the one that is counterfeit,
especially so clear a difference as a difference in the
place of location. A difference, then, between any
body of people and the body of Christ so striking, as
originating in Rome, and originating in Jerusalem, or
the difference between being founded in Rome,
and being founded in Jerusalem, proves that which
was founded in Rome, London or Geneva to be
counterfeit. The Church of Christ was first planted
in Jerusalem, and all churches first planted or founded
anywhere else are certainly *spurious.* They are
not genuine.

Nor is it any matter how many points of resemblance there may be between the genuine and the counterfeit—they are not the same; but the counterfeit is
only the more dangerous, and likely to deceive. When
trying them, to determine which is the true or the
genuine Church, look for this mark on it: "In
Jerusalem."

III. A community not founded at the *right time*
is not the kingdom of God, or body of Christ. This
test is a severe one. It is unambiguous. The community which the Lord calls "my Church" (Matt.
16: 18), was certainly not built when he said: "On
this rock I *will* build my Church." He alluded to what
he intended to do in the future, and not to what he
had done in the past, when he said, "I will build my

Church." He taught his disciples to pray, "Thy kingdom come"; but certainly did not teach them thus to pray after the kingdom *had come*. "There be some standing here who shall not taste death till they see the kingdom of God come with power." Many Scriptures like these show that the kingdom had not yet come, or that the Church was not yet established. In the apostolic letters, we find numerous references to the Church, kingdom, body, house of God, temple of God, etc., as then in existence, showing that the Church, or kingdom, was established. This, then, proves that it was founded in the time of the apostles.

This is sufficient for my purpose now. The true Church was, then, founded in the time of the apostles. This is a mark of the genuine Church not to be found on any counterfeit in the world. A community not founded in the time of the apostles, is not the one which the Lord called "my Church," or is not the Church of the living God. I care not where the history of a community of people may lead us. If it lead not to *the* time of the apostles, it does not lead us to the founding of that body, purchased and cleansed by the blood of Christ.

When did the Church of Rome originate? It did not originate in a day or a year, but gradually subverted the apostles' teaching, and, in centuries, inaugurated full-grown popery. But there is not a trace of a "Pope or Universal Father," to say nothing of "Vicegerent of Christ," or "Lord God the Pope," nor popery, in the history of the first three centuries of the Christian era. Popery was inaugurated too late, by at least three centuries, to be the true or genuine Church. It is one of the basest and most impudent counterfeits ever imposed on, the credulity of man. If popery was born *too late,* or is *too young* to be the true Church, what shall be said of those communities born in the past three centuries? They are all too young by largely more than a thousand years. No church that came into existence since the death of the apostles can be the Church of the living God.

IV. No church can be the true Church that was not founded by Christ and the apostles. Churches founded by other persons, or originating with other persons, are simply not the Church of Christ. All books, all parties, and all men agree that Christ and the apostles founded the community called "the body of Christ"—the "one body" of Paul. What shall we say, then, of a church that traces its history to George Fox, and finds not a trace of its existence beyond him. There never was a Quaker before George Fox, nor a Quaker Church. The history of the world does not refer to the existence of a Lutheran or a Lutheran Church before Martin Luther lived. The Lutheran Church originated with Luther. The body of Christ existed from the apostolic day till the time of Luther, before there was any Lutheran Church. The Presbyterian Church originated with John Calvin. Before the time of Calvin there never was a Presbyterian, nor a Presbyterian Church. The Church, or body of Christ, existed from the time of the apostles till the time of Calvin, and consequently could not have been established by Calvin. Presbyterianism was, therefore, born many long centuries too late to lay any claims to Christianity. It may have incorporated some Christianity in it, but it is still carefully and very justly labeled "Presbyterianism." The Methodist Church originated with John Wesley. Before the time of Wesley there never was a Methodist Church or a Methodist. But the Church of Christ existed from the time of the apostles till the time of Wesley. Hence, Methodism originated with the wrong person to be the Church of Christ. The body of Christ originated with Christ and his apostles, and not with Wesley. Any body or community that did not originate with Christ and the apostles, but with some more modern person or persons, is manifestly not the body of Christ.

V. A kingdom or community, with any other law than the one given by the Lord, the great Head of the Church, is manifestly not the kingdom of Christ. The law of the great King is clearly laid down in the Bible. The Bible contains the constitution and law of the King for his kingdom. This was the only law ever authorized by the great King and Head of the Church, or adopted, approved, and practiced under in the time of the apostles. Any church or body of people, who have substituted any *other law,* no matter how many resemblances there may be between it and the law of God, is not the body of Christ. He never authorized a living man even to alter his law, add anything to it, or take anything from it, to say nothing of *substituting another law for it.* It may be replied that these other laws are like the law of God, or taken from it. This, these parties do not believe themselves. A Presbyterian does not believe that the Methodist "Book of Discipline" is the Divine authority; has no regard for it; and probably never reads it. A Methodist does not believe that the Presbyterian Confession of Faith is of Divine authority, and has no regard for it. There is not a party in the world that has any regard for the Presbyterian Confession of Faith, except the Presbyterian party. The same is true of the creed of every other party in the world. But all good people have respect for the law of God. The law of God is supreme, and those loyal to it, united under it, and keeping it, are his people—the body of Christ. But those formed into parties, under other laws, are new settlements not indorsed by our King.

VI. Any community labeled with some foreign name, or some name unknown to the New Covenant, must be a new and strange body. There can be no use in a *new* name for the *old* body or community. There must be a new idea, or something different from the old community, to create the necessity for a new name. If we have nothing they did not have in apostolic times, we need no other names than they had. If we have the kingdom of God, the Church of God, the body of Christ, and nothing else, there is no need of calling it anything else. But the truth is, new names come from new ideas, and are intended to express something new. A man may read of the Church of God, the body of Christ, the kingdom of God, etc., for a month, and it never suggests a Methodist Church, a Presbyterian Church, or a Baptist Church, unless in contrast. He knows that he is not reading about these latter bodies, as they were not in existence at the time of the writing. The new and foreign name shows that it does not refer to the body of Christ, but something else.

Now, there are so many notions about succession of churches, preachers, officers, ordinations, ordinances, and the like, that I know that many will inquire for a succession in some of these respects. It will, therefore be necessary to make a few observations touching this subject:

1. The attempts at making out a succession of Popes on the part of Romanists—the wicked Popes through which their pretended succession runs, and the will, therefore, be necessary to make a few observations successions attempted to be shown in the Greek and Episcopal churches—are sufficient to cover the face of a man of conscience and sense with utter shame and confusion.

If there is no grace to be found unless these successions, or any one of them, can be made out, the world is lost. But I am thankful that the New Testament knows as little of any of these successions, or any necessity for them, as it does of a Romish, Greek, or Episcopal Church. The Church of Christ is not built on a succession of any kind, Romish, Greek, or Episcopal, but on the truth concerning Jesus, that "he is the Christ, the Son of the living God." The souls of the saints rest not on the difficult and doubtful task of making out successions of any kind. They turn their hearts to the truth concerning our Lord, which he compares to a *rock,* on which he said, "I will build my hurch" Th fi h hurch huil on tha foundation-truth, and it receives all its members on that truth, as it did at the beginning, in the *right place,* in Jerusalem; at the right time, on Pentscost; originating with the right persons, Christ and the apostles; having the right law, the law of God; and with the right name, the body of Christ, the kingdom or Church of God, with the original worship and all things as they were at the first. Having come into the school of Christ, they are now his disciples, learners, pupils, and he is their Teacher. They are so busily engaged in the lessons given them by their Great Teacher, and so enraptured with them, that they have no time for examining musty records about successions of churches, men, or ordinances. They depend not on succession, but fellowship with the Father, and his Son Jesus the Christ. They listen to no unregenerated men, prating about a succession which never was, and never can be made out, but to the law of their glorious King. If these successions ask where the Church was in the dark ages, tell them you know not; that the Lord took care of it, and you are thankful to know that it is here still, full of life, power, and determination, and destined to do a greater work than ever before. Tell them that, with God's blessing, we intend to restore the sure foundation which the Lord laid, and build on, sweeping away everything in the way of the work; that we intend to reinstate the authority —the supreme authority—of our only Potentate, Jesus the Messiah, head over all, blessed forever and ever, and sweep from earth all opposing authority of men; that we intend to restore the law of God to the people of this generation, reinstate it fully, where the clergy had set it aside by the doctrines and commandments of men, at the same time sweeping away all creeds, confessions of faith, disciplines, etc., in the way of the full and free administration of the law of God. Tell them that we intend a complete restoration of the faith, practice, worship, and all things as they were at the first.

Here is clear and definite work. That body, which the Lord called "my Church," which was "everywhere spoken against," in the time of Paul, is here, alive, standing on the old foundation, with the same Head, creed, or law, and the same name; nor does it fail to be "everywhere spoken against" still; nor is it a matter of importance whether it can trace a succession back through the dark ages or not; it is here and alive, and as determined as ever to live and maintain its rights. It was dead during the dark ages; God has raised it from the dead, and breathed new life into it. What we want now, is to know *who its friends are?* We want to see every man who intends to stand for the Head of the Church, the foundation, the apostles' teaching and all things as they were at the first, to stand out on one side. If there are those who do not intend to stand to this, we want them to stand on the other side. We desire to know who is on the Lord's side, and who is not; who is for us, and who is against us; who is loyal, and who sympathizes with the enemy.

We are occupying the most responsible position of any body of people on the earth. We are bound to the

Lord Jesus, in the new and everlasting covenant, sealed by the blood of Jesus, and confirmed by the oath of the Almighty, as well as by all the veracity and honor there is in us, to be true to this great work. Let us, then, make a glorious record, one that we shall be happy to contemplate at death, and that shall be a credit to us in the day of judgment.

To the King eternal, immortal, and invisible, the only wise God our Saviour, be glory and dominion, majesty and power, forever and ever.

A DISCOURSE ON CONVERSION.

BY J. M. MATHES.

James M. Mathes was born in Jefferson County, Ky., July 8, 1808. Died June 16, 1892.

My Christian Friends and Fellow Citizens:

I count myself peculiarly happy to-day in having the privilege of addressing so many of you as I see before me. The subject which I have chosen as the theme of the present discourse is one of much importance, according to the acknowledgment of all. It is the great subject of CONVERSION.

There is not, I believe, a sect in Christendom which does not teach that sinners must be converted. We may differ widely about what it is, and how it is effected, and when and where it takes place; but as to the necessity of it, there is no debate. The Calvinist preaches that sinners must be converted; but he tells us that it is a miraculous work, wrought on the elect only, by sovereign grace, and this God will perform in His own good time; while the non-elect are passed by, and no provision made for them in the covenant of grace; and they, of course, can not be converted. Universalists admit that men must be converted, but some of them think it will take place in the resurrection of the dead, and that all men, without distinction of person or character, shall enjoy this conversion.

276

And I would further remark, that from a pretty extensive acquaintance with the religious world, I am satisfied that this subject is not as well understood as it ought to be. We therefore propose to discuss it in a plain and familiar manner, so that every one may not only know what we mean by it, but understand the great doctrine of conversion as taught in the New Testament. I intend to make it so plain that the little boys and girls in the congregation can understand it. As a foundation for what we shall say upon this subject we will read the following texts of Scripture:

"For this people's heart is waxed gross, and their ears are dull of hearing, and their eyes they have closed; lest at any time they should see with their eyes, and hear with their ears, and should understand with their heart, and should be converted, and I should heal them."—Matt. 13:15.

"And Jesus called a little child unto him, and set him in the midst of them, and said, Verily, I say unto you, except ye be converted, and become as little children, ye shall not enter into the kingdom of heaven."—Matt. 18:3.

"Repent ye, therefore, and be converted, that your sins may be blotted out, when the times of refreshing shall come from the presence of the Lord."—Acts 3:19.

In the discussion of this subject, I shall observe the following order:

1.   We shall inquire, what is conversion?

II.   We shall inquire, how is it effected?

III. Speak of the glorious privileges and blessings of those who are Scripturally converted to God, and the awful consequences resulting from a want of conversion, and a life of sin and rebellion against God.

According to the order proposed, we are to inquire—

I. What is Conversion?

Now, I suppose, if I were to ask every member of my auditory the question, What is conversion? I should receive diverse and contradictory answers. A large proportion of our co-religionists use the term as synonymous with *pardon*. How common to hear expressions like this, from a certain class of professors of religion: "Twenty persons were converted at the camp-meeting this week." By which they simply mean that twenty persons were pardoned; or got religion, to use a more common phrase. Now we expect to prove conclusively in a few minutes, that such a form of expression does not convey the Scriptural idea of conversion. Indeed, conversion is one thing in which the sinner is active, and pardon is another and different thing, in which he is passive.

To prove this, it is only necessary to notice the form of expression in the text, "Lest they should see with their eyes, hear with their ears, understand with their heart, and be converted, and I should heal them."

Now, you will observe that the conversion takes place first, and the healing follows after. But what is the healing spoken of in the text? By reference to the parallel passage in Mark 4: 12, the matter is plain. Here it reads: "That seeing, they may not perceive; and hearing, they may hear and not understand; lest at any time they should be converted, and their *sins should be forgiven them.*" The healing, then, means forgiveness of sins. According to the teaching of the Saviour, then, men have to be converted in order that their sins may be forgiven them. But take another example. Peter says, "Repent and be converted, that your sins may be blotted out." The blotting out of sins is pardon or forgiveness of sins, as all will readily admit. It follows, then, with the clearness of demonstration, that conversion is a different thing from pardon. Men have to be converted in order that their sins may be pardoned. That the sinner is active in conversion is clear from the form of the command, "Repent and be converted;" literally, "repent and convert." That they are passive in receiving remission of sins, is clear from hundreds of Scriptures where the matter is spoken of. "And I should heal them," "that your sins may be blotted out," "It is God that justifies," "have received redemption through his blood, the forgiveness of sins."

Well, if conversion is not remission of sins, what, then, is it?

1. The Greek word *epistrepho,* in some of its forms, occurs some thirty-nine times in the New Testament. And it is rendered conversion one time, converteth one, be converted six, again three, turning two, turn ten, returned two, turned ten.

Now, from these renderings it is evident that the word means simply to change, to turn. We use it in this sense every day. When we say that A has converted his farm into money, we simply mean that he has changed his farm for its value in cash. The materials of which this book is composed have been converted. The paper was made of rags, and the process of manufacturing it was a conversion. The binding was once sheep skin; it was converted to leather, and then to a book cover.

But the conversion of the sinner is a great moral change, by which he is translated from the kingdom of darkness into the kingdom of God's dear Son. In order to understand the nature of this great change called "conversion," we will look for a moment at the moral condition of all unconverted men. They are represented in the Scriptures as rebels against God, and enemies to his moral government. At an early period in the history of our race, man rebelled against his God, and became a sinner. His sins separated between him and his kind Heavenly Father, and as a dark cloud shut out the light of His countenance from him; doomed to death, and condemned to toil in the sun, a slave to his appetites and passions, without the ability to redeem himself from the dominion of sin, and the sentence of death.

At the fall of man, Satan erected his empire on earth, and man became his subject, and was led away captive by the devil at his will. Satan, himself a fallen spirit, rejoiced in the degradation and misery of man, and bound him fast in the slavery of sin. Man, thus degraded and depraved, could not look up to God and claim his Divine protection and love; all this he had forfeited by his voluntary act of rebellion.

How fearful is that abyss of misery and woe, into which man was plunged by sin? God looked down from heaven and saw that there was none that did good—no, not one! They had all gone astray. And Paul describes the condition of the sinner before his conversion thus:

"That at that time ye were without Christ, being aliens from the commonwealth of Israel, and strangers from the covenants of promise, having no hope and without God in the world."—Eph. 2: 12.

This sad state of things lasted some four thousand years, till the time of reformation. But deep as was man's helpless misery, he was not left without a promise of future good. The declaration of God, made to the serpent at the time of the transgression, that the seed of the woman should bruise his head, is generally understood to have reference to the great Messiah, and his triumph over the great enemy of God and man. And to Abraham he made a direct promise of Christ, which the apostle Paul calls "the gospel preached before to Abraham, saying, in thy seed shall the families of the earth be blessed."

With the love of sin in his heart, and practicing it in his life, and without strength to save himself, the sinner must be regarded as ruined and undone. In this condition he must be lost forever. But God has provided means for his recovery. He must be converted, or he can not enter into the kingdom of God. This brings us to consider—

II. How is the sinner converted to God, and by what means is it effected?

In considering the subject of conversion under this head, I shall speak of conversion in reference to the heart, the life and state of the individual in this life, and his final deliverance from the bondage of corruption into the glorious liberty of the children of God.

1.   The conversion of the heart. The heart being the center of all our desires and labors, must first of all be converted.   "The heart is desperately wicked, and deceitful above all things; who can know it?" And the Psalmist says, "The wicked work wickedness in their heart."—Ps. 58. The heart may be regarded as the great laboratory or workshop of the mind. In the heart thoughts are matured and plans and purposes of future action are conceived and arranged. In the heart sin reigns as a tyrant, bringing the whole man into subjection to his unholy rule. On this subject the apostle Paul remarks:

"I speak after the manner of men, because of the infirmity of your flesh; for as you have yielded your members servants to uncleanness and to iniquity, unto iniquity; even so now yield your members servants to righteousness, unto holiness."—Rom. 6: 19.

Before any one can become a Christian, then, the tyrant sin must be dethroned in the heart—his reigning power must be destroyed. How is this to be done? We answer, the heart must be converted—that is, it must be changed from the love of sin to the love of righteousness. How is this conversion of heart effected? To this question several diverse answers are given. The Predestinarian says that God, having foreordained whatever comes to pass, has fixed the time irrevocably, at which each one of the elect shall be converted, and that when the time comes, he will convert them by His almighty power, without any condition being performed on the part of the creature.

To this theory of conversion we have several objections. 1. It makes salvation unconditional, while the Scriptures everywhere represent the whole matter as conditional. "He that believeth and is baptized shall be saved; and he that believeth not shall be damned." "Men and brethren, what shall we do?" "Repent and be baptized, every one of you, in the name of Jesus Christ for the remission of sins, and you shall receive the gift of the Holy Spirit." "Sirs, what must I do?" "Believe on the Lord Jesus Christ, and thou shalt be saved and thy house."

2. It destroys man's moral agency. For if God has foreordained whatever comes to pass, it extends to all the actions of men, and if no man can act differently from what he does, he acts not from choice, but from necessity—he has no choice in the matter! But the Bible everywhere teaches us that men are moral agents and act freely under the influence of their own choice, in receiving or rejecting the mercy of God. "Come unto me all ye that labor, and are heavy laden, and I will give you rest; take my yoke upon you and learn of me, for I am lowly in heart, and you shall find rest to your souls, for my yoke is easy and my burden is light." Again, "Ye will not come to me that ye might have life." "Look unto me all ye ends of the earth, and be ye saved." "Who-

ever will be my disciple, let him deny himself, **and** take up his cross and follow me."

3. But worse than all, it makes God the *author* of *sin!* For if God has foreordained whatever comes to pass, the wicked acts of man are as much the subject of his predestination as any thing else. For if man is not a moral agent, but acts under the law of necessity, he is not to be blamed for any wicked act, since he could not in the nature of things avoid it. And we ask, why are not all men converted? The answer is, God withholds the Divine power necessary to the conversion of the elect, and they can do nothing to superinduce those Divine operations so necessary to their conversion, and consequently they **are** living in sin. Now, I ask who is to blame? Not the sinner, for he could not do otherwise than he does; and consequently, if the theory be true, God must **be** the author of all the sin in the world. How monstrous!

But the predestinarian theory also destroys the doctrine of forgiveness altogether! Pardon always looks to the act of the creature, and recognizes man's moral agency. But if the doctrine be true, man has no moral agency, performs no voluntary actions, and of course is just as incapable of sinning as a horse or an ox; and therefore he can commit no sin to be forgiven! But the Bible teaches us that God pardons the believing, penitent, obedient sinner. Indeed, the text affirms this. But I need not elaborate this point, as we suppose but few, if any, of our hearers are troubled with this doctrine.

But Arminians generally give a very different answer to the question. They tell us that Christ died for all men, and thus opened the way for the salvation of all; but no man can be converted, or changed in heart, without the direct personal agency of the Holy Spirit.

Now this is but little less objectionable than the former. If we ask, why are not all men converted? the answer is, according to this hypothesis, sinners can not convert themselves, and God has not afforded to them the immediate gracious influences of his Holy Spirit; and therefore they remain in their sins. And suppose God should never send to them these direct influences, and they should die in their sins and appear before the judgment seat of Christ, might they not excuse themselves thus, "Lord, I am here in my sins; but I have done what I could to avoid it. I was willing to be converted, but had no power to effect it. I have waited all my life for the direct agency of the Holy Spirit to change my heart; but it came not?" Now, it seems to me, that such an excuse, if it can be fairly made out, would be taken at the judgment of the great day. But the Scriptures abundantly teach that man has something to do in his conversion, and that he must be active in coming to Christ.

But I shall now undertake to show briefly, but clearly, how the heart is converted. According to the text it is effected by seeing with the eyes, hearing with the ears, and understanding with the heart. God has given us our eyes to see, our ears to hear, and our hearts to understand, and our judgments to decide, and our reason and conscience enlightened, to guide us in obedience to the law of the Lord. The heart is affected by what we see and hear and understand; this no one will deny. God has therefore given us His Word; and the effect which it produces upon our heart is the same, whether we see it or hear it. It is like this: Suppose at this moment a well-known friend from the city of Indianapolis should step into this house and announce to me the death of my wife, since I left home; if I believed the report, it would immediately affect my heart, and sorrow would be depicted in my countenance. Or, if I should receive a letter from the city in the well-known handwriting of my son, giving me the same sad intelligence, it would have the same effect upon my heart; of course, in either case, I must understand the communication, and believe it, too.

Now, God has addressed to us, through our eyes and ears, the sublime and wonderful truths and facts of the gospel, designed to affect our hearts, and work in us a great moral change. "I am not ashamed of the gospel of Christ, for it is the power of God unto salvation to every one that believes." Again: "It pleased God by the foolishness of preaching, to save them that believe." And as the conversion of the heart is the very first step in our salvation, it follows that the heart is changed, or converted, by the gospel preached in its simplicity.

In the gospel we learn that we are undone and helpless sinners; but that "God so loved the world that he sent his Son into the world, that whosoever believeth on Him should not perish, but have ever-lasting life." Brought to see ourselves sinners, we look into the gospel, and there we contemplate with astonishment the philanthropy of the heavenly Father, in the rich provisions made for our salvation in the gospel. We approach the cross of Christ, and behold a demonstration of the love of God to man. And while we contemplate the wonders of the cross,

>"Our stubborn heart
>Feels its own hardness soon depart."

The enmity of the heart is slain, and with John we can say, "We love him because he first loved us." The love of sin in our hearts is destroyed, and in heart we are turned from the love of sin to the love of holiness.

To prove that I am correct in this, let me bring for-ward an example or two. Go to the day of Pentecost. Peter stood up with eleven, and preached the gospel to the astonished crowd. He told them of the death, burial and resurrection of Christ, and of His exalta-tion to the right hand of God. "And when they heard this they were pierced in their heart." What was it that affected their hearts? Why, what they heard. When Christ was transfigured upon the Holy Moun-tain, the voice which came from the excellent glory said, "This is my beloved Son, hear ye him."

But perhaps some one is ready to object and say that this view of the subject gives the sinner too much to do in his own conversion, and certainly the Saviour

says, "No man can come to me, except the Father
who sent me draw him, and I will raise him up at the
last day." Yes, and so say we; but how does the
Father draw men to Christ? Jesus tells us in the
succeeding verse (John 6: 44, 45), "As it is written,
and they shall be taught of God; every man, therefore, who hath heard, and hath learned of the Father,
cometh unto me." So, then, men are drawn to Christ
by being taught of God—by hearing and learning of
the Father. God teaches men by His word, and thus
prepares them to come, and draws them to His Son.

But, says another objector, the Holy Spirit certainly has something to do in the conversion of a sinner to
God; for Jesus promised His disciples that "When he
(the Holy Spirit) comes, he shall convince the world
of sin, of righteousness and of judgment."

Very well; and so he did, and so he does now;
upon this point there is no debate. The question is,
how does the Holy Spirit do the work? We answer,
when he came on the day of Pentecost, he was in
the apostles, and gave them utterance, and the words
which they spake were the words of the Holy Spirit;
and what they preached on that occasion was the
gospel. Then, the matter may be stated thus:

The Holy Spirit is the agent, and the Word of
God, or gospel, the instrumentality employed for convincing the world of sin, of righteousness, and of
judgment; and hence it is that Jesus commanded that
the gospel should be preached to every creature; and
hence it is, also, that no man was ever convinced of

sin and converted to God, without hearing the gospel in some way.

Thus it will be seen that our faith in the crucified Redeemer destroys the love of sin in our hearts and prepares us for the obedience of faith. "Without faith it is impossible to please God," but with faith, which is a firm belief of the truth with all the heart, we may please God by obeying Him as our heavenly Father.

I am aware that most of our religious friends and orthodox neighbors would consider a man thus changed in heart as a converted and pardoned man. So you see that we contend for all that the sects do, and more, too.

2. A man thus converted in heart, before he can be pardoned Scripturally, must be converted in life. For this purpose, "God has commanded all men everywhere to repent."

This gospel repentance which changes or converts the life may be considered in reference to two or three particulars. 1. Repentance signifies a change of purpose. In this sense it frequently occurs in the Old Testament. It is sometimes said that God repented. "If that nation, against whom I have pronounced, turn from their evil, I will REPENT of the evil that I thought to do unto them." "If it do evil in my sight, that it obey not my voice, then I will REPENT of the good wherewith I said I would benefit them" (Jer. 18: 8-10).

Now, we can not suppose that God repents in the sense of sorrow; but in the sense of changing his purpose, it is easily understood. In this sense, too, it occurs in Paul's letter to the Hebrews. He says, "For you know how that afterward, when he would have inherited the blessing, he was rejected; for he found no place of repentance, though he sought it carefully with tears" (Heb. 12:17). That is, Esau was not able to effect a change in the purpose of his father Isaac, concerning the blessing of Jacob, though he carefully sought to do so with tears. (See Gen. 26:31-38.)

But repentance also signifies reformation, or amendment of life; and this reformation grows out of a change of purpose, and sorrow for the past wrongs of our lives. It occurs in all these senses in the following passage: "But what think ye? A certain man had two sons: and he came to the first and said, Son, go work to-day in my vineyard. He answered and said, I will not; but afterward he repented and went" (Matt: 21 :28, 29). Here, you see, this son purposed in his heart not to obey his father, but afterward, upon reflection, he became sorry for his wickedness in saying "I will not," and he changed his purpose; and as a result of this, and as evidence that he was sincere, he reformed; that is, "he went." So it is with the sinner. God has been saying to him, "Go into my vineyard and work." But the sinner has said, "No, I will not go." But upon reflection, he sees the evil of his way, is sorry for his past sins, and this leads him to amendment, or reformation of life, and his change of purpose is proven by his going forward in obedience to the commands of God. In the sense of amendment of life, it often occurs in the Christian Scriptures.

Take one example: On the day of Pentecost, the three thousand were pierced in their hearts, and cried out and said, "Men and brethren, what shall we do?" "And Peter said unto them, REPENT," etc. Now, these persons were evidently penitent—sorry for their past sins, which led them to inquire what they must do. Peter's command to them to repent was therefore equivalent to "Reform, amend your lives, every one of you."

But there is still another view of the doctrine of repentance that we consider quite important. It is the idea of restitution. We have no confidence in any man's repentance who does not, as far as may be in his power, make restitution for any injuries he may have inflicted upon any one. Suppose a man has defrauded his neighbor to the amount of fifty dollars, or any other amount, and afterward he repents; he will surely make restitution to his neighbor. And this doctrine is recognized by the Lord himself. Take an example: "And Zaccheus stood, and said unto the Lord: Behold, Lord, the half of my goods I give the poor; and if I have taken anything from any man by false accusation, I restore him four-fold. And Jesus said unto him, This day is salvation to come to this house, forasmuch as he also is a son of Abraham" (Luke 19 : 8, 9).

Now, every one can see that a sinner that truly repents is converted in life. That is, his life and character are so completely changed that he no longer purposes to do evil, and therefore he does not practice it; but he now purposes to do right, and therefore he breaks off his sins by righteousness, and his iniquities by turning to the Lord. The things which he once loved he now hates, and loves the things which he once hated. He is no longer willing to continue in the state of sin, and he inquires, How shall I escape from the state of sin?

3. A man thus converted in heart and life is prepared for a conversion of state. That is, he must be "translated from the kingdom of darkness into the kingdom of God's dear Son." How is this effected? I answer, by Christian immersion. Now, the audience will not mistake me; I do not say that Christian immersion will change the heart or life; far from it, indeed, unless a sinner's heart and life are changed or converted he is not a Scriptural subject for baptism. But what we affirm is this: The sinner who has believed the gospel with all his heart, repented of his sins, and confessed the Saviour before men, is changed, or converted in heart and life, and is a fit subject for baptism, in which ordinance he puts on Christ. As evidence of this, Paul says:

"Know you not, that so many of us as were baptized into Jesus Christ, were baptized into his death?" (Rom 6:3). And in the same connection, alluding to this baptism as the "form of doctrine," he says to the Roman brethren, "But God be thanked, that though you were the servants of sin, yet you have obeyed from the heart that form of doctrine which was delivered you. Being then made free from sin, ye became the servants of righteousness." It follows, then, with the clearness of demonstration, that every penitent believer, who obeys from the heart the form of doctrine here referred to, namely, Christian immersion, puts on Christ, and enters into a new relation with God and the Lord Jesus Christ. Paul says of every such person, "There is therefore now no condemnation to them who are in Christ Jesus," etc. (Rom. 8:1). And this change of relation we call a conversion of state. And every person who comes into this new relation has the promise of REMISSION OF SINS. "Repent and be converted, that your sins may be blotted out." The phrase "be converted" comprehends all that we have said of the change of heart, life and state; and every such individual is prepared to enjoy the remission of sins. To prove this, we may only quote a text or two.

"Except a man be born of water, and of the Spirit, he can not see the kingdom of God." "Not by works of righteousness which we have done, but according to his mercy he saved us, by the washing of regeneration, and renewing of the Holy Spirit." "That he might sanctify and cleanse it (the church) with the washing of water by the word." "For as many of you as have been baptized into Christ, have put on Christ. There is neither Jew nor Greek, there is neither bond nor free, there is neither male nor female; for ye are all one in Christ Jesus. And if ye be Christ's, then are ye Abraham's seed, and heirs according to the promise." "And why tarriest thou? Arise and be baptized, and wash away thy sins, calling on the name of the Lord." "And Peter said unto them, Repent, and be baptized every one of you, in the name of Jesus Christ, for the remission of sins, and you shall receive the gift of the Holy Spirit." The application of these Scriptures is easy, and I need not further elaborate this point now.

One objection we must consider before we leave this part of the subject. Some persons who do not understand the gospel, think that we undervalue the blood of Christ, and place too much reliance on water. Now, it is only necessary that I should say, it is the blood of Christ that gives efficacy and virtue to faith, repentance and baptism. Without the blood, neither would secure for us the pardon of sins. "The blood of Jesus Christ his Son, cleanses us from all sin." Those whom John saw standing before the throne, who had come up through great tribulation, had "washed their robes and made them white in the blood of the Lamb."

III. Every such converted person, being wholly dedicated to the service of God, and sanctified in soul, body and spirit, enters upon the enjoyment of new privileges and blessings. They now have the privilege of crying "Abba, Father!" in a sense in which they dared not approach him before. And what a glorious privilege is this, to call God our Father. When way-worn and sad, persecuted and despised, to be permitted to come to the mercy-seat in the name of our great High Priest, and there present our petitions, with the divine assurance that we shall be heard. "Ask, and you shall receive; seek, and you shall find; knock, and it shall be opened unto you."

We have the glorious privilege also of being associated with the family of God in heaven and on earth.

All Christians are our brethren and sisters. Angels are our ministering spirits, and Jesus Christ is our elder brother. What a noble companionship! How honorable the station! All children of a King, and belonging to the royal family! But it is also our privilege to come to the Lord's Table, and openly publish our faith in his death and coming. But we have not time to speak of all the blessings and privileges of the children of God. They are blessed with all spiritual blessings in Christ Jesus, and can rejoice with joy which is unspeakable and full of glory. They know that they have passed from death unto life because they love the brethren. Paul speaks of the valuable inheritance of the Christian thus: "All are yours, whether Paul or Apollos, or Cephas, or the world, or life or death, or things present, or things to come; all are yours; and ye are Christ's, and Christ is God's" (I. Cor. 3:22). Again, he declares that we are heirs of God, and joint heirs with Christ. Indeed, all the substantial pleasures, blessings and enjoyments of this life belong to the Christian, and he has the promise of a "crown of life" beyond the grave. In a word, "he is rich in faith, and an heir of the kingdom."

(THE END.)